The Light of Imagination

Mavis Gallant's still growing reputation as one of the finest living fiction writers in English rests on her work over the last thirty-five years. A Canadian who has long made her home in Paris, Gallant has published over one hundred stories—most of them in *The New Yorker*—as well as two novels, a play, and several important essays.

The Light of Imagination is the first book to consider the entire range of Gallant's fiction. It includes biographical detail, discussion of her non-fiction writings, and substantial analyses of her books of short stories and her two novels. Besner shows how Gallant's fiction evokes the tensions between North American and European social, political, and historical perceptions more fully and subtly than the work of any writer since Henry James. In Gallant's stories the misapprehension of the past emerges from the various cultural, social, and political upheavals which both precipitated and followed World War II. Her North Americans abroad encounter a postwar European landscape which shows them to be living largely unaware of history's more immediate European legacies. Her vision of North American and European perceptions of history provides one framework for Besner's discussion of her work.

Another line of analysis traces the importance of figures of "return" when characters and cultures grapple with the past as it inhabits the present. Because her stories often eddy around significant moments in a character's memory or a culture's history, the plot device of the return exerts a strong shaping influence on her fiction. The book culminates by showing that Gallant's stories can be read as explorations of human time, stories which call the fragmented imaginative being of the past into full fictional presence.

The title originates in a passage from a Gallant story when "the light of imagination" momentarily illuminates and unifies the central character's perception of the past. The significance of this "light of imagination," in Besner's study, opens a way for the understanding of the form and function of similar moments throughout Gallant's fiction.

NEIL K. BESNER is a member of the English Department at the University of Winnipeg. He is currently working on a book on contemporary short story theory and practice in Canada.

The Light of Imagination

Mavis Gallant's Fiction

NEIL K. BESNER

University of British Columbia Press

VANCOUVER 1988

This book has been published with the help of a grant from the
Canadian Federation for the Humanities, using funds provided by
the Humanities and Social Science Research Council of Canada.

Canadian Cataloguing in Publication Data

Besner, Neil Kalman, 1949–
   The light of imagination : Mavis Gallant's fiction

   Includes bibliographical references and index.
   ISBN 0-7748-0297-9

   1. Gallant, Mavis, 1922–   – Criticism and interpretation.
I. Title.
PS8513.A593Z58 1988   c813'.54   c88-091149-2
PR9199.3.G34Z58 1988

International Book Standard Number 0-7748-0297-9

Printed in Canada

For Carlene

Contents

Preface

Since the appearance in 1979 of *From the Fifteenth District,* the book of stories that firmly established her growing reputation in Canada, Mavis Gallant has often been praised as one of the finest living writers of fiction in English. Yet if there has been agreement among many of her readers about the merits of Gallant's fiction, this praise has most often emerged in reviews, and in quite general terms. The history of more sustained critical attention to Gallant's work in Canada is all too quickly told. Although Gallant published her first short stories in *Preview* in 1944, the first article on her fiction, a study by Peter Stevens, appeared in 1973. The first Master's thesis was completed in 1975; there have been several others since and a Ph.D. dissertation in 1983. In 1978, an entire issue of *Canadian Fiction Magazine* was devoted to Gallant, with an interview by Geoff Hancock, articles by Robertson Davies, George Woodcock, and Ronald Hatch, and a bibliography compiled by Douglas Malcolm of works by and about Gallant. This issue remains the single most valuable source of material on Gallant's work. In addition to Ronald Hatch's several other articles on Gallant, there is a 1978 monograph by Grazia Merler (*Mavis Gallant: Narrative Patterns and Devices*), a 1982 article by David O'Rourke, a 1983 study by Michel Fabre, and five recent essays, two by Donald Jewison and three by Janice Kulyk Keefer.

What this paucity of critical discussion might indicate about Gallant's fiction or about the Canadian critical community is a difficult question to answer. On one hand, the circumstances of Gallant's chosen life have intrigued Canadian readers since the beginning of her career. Two issues, both peripheral to her fiction itself, have troubled our encounters with Gallant's work. How, Canadian readers have asked, are we to understand Gallant's leaving Canada at twenty-seven in 1950? In what senses is Gallant an expatriate writer? Or an exile? And how are we to look at Gallant's thirty-five-year association with *The New Yorker*? Since the appearance of *From the Fifteenth District,* these generally unproductive questions have gradually given way to a more appropriate focus on the art of Gallant's stories themselves.

The other difficulty has been that Gallant's stories seem to resist interpretation. After praising her as a fine realist and for her faithful, exacting transcriptions of setting, her precise renditions of the nuances of cultural surrounds, her

fine ear for dialogue and her sharp eye for detail, much interpretation has come
to a dead end. Close readings of Gallant's stories run the risk of bogging down
in a mass of details, all significant, none representative. Thematic interpretation,
which often calls attention to Gallant's recurring focus on exiles, expatriates,
and refugees, adrift in European *pensions,* villas, and hotels, runs the risk of
leaving too many unanswered questions about form and style in Gallant's fiction. Yet form and style are precisely the qualities of Gallant's fiction which first
meet the eye.

Gallant's stories range over a wide domain. Children's relations with their
parents, servants' relations with their households, and the subtle shifts within
unstable relationships form at times the foreground—in her later stories more
often the background—for the most detailed fictional evocations of the tensions
between North American and European social, political, and historical visions
since the work of Henry James. Gallant shares with James an exquisitely sure
sense of significant detail, imparting to her stories their dense particularity; but
Gallant's fiction differs from James's because of her eminence in the short story
form rather than the novel, and this is a crucial difference, predicated as it is on
the formal designs which shape Gallant's stories. Woven from complex repetitions and variations, Gallant's stories reflect, paradoxically, the fragmentation
of historical reality in the West over the last seventy years. In Gallant's fiction,
form evokes the traces of the past as history, as memory, as fiction, and as what
is often referred to in her stories as "invention." No other contemporary writer
in English conceives of this recent past—the past as social, cultural, and political
history and the past as recreated in individual and in cultural memory—in as
varied and significant a manner as Gallant.

Because her stories often eddy around significant moments in a character's
memory or a culture's history, the plot device of the return exerts a strong shaping influence on Gallant's fiction. Its form reflects her stories' tendencies to return to moments of potential insight—readers', characters', and cultures'—which might restructure the "locked situation" in which Gallant says
many of her stories begin. The centre of a Gallant story often consists, not only
of a "locked situation," but also of a moment of potential revelation; but the
significance of these revelatory moments is often missed by characters and cultures deafened amidst their many-voiced dialogues with the past, and the
pastward gaze in Gallant's stories is one which mesmerizes or transfixes more
often than it illuminates.

One of the most important interpretative journeys for Gallant's readers,
therefore, involves constructing the potential revelations in these moments of return. Gallant's stories invite readers to consider characters' missed moments of
insight, dialogue, and contact, and to conceive of these moments as elements of
plot. Reading the stories in this manner becomes less a matter of choice than of
necessity: close readers wishing to take interpretative revenge on Gallant's art

may find themselves lost in a labyrinth of particulars which seem to refuse to lead toward generalization. Gallant's fiction invites readers to attend first to its surface and style; interpretation becomes a form of attention rather than a process of inference or deduction. The kind of attention Gallant's stories cultivate, this study suggests, illuminates our readings of the past as documented, narrated history, as recorded, reported memory, and as imagined, fictional presence.

Acknowledgements

I owe thanks to a number of individuals and institutions for help with this book. I am grateful to the Social Sciences and Humanities Research Council of Canada for granting me doctoral fellowships in 1979 and 1981. In the book's germinal stages as a dissertation, Professors Bill New, Ronald Hatch, Laurie Ricou, and Donald Stephens of the University of British Columbia offered critical guidance and encouragement with unstinting generosity. I am indebted in particular to Ronald Hatch, whose own readings of Gallant's work showed me directions I would never have found on my own, and to Bill New, who listened to my early fumbled formulations with what seems in retrospect to have been endless patience and tact. I would also like to thank Professor David Staines of the University of Ottawa, who gave me invaluable critical advice, supported by exemplary editorial acumen, at several stages in my research. Tirthankar Bose and Jane Fredeman of the University of British Columbia Press were very helpful in the final editing stages. All responsibility for the inadequacies and inaccuracies of this book, of course, remains my own.

I am grateful to the staff of the Interlibrary Loans division at the University of British Columbia, who proved endlessly and cheerfully resourceful in helping me to secure copies of Gallant's early journalism, and to the National Library for allowing me to use its microfilm copies of the *Montreal Standard.* Mrs. Rachel Grover and Mrs. Katharine Martyn of the Thomas Fisher Rare Book Library, University of Toronto, were most helpful in making the growing collection of Gallant papers available to me. CBC Radio in Vancouver and Toronto generously allowed me access to several taped interviews with Gallant, and Centaur Theatre in Montreal kindly sent me a number of documents connected with its production of Gallant's play, *What Is To Be Done?*

Over the last eight years, the many individuals who have given me various kinds of help, advice, and support are simply too numerous to mention here. But I would like to acknowledge the generosity of Mavis Gallant, who was unfailing in her prompt and detailed responses to my many letters and questions, and who went out of her way to provide me with information about her years in Montreal with the *Standard,* to give me the names of friends and associates who provided me with additional information, and to personally show me some of the Montreal streets, houses, and ambiences that she remembered from the forties and has recreated so vividly in recent years.

For their help and for sharing their recollections, I am grateful to May Cutler and Dusty Vineberg-Solomon of Montreal and to Doyle Klyn of Sydney, B.C. Professor John Xiros Cooper of Mount Royal College, Calgary, who read and reread sections of the manuscript, brought a passionate intelligence to bear on my approach, taught me how to begin thinking about European history, and has given me valued years of friendship and support. And Professor Fred Miles of Mount Royal College listened to it all, at any time, everywhere, over and again; his generosity remains an inspiration to me.

I owe my children, Daniel and Barbara, gratitude for their long patience with my distracted absences. And first and last, I am indebted without measure to my wife Carlene, who for eight years listened to every word I wrote and many I didn't, who remains my first and most faithful reader, critic, and editor, and who has been at all times, and in all ways, my constant and loving companion. There would be no book without her.

1

The Other Paris

Memory's Fictions
Against History's Reports

Mavis Gallant's stories and novels are distinct from the fiction of her English-Canadian contemporaries—among them, several writers of the first rank—by virtue of their form and style, the nature of their intelligence, and their breadth and depth of vision. Alice Munro's stories reveal a similar command of craft, but Munro's style and vision evoke a fictional world most powerful in its regional resonances. Margaret Atwood's irony can be similarly incisive, but most often in the service of more particularly Canadian and North American ends; Gallant's irony, which can construct a hard-edged comedy of manners as skilfully and effectively as Austen's, can also lay bare the workings of memory, of a relationship, a family, a society—most often in the wider context of postwar Western history. Margaret Laurence's rendering of Western Canadian women's lives is more complete; but when Gallant's stories recreate Canadian life, her intelligence is typically more politically informed, and her vision remains comprehensively North American and European. It is the pervasive European colouration of many of Gallant's stories, which emerges from her close attention to European post-war history and culture, that distinguishes her fiction from the work of such accomplished Canadian writers as Clark Blaise, Hugh Hood, John Metcalf, and Audrey Thomas. Gallant's distinctively alloyed North American and European vision, which is inseparable from the most highly finished and economical style in contemporary English-Canadian writing, challenges, engages, and educates her readers at the same time that it invites sustained critical study.

Before proceeding directly to such a study, it is best to summarize what is known about Gallant's early life, since the few details that are public have already begun to be mythologized. The six Linnet Muir stories in particular, which develop episodes in the life of a girl growing up in Montreal and then returning there at eighteen to work during the war years, have helped to create a legend that obscures as much as it reveals. Gallant has called Linnet a "semi-autobiographical" character, and certainly there are parallels between the lives and experiences of Linnet and the younger Gallant. But these parallels should not be taken as exact correspondences between fiction and life: citing Linnet's name, George Woodcock remarks that "Linnet Muir is about as near to Mavis Gallant as her namesake bird (a modest British singing bird) is to the Mavis, which is the Scottish name for the magnificent European song thrush."[1] As fictions, the Linnet Muir stories are remarkable evocations of the childhood and adolescence of a forceful, sensitive, but strong-minded character who narrates and transforms her experience into insight. But the stories are not only, or not purely autobiographical fictions, and even if Gallant had set out to write "true" autobiography, it would still be an obvious mistake to *identify* her with Linnet's various incarnations. Given the sharp focus in much of Gallant's fiction on the dangerous crosscurrents of memory and imagination swirling around the past, it is best to read the Linnet Muir stories first as fictions, and then as "semi-autobiographical" fictions.

Gallant, an only child, was born Mavis Young in Montreal in 1922. Her family lived in a modest two-storey house (still standing, but remodelled) on Sherbrooke Street across from McGill, where she was taken occasionally to play on the campus. Shortly after her fourth birthday, her parents placed her in a Catholic convent school on Sherbrooke Street East—a "very very severe institution," Gallant recalls—the first of what was to be a series of schools, some Catholic in Montreal, some Protestant in Ontario, some boarding schools in the United States. The number of schools in Canada and the United States that Gallant attended is usually cited as seventeen. Of her peripatetic school years, Gallant has remarked:

> It has a different effect on different people, doesn't it. If I had children, I would not have put my child through that. I imagine some children could take it, but it would absolutely break another kind of child. But it did something positive for me—there's no milieu I don't feel comfortable in, that I don't immediately understand.[2]

Commenting on her experience as the only English Protestant student in a French Catholic institution in Montreal, Gallant has said that although she never understood why her parents placed her there—they were "very young," she remarks—she was "grateful for one thing":

> I never looked upon Catholics as peculiar people or anybody who was anything other than I was as peculiar. I would be incapable. It doesn't even

cross my mind. And I am incapable—really and truly—this isn't a pose—of understanding racism. It isn't that I don't approve of it. I really and truly don't. I have got a piece missing where it is concerned.[3]

Gallant's inability to understand racism may explain in part her motivation for writing the stories in *The Pegnitz Junction* (1973), a book which she says helped her to understand the roots of Fascism. These so-called "German stories" show Gallant's talent for evoking general political or historical climates through small-scale revelations, through the careful development of character traits woven into a significant pattern of detail. Gallant has remarked that *The Pegnitz Junction* is the favourite of her books because in it she was able to particularize a historical moment and movement: the stories, she has said—in a remark which points to a crucial element in Gallant's art—allowed her to see Fascism's "small possibilities in people."[4]

Gallant has been quite reserved about the details of her childhood and her feelings for her parents, and the people who remember Gallant from earlier years date their recollections from her years with the *Montreal Standard,* where she began working in 1944. Again, it is tempting to read Gallant's stories—in which communication between parents and children is typically blocked and misunderstandings are the norm—as deriving in part from her own experience with a mother who in some measure abandoned her to various schools and to foster parents in Ontario, and with a father who may have served as a model for the remote, vaguely ineffectual man who takes his daughter Linnet to visit his mistress in "Voices Lost in Snow." Gallant's father died when she was a girl, and by the time she was a teenager she had in effect broken contact with her mother. Perhaps the most that can be said is that Gallant's early years with her own family may have forced her into a premature and troubled independence in order to survive.

Gallant returned to Montreal from New York at the age of eighteen. For most of her teenage years, she had lived with a psychiatrist and his wife in New York who had become her legal guardians after meeting her at one of the boarding schools Gallant had attended in the United States. "In Youth Is Pleasure" (1975), the first of the Linnet Muir stories to be published, recalls Linnet's return to Montreal, also at eighteen, also from New York. Gallant may have returned for reasons similar to Linnet's—to begin her own adult life and to find out more about the circumstances of her father's death. But Linnet, who hears a number of versions of her father's death, finally learns more about her own life than about her father's, discovering that her changing perceptions of how memory recalls and recreates the past also signal the end of her childhood. It is typical of the way in which change is evoked in Gallant's stories that Linnet's developing insight should be intimately related to her perception of memory's power to work the past into fiction. When Linnet, standing on a Montreal street corner, realizes that she can no longer conjure a Montreal faithful to her past and also live fully in the actual Montreal of the present, she senses that her "youth" has ended, and with it the pleasure of imagining that the private palaces she has erected in memory can share equal (and equally significant) space with the stone schoolhouses she sees in front of her in the historical world.

After a short stint with the National Film Board in Ottawa in the winter of 1943–44, Gallant landed a job in September 1944 as a writer for the *Montreal Standard,* where she worked until August 1950, writing over sixty feature articles as well as photo-stories, reviews, captions, and (from October 1947 to June 1949) a weekly column about radio, "On the Air."[5] Two of the Linnet Muir stories,"Between Zero and One" (1975) and "With a Capital T" (1978), offer what might be read in part as fictionalized versions of these years. Within a wider historical perspective, Gallant's 1982 play *What Is To Be Done?* vividly evokes the claustrophobic atmosphere of wartime Montreal as the play's principal characters, at a distance from developments overseas, hold political visions dimly conceived, but fervently embraced.[6]

Gallant's experience at the *Standard* was probably not quite as bleak as Linnet's experience in the exclusively male world of the office in "Between Zero and One." Although Gallant sometimes chafed at being paid less than the paper's male writers for the same work, she was generally delighted at the freedom she was given to pursue her own ideas for feature articles. The first feature Gallant wrote for the *Standard,* "Meet Johnny," developed from her idea to follow a Montreal street kid around on his daily routine—an early indication, perhaps, of her lifelong fascination with the patterns that the ordinary, the solitary, and the marginal life might reveal.

Some quite general connections can be inferred between Gallant's *Standard* work and her fiction. "My Heart Is Broken" (the title story of her second book of stories, which appeared in 1964), "The Legacy" (1954) and "Up North" (1959) all developed in part out of research Gallant was doing for *Standard* features, and other stories will occasionally sound echoes of material originally cast in the form of feature articles for the *Standard.* Some of the features, written for a general audience, obviously reveal very little about Gallant's own interest in or knowledge of the topic at hand. Her article "Freud or Doubletalk," for example, is a simplified and generalized report on basic Freudian tenets; Gallant herself, raised for a time by a psychiatrist who had been analyzed by Freud, was deeply interested in Freudian psychoanalysis at one stage in her life.[7] In other articles Gallant's comments on her material are more revealing, giving readers a sense of her encyclopaedic range of interests. These include more than a passing acquaintance with both English- and French-Canadian writing, as well as with the French-Canadian cultural scene of the times. Gallant wrote features for the *Standard* on Hugh MacLennan, Dorothy Duncan, W. O. Mitchell, Paul Hiebert, Roger Lemelin, Louis Hémon, and Gabrielle Roy.[8] For her photo-story on Roy's

Bonheur d'Occasion, a novel she admired deeply, she had actors stage scenes from the book in Montreal's St.-Henri district, Roy's original setting.[9] "Above the Crowd in French Canada," published in *Harper's Bazaar* in 1946, surveys the personalities and developments in French-Canadian art.[10] Gallant wrote several features on war-brides, on refugees, immigrants, on displaced people in an alien culture—the kinds of figures who populate many Gallant stories.[11] She also wrote several features and shorter articles on the power politics within families, a theme which was to figure importantly in many of her stories.[12]

In her work for the *Standard,* Gallant sometimes reflects on plot, character, dialogue, and fiction, throwing light on her practices as a writer. Gallant's sentences are among the most rhythmically balanced in contemporary English fiction; some readers speak of the "melody" of Gallant's prose. Commenting on a Saturday night program, "Canadian Short Stories," Gallant writes:

> [I]t gives the writer the experience of hearing rather than seeing his own work, which can be a valuable lesson. There is something relentless about a story read aloud. Lack of rhythm, vagueness and faulty characterization are glaringly obvious because you can't skip and you can't reread.[13]

In other columns, Gallant takes sharp measure of Canadian intellectual life. Scoffing at a program called "Critically Speaking," for example, Gallant presents her view of Canadian criticism *circa* 1949:

> In voice and opinions most of the speakers vary from the academic whine to the petulant groan. Over everything they say, in the case of the book critics, lies that terrible pall of Canadian literary pedantry, that feeling that the speaker has read all the back issues of Partisan Revue [sic] and is just as smart as anyone else, see?[14]

Panning an album of records, "I Can Hear It Now," Gallant complains of reviewers who fail to mention the "overbearing commentary" by Edward Murrow as he interrupts speeches by Churchill and Stalin; Murrow, writes Gallant, becomes "embarrassingly emotional about events which have enough emotional value in themselves to get by without adjectives."[15] Gallant's own fictional idiom gains much of its intensity from compression and restraint; almost forty years later, she comments again on her wariness of adjectives, recalling the manner in which she tried to describe the first pictures of the concentration camps sent to the *Standard* after the war. She remarks in an interview that she had decided that adjectives would blur the pictures' significance, and so there "would be no descriptive words in this, no adjectives. Nothing like 'horror,' 'horrifying' because what the pictures are saying is stronger and louder."[16]

Gallant's sense that literary form must sometimes accommodate the less formal patterns of real people's "case histories" emerges in another "On the Air" column. Describing Len Peterson's radio plays, broadcast on "In Search of Ourselves," she writes:

> Although these short dramas deal with emotional problems, they are not relentless. They combine humour with insight, details which detract from the occasional grimness. Unlike the ordinary radio play, they don't come to the traditional fictional climax. After all, the people portrayed here are real and their stories are case histories. Real problems do not always resolve themselves tidily, and if the stories sometimes seem incomplete it is because they are true.[17]

But the most significant aspect of Gallant's *Standard* work is that it prefigures the more important essays Gallant wrote later in her career, after she had left Montreal and devoted herself to writing fiction. Some of these essays have recently been collected in *Paris Notebooks*.[18] For some readers, these essays share many of the virtues of Gallant's fiction and few of its difficulties—its elusiveness, its indirections, and its veiled or opaque endings. Six of these essays in particular reward close attention: Gallant's two-part diary, "The Events in May: A Paris Notebook" (1968), which records day-to-day life in Paris at the time of the student uprisings; "Annals of Justice" (1971), her long essay on the infamous Gabrielle Russier case, in which a French schoolteacher committed suicide after being prosecuted as a result of her affair with a minor; her introduction to Joyce Hibbert's *The War Brides* (1978); her essay "Paris: The Taste of a New Age" (1981); her introduction to her 1981 book of stories, *Home Truths*; and her essay, "What Is Style?", published in 1982. The three essays on French institutions—political, social, legal, educational—demonstrate Gallant's comprehensive grasp of the details as well as the cultural norms that inform French life. "Paris: The Taste of a New Age" documents Gallant's close knowledge of the history and the recent transformations of French architecture, and all of the essays show Gallant's familiarity with the customs of French domestic life. Gallant's thoroughness as a reporter, evident in her repeated references to statistics, documents, to the history of particular pieces of legislation, is complemented in these essays by the rewards of her keen curiosity about "foreign" conduct and by a challenging directness of observation. Her essays clarify complex situations and developments by placing them within as complete a historical, political, social, and domestic context as possible; but they also move beyond explication to evoke the particular quality of the events, to reveal how they characterize the way a society lives and breathes in the atmosphere of its culture. Gallant examines Gabrielle Russier's case, for example, for what it reveals about French attitudes (as distinct from generally European, as contrasted with North American attitudes) to women involved with younger men—in this case, a minor. But in the course of the essay, the reader also learns much about the French educational system and the French class structure (Gabrielle Russier was a teacher, and the parents of the boy are both university professors), about the relations between French parents and children (relations quite different from those in North American families), about the workings of the French media—again, quite different from North American practices. The intelligence which informs these essays characteristically analyzes its subjects from within; but Gallant also communicates a paradoxical sense of French life as at once strikingly foreign and yet also familiar to her (and accessible to North American readers). Often, Gallant seems at once steeped in and also removed from her objects of inquiry—a natural enough stance, perhaps, for a writer who was raised and educated in North America but has lived and worked in Europe for most of her adult life.

By the spring of 1950 Gallant had given notice to the *Standard* that she would be leaving in the fall. She had begun to feel that she was not going forward any more at the *Standard,* that she had begun to repeat earlier assignments; she also felt that as she neared thirty, she was reaching what she thought of as "a deadline, a trench across [her] life."[19] Gallant had been writing fiction while she was working for the *Standard,* collecting her stories in a large picnic hamper often mentioned in her recollections of the *Standard* years and her departure for Europe. She chose a story from the hamper and sent it to *The New Yorker,* a magazine which many thought of, then as now, as the best in North America. *The New Yorker* returned the story to her as "too specifically Canadian" but asked if Gallant had anything else. She then sent "Madeline's Birthday," which was published in September 1951, marking the beginning of Gallant's longstanding association with *The New Yorker.* The "Canadian" story, "The Flowers of Spring," was published by John Sutherland in the summer of 1950 in *Northern Review.*

The reasons why Gallant left the *Standard* and Montreal for Europe are not simple. She was determined, after a brief and unsuccessful marriage to Johnny Gallant, a talented pianist who played in nightclubs in Montreal and New York, to live independently, and felt that Montreal was too restricted for a single woman (she was to find the same of Rome and of London in the early fifties). She had always been "very European-minded," had grown up "European-minded"—for which she credits her parents in part—and she "felt the war as something very claustrophobic."[20] She was also reacting against what she characterized later as "the whole Eisenhower mentality," which she saw as " . . . so stupid, political and materialistic, [with] something awfully wrong."[21] Gallant has often said that she wanted to go to Europe to see if she could live on her own terms, and live from her writing. Perhaps her most interesting comments in this regard, particularly as they relate to her fiction's tendencies to explore the various connections between people's senses of their past as "true," "invented," "real," or "imagined," focus on her sense of Canada in the late forties. In Europe, Gallant remarks, "you can't invent" because "everyone knows too much"; but she says of Canada:

> I've never been in a country where there was so much gap between reality and dream. The people's lives don't match up to what they seem to think they were and the people invent things or they invent backgrounds or they invent families. Canada is a fascinating place . . . in Canada you move from Halifax to Vancouver and suddenly your father was something else, your mother was something else.[22]

Finally, Gallant has explained that she did not leave for Europe on impulse, or because *The New Yorker* had accepted a story; it was a move that she had been planning for some time. Nor is it quite true that Gallant had not published anything before she left for Europe. She had published one story, "A Wonderful Country," in the *Standard Magazine* in 1946; this story is not particularly strong stylistically or formally, but it reflects Gallant's abiding curiosity with displaced individuals, disoriented in a foreign culture—in this case, Hungarian emigrants hunting for accommodation in Montreal. The two stories, "Good Morning and Goodbye" and "Three Brick Walls," which appeared in *Preview* in December 1944, however, are more significant. Gallant, apparently, was not very happy with these stories, and asked Robert Weaver, who was editing a collection of her stories for the New Canadian Library in the early seventies (*The End of the World and Other Stories,* 1974) to ignore them. But these linked stories define a typical Gallant figure's sensation of being foreign and voiceless, silenced by what passes among characters and families in the "home" culture as dialogue.

In "Good Morning and Goodbye," Paul, a young Jewish-German boy, is doubly estranged from the Trennans, the family that has taken care of him during the first year of his North American initiation. The story focusses on Paul's last day with them, a day on which the only words Paul says are those of the story's title as he ironically frees himself into a silence beyond the family's inane chatter. "Three Brick Walls" follows Paul to his new "freedom" in the silence and anonymity of a working class district in an unidentified big city. Both stories take as their crucial moment a break in the ordered but sterile patterns of Paul's life. These moments, like the moments typical in many of Gallant's stories, both promise and threaten. They promise a break from the stifling patterns which have imprisoned Paul, a victim of political and historical developments obviously beyond his control, in a silent but ordered isolation; but they also threaten him with the "vacuum" which the absence of a pattern, of order, will confer: "He had learned in his life of many changes never to say 'This is the last time I walk down these stairs to breakfast' and 'This is the last time I say "Good Morning".' But it was there, the sense of ending, and the slipping into the vacuum that lies between the patterns in a life."[23] Paul's sense of freedom in silence is ironic, but no more so than the family's sense of engagement and communication through chatter.

A character very much like Paul, and with the same name, reappears in a minor role in "Madeline's Birthday," a story in which the isolation resulting from cultural displacement is replaced by the isolation resulting from children being abandoned by their parents. The central figure in this story is Madeline, who finds herself on her seventeenth birthday at the summer house of a friend of her mother's. Madeline deeply offends her hostess and antagonist, Mrs. Tracy, by crying on what should be a festive occasion. The story turns on the opposition Gallant creates between Mrs. Tracy's tightly defined sense of social order and routine and Madeline's spontaneous and unsettling unhappiness, which momentarily isolates Mrs. Tracy in her determination to see that everyone behaves predictably. Mrs. Tracy's response to this threatening moment, this rupture in her conception of proper reactions to events such as birthdays, is skilfully handled in the most suggestive ending in Gallant's uncollected early fiction. Mrs. Tracy tells her daughter Allie that her summers "have always been so perfect, ever since I was a child"; she then bursts into tears and runs out to the garden, where she makes a gesture toward reestablishing the carefully cultivated order which Madeline has disrupted. As Paul watches from a window, Mrs. Tracy "stopped and bent down to pull three or four bits of wild grass from a flower bed. Then she wiped her eyes with her hands and walked calmly to the house."[24] It is Mrs. Tracy, with her nearly inviolable sense that life is orderly and that people in her house must be happy on their birthdays, who carries the day.

These early stories suggest the scope of some of Gallant's themes and point to the directions which her form will take. Gallant's fiction continues to take as its principal focus the study of refugees, expatriates, and exiles of different kinds and degree, although as she begins to set her stories in postwar Europe, an emerging fiction concerning North American versus European visions of history evolves, elaborated through Gallant's developing exploration of memory's interrupted dialogues with the past.

By the time Gallant's first book of stories, *The Other Paris*, appeared in 1956, Gallant had published eighteen stories, eleven of them in *The New Yorker*, and the outlines of her career as a writer of short fiction were beginning to emerge more clearly. The title story of *The Other Paris* opens up fissures between memory and history, between self's fictions and world's facts, and between Gallant's "North America" and Gallant's "Europe." These ruptures and discontinuities riddle the surface and structure of many of Gallant's stories. In "The Other Paris," her finest and most representative early story, memory flees from history, North America flees from Europe as Carol Frazier finds a postwar Paris that threatens her ahistorical vision. As the narrator of "The Other Paris" makes painfully clear, we must read Carol's resolution of the polarities of her double vision ironically: Carol constructs a romance, a fiction which will allow her to retreat into a comfortably private, privileged selfhood.

Along with this first major expression of the broken dialogue between memory and history in Gallant's fiction, the stories of *The Other Paris* begin to suggest many of Gallant's other major themes. "About Geneva" is a fine early example of a story about the subtle but also savage battles within families, and "Señor Pinedo" is in its way as political a story as those collected in *The Pegnitz Junction*. "The Picnic" is representative of those stories which bring domestic codes of conduct into sharp focus by displacing characters in alien settings, most often in Europe; two other stories, both set in Canada, read almost like reminiscences with light, comic resolutions ("Wing's Chips," "The Deceptions of Marie-Blanche"). Like all of Gallant's fiction, these early stories record a closely observed surface of details, of atmosphere and setting, without shading into forms like the memoir, the documentary, the personal narrative, or the essay.

Most of the narrators of *The Other Paris* are ironic and detached, taking up an objective or a dispassionate stance, framing characters in settings, establishing situations. When first-person narrators remember, they report their memories, rather than reflect on memory's process or meaning. As Gallant's fiction develops, reporters and documentary reports, objective narrators and distanced, ironic narration begin to evolve into more inventive and reflexive structures, implicitly or explicitly raising questions about narrative perspective, narrative truth, the significance of memory, history, and the recreation or recollection of the past.

"The Other Paris" turns on the moment of Carol Frazier's encounter with history in the postwar Paris of the fifties, followed by her retreat into memory's fictions. The narrator invites us to read the story Carol tells herself about Paris as an evasive romanticization, one that will form her "disappointing" experience into a pleasant fiction, a "coherent picture, accurate but untrue."[25] Carol is one of the first of Gallant's characters to suffer the ambiguities of a doubled vision: "The Other Paris" follows the course of Carol's engagement to her American boss, an engagement which has to survive Carol's attempts to bridge the gulf between the possibilities of love in the real postwar Paris and her romantic vision of love in the Paris of her dreams.

Carol, twenty-two, has come to work in Paris and quickly becomes engaged to Howard Mitchell, who is "sober, old enough to know his own mind, and absolutely reliable" (4). A young North American girl abroad, Carol brings to Paris and her engagement an unworldliness nurtured by the "helpful" practicality of classroom talks:

The fact that Carol was not in love with Howard Mitchell did not dismay her in the least. From a series of helpful college lectures on marriage she had learned that a common interest, such as a liking for Irish setters, was the true basis for happiness, and that the illusion of love was a blight imposed by the film industry, and almost entirely responsible for the high rate of divorce. (3–4)

The sharp irony here is directed first at the nonsensically commonsensical worldview which would dispense this kind of practical classroom wisdom; by extension—although already tempered with an allowance for Carol's innocent sincerity—the irony is also directed at her character. The narrator lays bare Carol's naïveté and the contours of the worldview that serves as the cornerstone for Howard's "absolute reliability"; the price that Carol must pay for her distinctively North American brand of determined innocence is the radical separation of the banished "illusion of love" from the precincts of the real Paris, a dull, rainy city which repeatedly disappoints her.

The comic disparity between Carol's romanticized Paris and the Paris she encounters daily provides the simplest of the story's oppositions. On this level, Carol's disappointments are unambiguous: waiting for love to unfold as it properly should, Carol searches for a Paris of "famous parks," "read about" rather than lived in, its men characters in the books of "English lady novelists"; she finds transplanted Coca Cola signs, "men who needed a haircut," and "shabby girls bundled into raincoats" (6–7).

Carol looks and waits for the appropriately romantic (and at the same time comfortably middle-class) environment in which love will naturally blossom: retrospectively (and hypothetically) she "sincerely imagines"—which in this story is closely linked with believing—romantic contexts for romantic events: "If anyone had asked Carol at what precise moment she fell in love, or where Howard Mitchell proposed to her, she would have imagined, quite sincerely, a scene that involved all at once the Seine, moonlight, barrows of violets, acacias in flower, and a confused, misty background of the Eiffel Tower and little crooked streets." (3)

The comedy of Carol's engagement is played out against a background which continually threatens to become foreground—the real postwar Paris, a city in which Parisians themselves are out of time and place. Odile, a secretary in Carol's office, is a representative figure, complaining to Carol over lunch about her family's economic decline since the war; like so many of Gallant's postwar Europeans, Odile "touche[s] on the present only to complain in terms of the past" (8).

Felix, Odile's young lover, completes the quartet. He is closest to Carol in age, but most removed from her by dint of her perception of his status and class.

Unemployed, without working papers, Felix is a product of the massive displacements resulting from the war. He, as much as Odile, is a "typical" postwar Parisian—a refugee. Anticipating her moment of contact with Felix at the end of the story, Carol compares his situation with hers but then "los[es] track" in a passage through which we hear how effectively this narrator's tonal variations can modulate: "She and Felix, then, were closer in age than he was to Odile, or she herself was to Howard. When I was in school, he was in school, she thought. When the war stopped, we were fourteen and fifteen . . . But here she lost track, for where Carol had had a holiday, Felix's parents had been killed." (10) For Felix, for Europe, the war did not simply "stop"; there was no North American "holiday" from the more immediately apparent effects of history.

Carol's fictionalizing—what she imagines, what she reconstructs through memory and will finally believe—must be understood in the double context of what she brings to Paris and what she finds there. The narrator persistently calls our attention to this attempted synthesis of dream world and real world, inviting us to read Carol's kind of storymaking as a process closely linked with the manoeuvres of North American memory reshaping European history. These connections between events and characters' transformations of events into ironic stories form the structure of "The Other Paris," so that its plot becomes a double one.

There are four major events in the story. The story opens at Madame Germaine's; she is fitting Carol for her wedding dress. Looking out the window of the flat, Carol sees a dreary, unpromising spring. The story then cuts away from the narrative present as the narrator fills in the events of the past six months and describes the four principal characters. The second episode takes place the previous Christmas, when Carol had pleaded with Howard to take her to hear the carols sung at Place Vendôme. Predictably, the excursion results in one of Carol's disappointments at the actual event's unromantic nature. Then, near the end of winter, Odile invites Carol and Howard to her sister Martine's recital. Carol is excited at the prospect of finally gaining entrance to her romantic Paris, but again, reality disappoints, and Carol dimly realizes that her conception of Paris and what she actually encounters are in some sense irreconcilable. Returning to the narrative present, we rejoin Carol and Odile, who have just left Madame Germaine's flat. Odile persuades Carol, against her will, to visit Felix, and they walk to Felix's disreputable Left Bank apartment. Carol, ill at ease, is left alone with Felix when Odile unceremoniously falls asleep on the bed. Felix escorts Carol to the Métro, where in a final confrontation they come together briefly and then part for good.

These are the story's four principal events. Their importance in themselves becomes subsumed in their significance as occasions for storytelling, or as the factual bases for stories, or as theatres, stages for the melodramatic collision of two spectacles. This set of oppositions between events and their recreations pro-

vides an important context within which to read the story, a context which
meshes with the set of oppositions between the real Paris and Carol's moonlit
fantasies.

The opening scene provides Odile with an occasion to tell the dressmaker the
story of Carol's engagement to Howard. Carol herself is detached; there is "evidently no conversation to be had" with her (2). Odile's exchange with the
dressmaker is a melodramatic excerpt from a modern fairy-tale:

> "Just imagine! Miss Frazier came to Paris to work last autumn, and fell
> in love with the head of her department."
> "Non!" Madame Germaine recoiled, as if no other client had ever
> brought off such an extraordinary thing.
> "Fell in love with Mr. Mitchell," said Odile, nodding. "At first sight, *le
> coup de foudre.*"
> "At first sight?" said the dressmaker. She looked fondly at Carol.
> "Something no one would have expected," said Odile. "Although Mr.
> Mitchell is charming. *Charming.*"
> "I think we ought to go," said Carol. (2)

Odile mildly protests as they walk away ("I didn't say anything that wasn't
true . . . it's such a wonderful story. . . . It was terribly romantic" [2–3]); but "it
penetrated at last that Odile was making fun of her" (3). Carol finds Odile's
"slight irony" perplexing, as she should. Carol is the subject of a story which
Odile is narrating to Madame Germaine. The exchange between Odile and
Madame Germaine mirrors the structure of the larger story, in which a narrator
skilled in the uses of irony is describing Carol to readers who are being invited to
interpret her actions and her character in order to understand the story. Odile
modulates the narrator's sharper ironies; her minor-key variations on the major
theme begin the process of teaching us to read the larger story in which she herself takes a part.

The next "story" has more complex implications. Carol goes to the carol
singing at the Place Vendôme hoping to find the raw content for a "warm
memory": "Here, she imagined, with the gentle fall of the snow and the small,
rosy choirboys singing between lighted Christmas trees, she would find something—a warm memory that would, later, bring her closer to Howard, a glimpse
of the Paris other people liked" (11–12).

But instead of snow there is rain; the singers are "testing voice levels for a
broadcast," and the whole scene is an empty media event. Carol and Howard go
on to finish the evening with friends, for whom Howard "made an amusing
story out of their adventure in the Place Vendôme" (13). In one of the story's
crucial moments, the narrator describes Carol's insight upon hearing Howard's
version of their misadventure:

She realized for the first time that something could be perfectly accurate but untruthful—they had not found any part of that evening funny—and that this might cover more areas of experience than the occasional amusing story. She looked at Howard thoughtfully, as if she had learned something of value. (13)

Carol *has* learned something of value; Howard makes an uncomfortable experience into an amusing story. Carol will soon begin to recreate her final, most troubling encounter with Felix—and more generally, her whole experience of Paris and her engagement—into a warm and coherent fiction.

The implications of these continuing references to storytelling and storymaking for the construction of the plot are significant. Discussing the plot of Joyce's "Eveline," Jonathan Culler speaks of identifying a "kernel" of plot and then awaiting a "structurally more important kernel"; in "Eveline," he suggests, the first kernel is "musing": " . . . we know that musing itself will not found a story but must be related to a central problem, decision or action on which the character is musing."[26] In "The Other Paris," the central problem or decision Carol is contemplating is two-fold. On one level, she must decide whether to continue with her engagement or to break it off. The narrator alludes to this decision directly following Carol's central "insight": "Temporarily, she put the question of falling in love to one side. Paris was not the place, she thought; perhaps it had been, fifty years ago, or whenever it was that people wrote all the songs. It did not occur to her to break her engagement" (13). We read the story on this level to answer the question of whether or not she will finally break off the engagement; but because of the stories created *around* this plotline, we read with increasing curiosity on another level. The central enigma becomes the question of how Carol will apply her lesson—how and if she will follow Odile's and Howard's leads in making stories. Culler suggests that "the goals towards which one moves in synthesizing a plot are, of course, notions of thematic structure";[27] when we articulate the plot of "The Other Paris," we construct a theme which has as much to do with the course of Carol's engagement as with its attendant transformations into the stories about Carol's engagement.

Before Carol's final encounter with Felix, Gallant interposes Martine's recital, an important scene on several counts. In this set piece, spaced off from the rest of the text to indicate its dramatic (and melodramatic) significance, two levels of make-believe clash in an "ordinary, shabby theatre," while outside the rain comes down as ever. Carol's fantasies about the concert and its *cachet,* of course, are shattered. Here as elsewhere, Parisians, like the theatre itself, are "shabby" (17). At this point, Carol has not yet fully grasped the art of making amusing stories out of disappointing experiences. Instead, she compensates for her growing disillusionment with a fantasy of her own to counter the thin spectacle of Martine's recital. But the symbolic collapse of the theatre itself intrudes upon her fantasy:

> She settled back and began furnishing in her mind the apartment they would have in Chicago.... Carol had just finished papering a bedroom green and white when Martine walked onstage, with her violin. At the same moment, a piece of plaster bearing the painted plump foot of a nymph detached itself from the ceiling and crashed into the aisle, just missing Howard's head. (16)

The cultural furnishings that are the settings for Martine's aspirations are crumbling like the statuary, relics of a past that has suddenly become as remote as the age of plump plaster nymphs or of "J. S. Bach," the name on a poster in the empty lobby. Martine and her family, like Carol, are playing roles in a rundown theatre; the play of Carol's mental closet drama against the shambles of Martine's recital shows them both up as inadequate dramas, private theatres from the past or the projected future.

This midwinter retrospective, narrated between the two scenes at the dressmaker's, fills in our understanding of Carol and Odile, so that when they emerge from the dressmaker's, they come out as more substantial figures than they were one moment (and twelve pages) earlier. So it is not incongruous that as she looks out the window, Carol sees no sign of spring, and yet a moment later she agrees with Odile that winter is finally over. Indeed, the whole final scene is charged with significance which has accrued from intervening episodes. Nuances of description and dialogue recall earlier descriptions, earlier dialogue. The setting of Carol's "sincerely imagined" proposal scene, for example, "a scene that involved all at once the Seine, moonlight, barrows of violets . . . and a confused, misty background of the Eiffel Tower and little crooked streets," ironically recalls the description of the neighbourhood Felix lives in, which Carol "did not like the look of": "They crossed the boulevard and a few crooked, narrow streets filled with curbside barrows and marketing crowds. It was a section of Paris Carol had not seen; although it was on the Left Bank, it was not pretty, not picturesque" (22).

What is picturesque in her imagination makes Carol uncomfortable when she finds its antithesis in the world. Appropriately, it is Felix's neighbourhood that most closely resembles Carol's picture-postcard Paris, just as it is Felix who comes closest to touching Carol. Here as elsewhere, descriptions of setting recall earlier settings: by ironically realizing one of Carol's "sincerely believed" visions, Gallant shows us the process Carol undergoes of successfully avoiding an education. We read of Carol's discomfort in Felix's dingy room, her "breathless . . . embarrassment" when it becomes clear to her that Felix and Odile are lovers; immediately we recall the earlier observation that "indeed, Carol rated the chances of love in a cottage or furnished room at zero" (4).

Now all of the earlier suggestions of relationship between Carol and Felix converge, and the inappropriateness of her engagement to Howard resurfaces as she reflects on the incompatibility of Felix and Odile. It is too much for Carol to believe that love can be a reality for this pair in this "slummy quarter." Standing with Felix at the entrance to the Métro, she experiences a fleeting sense "that she had at last opened the right door" as she holds Felix's hand; but at once she responds by withdrawing, correcting her intuition, and responding to Felix "with cold shyness" in the idiom she has learned from Howard:

> What she and Howard had was better. No one could point to them, or criticize them, or humiliate them by offering to help.
> She withdrew her hand and said with cold shyness, "Thank you for the coffee, Felix."
> "Oh that." He watched her go up the steps to the Métro, and then he walked away. (29)

Carol's antiseptic politeness to Felix sterilizes the immediate sting of the present—so much so that she sees herself "in a little scene," with "the gentle, nostalgic air of something past," making disquieting experience into sentimental fiction on the spot (29). Her warm memories of Paris will soon blur the sharp contours of her "disappointments": "Soon, she sensed, the comforting vision of Paris as she had once imagined it would overlap the reality" (30). The story's closing passage, with its echoes of Howard's "perfectly accurate but untruthful" storymaking, ironically resolves the tensions set up in this story between historical reality and historical romance, between painfully fragmented experience and reassuringly coherent fiction:

> She would forget the rain and her unshared confusion and loneliness, and remember instead the Paris of films, the street lamps with their tinsel icicles, the funny concert hall where the ceiling collapsed, and there would be, at last, a coherent picture, accurate but untrue. The memory of Felix and Odile and all their distasteful strangeness would slip away; for "love" she would think, once more, "Paris," and, after a while, happily married, mercifully removed in time, she would remember it and describe it and finally believe it as it had never been at all. (30)

The deliberate, mesmerizing phrasing reveals the process of Carol's soothing and lulling and smoothing away the harshness of her experience, transforming it into the faithful recitation of a vague, comforting memory—a memory which will be perfectly inaccurate to experience, perfectly true to Carol's fondly held vision. For Carol, the agency of memory imposes form and so creates order and meaning, but ironically, the "meaning" she creates denies history—denies the reality of postwar Paris, of "Felix" and Odile. Much like a writer recreating the past, Carol forms a coherent story out of incoherent experience, but she does so by suppressing history—her own and the world's—in order to make memory a more comfortable home. One might describe the writer's recreation of the past—a process which Linnet Muir explores as one of the major themes of her stories—as an art which loosely follows the sequence of Carol's "art": first the writer remembers "it" (remembers a subject, content, event, experience, sensation); then the writer describes (shapes, forms, structures, patterns—turns these nouns into verbs, turns static "content" into motioning form), and finally believes (the result of "sincerely imagining"). But Carol forms her story as an evasion, a retreat, and she is judged accordingly throughout "The Other Paris."

The strength of "The Other Paris" emerges in part from its near-documentary presentation of postwar Paris and its social, political, cultural, and historical climate. These cultural qualities inhere in tangible descriptions of shabbily-dressed Parisians, of gloomy restaurants, theatres, and apartments, and of course of the perpetual drizzle, which is so pervasive that it begins to seem figurative. These aspects of setting form the background and the foreground for Carol's trials; the story's strengths as realist fiction are complemented by its reflexive qualities, which begin with the attention paid to characters' stories about Carol's engagement and end with the sharply ironic focus on Carol's story-making memory. In "The Other Paris," memory is the means through which Carol transforms potentially educative experience into a lullaby. In this sense, the story is an account of an ambiguous initiation, one which is also a retreat—a recurring theme in Gallant's fiction.

The conflict between documentary versions and romantic visions is not always as sharp as it is in "The Other Paris." In several early Gallant stories, narrators transcribe settings without explicit reference to the shaping process of memory or of imagination. Artifice is muted, more conspicuous in its apparent absence. The shaping of actuality goes unnoticed—so much so that Gallant's editors and bibliographers disagree over whether or not these stories are more properly essays and discuss the close relation between the two forms in Gallant's work. The mediating, forming, reflexive patterns of artifice shape content into form—ironically—before our eyes in the stories within "The Other Paris"; this shaping process is less apparent in stories like "Wing's Chips" (1954), "The Deceptions of Marie-Blanche" (1953), "Señor Pinedo" (1954), and "When We Were Nearly Young" (1960). These stories, in which a first-person narrator remembers without commenting on the shaping force of memory, are at the transcriptive, documentary edge of Gallant's fictional world, with a straightforward, chronological narrative line and a narrator at once detached enough to observe and engaged enough to comment on social rituals in their settings.

"The Deceptions of Marie-Blanche" and "Wing's Chips" are set in Quebec, the former in East-end Montreal, the latter in an unnamed French-Canadian town where the narrator spent a summer with her father when she was a little girl. Both stories open by at once locating the setting and distancing the narrator from her report on the past. The narrator then reintroduces herself into the past as she remembers it; in "The Deceptions of Marie-Blanche" she never becomes more than a detached (if amused) observer, but in "Wing's Chips" she merges with her younger predecessor to become her father's young daughter once again. Unlike "The Other Paris" or the Linnet Muir stories, in which the process of remembering is explicitly part of the stories' theme, a subject to be explored even while it is the central technique employed to tell the story, the device of conflating an older narrator with her younger self in "Wing's Chips" is left largely unexamined; it is simply a convention used to enter the story proper. Nevertheless, we can see the typical Gallant concern with memory in the opening sentences:

> Often, since I grew up, I have tried to remember the name of the French-Canadian town where I lived for a summer with my father when I was a little girl of seven or eight. Sometimes, passing through a town, I have thought I recognized it, but some detail is always wrong, or at least fails to fit the picture in my memory.[28]

The narrator then quickly shifts from her momentary focus on the process of memory to address the more explicitly social themes of "Wing's Chips": the divisions between French Catholics and English Protestants in the small town, and the universal misunderstanding and distrust of her father, a painter, who as such is suspect, less than gainfully employed, less dutifully a breadwinner than he should be by rights. The story neatly and comically resolves, for French and English alike, the perceived conflict between profitable labour and esoteric foolishness, and at the same time reassures the daughter of her father's worth: the Wing family, Chinese owners of the local fish-and-chip store, commission her father to paint the sign from which the story takes its title. Gallant approaches the conflict in this story lightheartedly, from the outside, from the social point of view. The daughter-narrator stands at a point between her father's private world and the villagers' public one, seeing him both as a family member and through the villagers' eyes. The sharp-eyed older narrator's cutting social commentary, as she dissects the villagers' prejudices and social pretensions, is softened by the story's comic resolution, which reconciles the demands of the working world with the demands of art by interposing a commercial painting. Social commentary occupies the foreground; the story's strength lies in its report on a society in its setting, rather than in its development of character or motivation.

"The Deceptions of Marie-Blanche" is another good early example of Gallant's powers as a documentary realist. The first-person narrator remains detached throughout; she begins the story in her own present, identifying herself as an observer, placing herself in the context of the story she is about to tell, and advertising her amused detachment:

> Marie-Blanche wrote from Canada a few days ago to say that she was engaged again. . . .
> The reminder of her engagement is, for me, only a reminder of her deceptions. When I lived with Marie-Blanche and her mother in Montreal during the war, I saw the rise and fall of three love affairs in a very short time. Marie-Blanche is deception-prone the way some people keep bumping their heads or spraining their ankles.[29]

The narrator, an English Protestant in a French Catholic household, observes and reports on Marie-Blanche's repeated ritual of engagement and disengagement as suitor after suitor retracts his vows following a closely-supervised courtship. The Dumard apartment is on a street where "a French-Canadian parish merged with a Jewish district, full of kosher meat-markets and dingy shops" (126). The delightful mix of idioms which Marie-Blanche has at her command—a "singular kind of English, with a French-Canadian accent and a Yiddish lilt"—prepares for the story's ending: Marie-Blanche dismisses her latest suitor, a farmer more in love with his horse, Victorine, than with her, by handing him his snapshots of his horse and "addressing him in her perfect English . . . 'To heach 'is own, Monsieur Dancereau'" (140). Her mother invokes the traditional dismissal, a chorus repeated throughout the story (*"Il a un grand défaut"*), but Marie-Blanche cuts her off with multicultural asperity: "Défaut be damned. . . . He's just like the rest of them, nothing but a big schlemiel" (140).

The plot of the story consists of Marie-Blanche's deceptions, chronologically recounted; character development is confined to comically revealing details of appearance (Marie-Blanche, for example, emulates Shirley Temple), and the narrator herself, unnamed, draws little attention to her own interest in or involvement with the story she tells. She remains an observer, a boarder who enters a little way into the Dumards' lives and comments from the double perspective, focussing both on the larger social milieu which Marie-Blanche's suitors belong to and on the particular society of the French-Canadian family she lives with.

"Señor Pinedo" and "When We Were Nearly Young," stories which report on social and political environment abroad, reveal Gallant's early and sustained fascination with foreign cultures, the corollary of her sharp curiosity about her own. As is the case with "The Deceptions of Marie-Blanche," the narrator of

"Señor Pinedo" is an astute observer, both detached from and engaged with the society she observes. The opening locates the narrator at a point nicely balanced between public and private settings: "Because there was nothing to separate our rooms but the thinnest of partitions, it sometimes seemed as if the Pinedos—Señor, Señora, and baby José Maria—and I were really living to-gether."[30] The narrator's reports on the Pinedo family's private conversations balance with her commentary on the Pinedos in the context of the larger com-munity of the *pension*. She scrutinizes the various interiors of the *pension*—the communal dining room, the faded sepia etching of Franco in the entrance hall—reporting on furnishings in sharp and revealing detail, setting the Pinedo family and the other boarders among tangible artifacts which, like the Dumards' furnishings, communicate a cultural code more explicitly than more direct (and so more abstract) social commentary. At the same time, she describes the sensibility of the Spanish community as a crowd gathers in the *pension* court-yard to watch over the victim of an accident. The description prepares for the story's closing analysis of the Spanish temperament:

> The courtyard suddenly resembled the arena of a bull ring. There was the same harsh division of light and shadow, as if a line had been drawn, high on the opposite wall. The faces within the area of sun were white and ex-pressionless, with that curious Oriental blankness that sometimes envelops the whole arena during moments of greatest emotion. (213)

Señor Pinedo's portrait is double. He is a "Spanish husband and father, and his word, by tradition, was law" (202); but he is also a civil servant—for him, his most important identity—a patriot who volunteered at seventeen to fight with the Whites, a passionately politicized figure who distributes government pamphlets around the *pension* dinner table. In his double role as loving father and blindly committed servant of the state, Pinedo embodies the story's central irony: when a neighbour's child is crushed by an elevator's block-and-tackle as-sembly, Pinedo, in his happiest moment, proclaims to the gathered crowd that their child will qualify for a pension: "'I guarantee it!' Señor Pinedo said. He leaned over the railing and closed his fist like an orator, a leader. . . . 'I guarantee it . . . I work in the office of pensions'" (216). The narrator draws attention to technocrat Pinedo's "childlike" faith in his adopted political cause as she eaves-drops on his conversation with his wife following the accident. Finally, she presents Pinedo in public again, so that the story ends with his double portrait exposed in succession. Through Pinedo, the narrator evokes a national tempera-ment in its individual incarnation; her closing suggestion of the turmoil beneath the tenants' silent surface calm confirms her own observer's status and her un-easiness as witness to a spectacle at once intensely personal and intensely politi-cal:

Through the partition I heard him telling his wife that he had much to do that week, a social project connected with the hurt child. In his happiness, he sounded almost childlike himself, convinced, as he must convince others, of the truth and good faith of the movement to which he had devoted his life and in which he must continue to believe.

Later, I heard him repeating the same thing to the *pension* tenants. . . . There was no reply. . . . I could not have said whether the silence was owing to respect, delight, apathy, or a sudden fury of some other emotion so great that only silence could contain it. (216)

This closing shows the narrator's insight into the essential volatility of the Spanish character under Franco, a volatility masked by an ambiguous silence and by rigidly observed social decorum. When Pinedo proclaims his childlike reverence for the patriarchal state to his fellow boarders, they are, if not equally reverent, politic enough to seem properly deferential. Gallant brings the narrator's double perspective to a point in the description of Pinedo's reaction to the accident, a description which allows her to move effectively from particular incident to general cultural sensibility. "Señor Pinedo" is a fine early example of Gallant's power to communicate an acutely familiar sense of foreign conduct, public and private, in foreign settings— not only to report in detail on this conduct, but also to point to its significances in terms of a culture's history. The faded sepia etching of Franco in this story is a case in point, as it evokes the continuing (if faded) presence of Franco in the Spain of the early fifties, the complex and ambiguous Spanish attitude towards authority, and the lingering spectre of the Spanish Civil War. "Señor Pinedo," with its critique of the political impulse governing even Pinedo's private conduct, anticipates the wider-ranging analysis and critique of fascism's "small possibilities in people" in *The Pegnitz Junction*.

"When We Were Nearly Young," also set in Madrid, returns briefly to a *pension* similar to the one in "Señor Pinedo," but passes it over quickly because the main focus is on the companionship between four "nearly young" people, three Spaniards and the North American first-person narrator. Again, the narrator is both outsider and insider; the four friends' common denominator is their shared poverty, while what finally differentiates them is the narrator's status as a foreigner, free to leave Madrid forever when her long-awaited money from home arrives. The story transcends good journalism, transforming report into representation; even in this, arguably one of the flattest of Gallant's stories, the typical concern with memory's apprehension of time past is broached in the closing paragraph: "I don't know what became of them, or what they were like when their thirtieth year came. . . . Eventually they were caught, for me, not by time but by the freezing of memory. And when I looked in the diary I had kept during that period all I could find was descriptions of the weather."[31]

If memory can create warm and coherent pictures to comfort Carol Frazier, it can also freeze into cold fact. This narrator, more than Linnet Muir, speaks in the casual, anecdotal tone of the informal memoir, a tone sharpened by Linnet's more urgent demands for coherence and instruction from *her* memory. The narrator of "When We Were Nearly Young" also raises the issue of the connections between autobiography, fiction, and "true" memory, an explicit concern in the Linnet Muir stories and an implicit concern in many others.

Although none of the remaining stories in *The Other Paris* is as powerful as the title story, taken together they complement "The Other Paris" by depicting a linked series of dissociations between past and present. Six of the seven remaining stories are set in Europe; one, "The Legacy," is set in Montreal. The focus in these stories ranges from the light thrown on the cultural, political, and historical rifts opened up across the postwar European landscape—rifts only dimly perceived, at a remove, by North Americans—to explorations of the rifts between generations, particularly of the gaps in communication between children and adults. At one extreme, a story like "The Picnic" (1952—originally entitled "Before the Battle") comically reports on the mannered dance of an American army family in postwar France, anxious to please their French landlady and their host country at a bicultural picnic the American brass has planned for "the most typically French town" they can find.[32] At the other end of the book's range, "About Geneva" (1955) is Gallant's finest and most representative early story about the impasses between children and adults. "About Geneva" demonstrates how Gallant can use a more muted irony to less comic ends: the "interrupted dialogues of the deaf" in Gallant's families constitute private analogues to the broken dialogues between memory and history and across continents.[33] In "About Geneva," this separation is imagined as the distance between adults' reports and children's inventions, between adults' demands for reliable witnesses and children's needs for imaginative reconstructions.

The family of "About Geneva" fights small-scale battles in which combatants speak to each other by accident, in between orders and refusals, retorts and subterfuges. The reports of the two children to their mother "about" Geneva comment more directly on the emotional politics of the family than on Geneva itself. Like so many other Gallant stories about children and adults, "About Geneva" sets children's fantasies, children's dreams and inventions, over against parents' codes and rules. Just as the shape of Carol Frazier's "other" Paris points to the implications of her storymaking, the various "crystallizations" of Geneva in this story invite readers to consider the dramatic tensions created by the family structure as both children and adults manoeuvre toward revealing or concealing themselves through various stratagems.[34]

Dramatically compressed into a small space and a brief time, "About Geneva" reads like a short one-act play. Its setting is claustrophobic—a "standard seasonal Nice *meublé*," the sitting room "hung with dark engravings of cathedrals" (191). The rented flat is "Granny's" winter retreat, shared with her recently divorced daughter and her two children. The children have just returned from their first visit with their father and his new lover in Geneva. Only the children, Colin and Ursula, are named: the important designations for adults in this story are their relations to each other within the family hierarchy—"father," "mother," "Granny"—positions of power in a corporate structure rather than names which confer more subjective identities. Granny's power over her three charges is evident from the opening lines: "Granny was waiting at the door of the apartment. She looked small, lonely, and patient, and at the sight of her the children and their mother felt instantly guilty" (190). The tensions in this family create a drama verging on both trauma and melodrama: Granny's old-world propriety clashes comically with her grandchildren's conduct, and the mother, who "at thirty-four, had settled into a permanent, anxious-looking, semi-youthfulness," transmits these tensions both ways (192).

The essentially private nature of Granny's theatre announces itself in the performance with which she welcomes her children home:

> "Darlings," said Granny, very low. "Home again." She stretched out her arms to Ursula, but then, seeing the taxi driver, who had carried the children's bags up the stairs, she drew back. After he had gone she repeated the gesture, turning this time to Colin, as if Ursula's cue had been irrevocably missed. (190)

As in "The Other Paris," details of language refer us to larger structures of meaning. Granny's quite clinical concern for her grandchildren shows through the empty theatricality of her "repeated gestures" and her assigning of "cues," as well as in the precise impersonality of the verbs used to describe her actions. She dramatically laments Colin's haircut, which has shorn him of his childhood; "releasing" him, she continues to complain to his mother. Her manner of teaching proper posture to Ursula is to "nicely cause" her to sit correctly: "She slumped on her spine (a habit Granny had just nicely caused her to get over before the departure to Geneva)" (193). Granny's manipulative control "just nicely causes" many of the tensions which organize the dramas of revelation and concealment over which she presides.

The main text of the drama, a text which her daughter has warned Granny not to announce openly, examines the children's reactions to their father's new relationship in Geneva. The subtext, which, because of the adults' purposefully indirect approach to their real interest, appears to be the main focus of the story, is first articulated through a bland and indirect ploy: "'Did you go boating, Ursula?' said Granny, not counting this as a direct question. 'When I visited Geneva, as a girl, we went boating on the lake.' She went on about white water birds, a parasol, a boat heaped with colored cushions" (192).

Thus begins one line of this family's "dialogue of the deaf," characteristic of the communication within families in Gallant's fiction. Granny "goes on" about a remote past, foreign to her grandchildren's experience. Her memory apparently does nothing to clear the air for a frank discussion of the visit; actually, however, subtext does comment on text, and the children *do* communicate something through their accounts "about" Geneva. Geneva's appearance announces several realities—the children's transformations as they begin to conceive identities which "name" them, transcending their status as members of a family, the implied details of their father's new life, and the mother's failure to understand why her husband has gone.

Ursula carries on the dialogue initiated by Granny's gambit by spontaneously crossing texts to proclaim that her father's lover is "not a good manager" (193). But after reporting this information to her very attentive adult audience, she crosses languages again to announce a more important revelation: Geneva is the place in which she has begun to write a play, encouraged by the Geneva adults. She quotes one line to her Nice audience: "'The Grand Duke enters and sees Tatiana all in gold'" (194). The Geneva adults have told her "it was the best thing they'd ever heard anywhere"; but although the women are gratified that Ursula appears to have inherited her father's imagination, apparently they have no real regard for its fictions. Again, details of language reinforce the sense of the mother's general distrust of imagination. "'It's lovely dear'. . . . 'It sounds like a lovely play'," she says; "'Were they lovely, the swans?'" she asks Colin after he has announced his image of Geneva (195, 198).

Colin's version of Geneva is more painterly than narrative, more an image than the temporal seed of a story. In response to Granny's question about his walks in Geneva, Colin remembers:

"I fed the swans," Colin suddenly shouted.
There, he had told about Geneva. He sat up and kicked his heels on the carpet as if the noise would drown out the consequence of what he had revealed. As he said it, the image became static: a gray sky, a gray lake, and a swan wonderfully turning upside down with the black rubber feet showing above the water. His father was not in the picture at all: neither was *she*. But Geneva was fixed for the rest of his life: gray, lake, swan. (196)

The swan at the centre of Colin's image is magically, memorably a swan at the moment of its transformation into an imagined swan, "wonderful" in its modality. Colin purposefully, emphatically edits out the Geneva adults: *they* will not interfere with the purposeful magic of selective memory. He will simply refuse to record his father's new relationship. Just as "gray, lake, swan" has fixed Geneva for Colin, Ursula, the mother thinks, "was too preoccupied with herself. Everything about the trip, in the end, would crystallize around Tatiana and the Grand Duke. Already, Ursula was Tatiana" (196). Because the children both have their own indirect revelations to create and convey, neither child can tell the mother anything she wants to know about her failed relationship. The children's creations and recollections are for themselves, revelatory of their own needs. They are too self-referential to serve their mother's needs for explanations, turning back towards their creators as much as opening out into the world: Ursula's romantic vision, for example, is almost totally self-centred, so that the creating, subjective self becomes its own sentimental object: "Ever since she had started 'The Grand Duke' she could not think of her own person without being sorry. For no reason at all, now, her eyes filled with tears of self-pity" (195).

The line between fictionalizing and lying, the narrator of this story suggests, is difficult for adults to draw; Granny and her daughter cannot distinguish one from the other. In Gallant's stories, "invention" is a term which signifies lying or imagining, depending on the context:

> Having delivered his secret he had nothing more to tell. He began to invent. "I was sick on the plane," he said, but Ursula at once said this was a lie, and he lay down again, humiliated. . . .
>
> "He never once cried in Geneva," Ursula said. But by the one simple act of creating Tatiana and the Grand Duke, she had removed herself from the ranks of reliable witnesses. (196–97)

If Ursula can write a play, then she cannot be relied upon to tell the literal truth about anything. The adults cannot reconcile dreaming and witnessing, literary and literal truth, although Ursula shows she is capable of both. The mother realizes, too, that Colin is another unreliable narrator, another separate keeper of secrets. She cannot even decide whether or not Colin was actually sick on the plane; Granny, over Ursula's protestations to the contrary, asserts that he was: "'That, at least, is a fact'" (198). The mother is left looking for reliable witnesses, unable to enter into the spirit of her children's visions. She wants Colin to make a story out of his static image, a narrative beginning with "the lake, the boats, the swan" and ending with "why her husband left her" (198).

The children's distillations of Geneva function similarly to Carol's fond vision of Paris. Carol's vision refracts postwar Paris into a city which, given time and her removal to her North American marriage, will conform once again to her dream city; in "About Geneva," the children respond to the adults' conflicting demands by "crystallizing" Geneva, sidestepping their mother's demand that they be witnesses, stolid statisticians of experience. Finally, "About Geneva" explores the insecurity and compensatory imaginative lives of the two children, as well as the loneliness and anxiety of their mother, a woman whose interior life has been hollowed out by the theatrics of propriety—propriety without much of a subtext, appearance without very much reality.

The twelve stories of *The Other Paris* established early in Gallant's career her talent for evoking a tangible cultural surround through meticulous attention to detail. In these stories, the concise descriptions of the interiors of apartments, of *pensions,* kitchens, dining rooms, hallways, balconies, create a sense of culture which seems to inhere in tangible things, in artifacts of various kinds, so that culture itself begins to seem tangible, taking substance from its association with a carefully recreated material world. The concrete in these stories is always evocative—the more concrete, the more evocative.

Less remarkable than the attention to detail is the treatment of narration and character. Because the narrators of *The Other Paris* are typically carefully distanced from the characters they develop, and because irony exerts such sharp control over readers' perceptions of characters and their situations, there is a tendency in these stories for narrative structure to overdetermine character, to seem to trap characters in narration. Later Gallant stories allow characters a greater measure of freedom; in the stories of her next book, *My Heart Is Broken* (1964), the observant but detached narrator's eye typical of *The Other Paris* evolves into a more reflective eye as Gallant's first-person narrators begin to speculate about their manner of seeing, and characters' memories become subjects as much as objects, recreations as much as recollections.

"The Other Paris," the most important and engaging story in this first book, outlines a vision of postwar European history as it is misapprehended by the North American imagination. The implications of this misapprehension will be more fully developed in later stories, and history, which will manifest itself as a more pervasive and unsettling presence, will not be so easily put out of mind through memory's artful evasions. Memory, too, will be made to bear more vigilant witness to its own duplicitous nature in later stories. But "The Other Paris," with its telling critique of a culture's wilful naïveté in the face of its own recent history, marks the beginning of the career of a major writer.

2

My Heart Is Broken
Ghosts in Memory's Mirrors,
Heartbreak in Memory's Voice

In the stories of *My Heart Is Broken* (1964), memory more ambiguously engages more complex characters in increasingly fissured relations with the past. Showing that the processes through which memory asserts its truths are always significant, these stories invite readers to consider inventions, recollections, and recreations of the past by attending to the forms of the stories Gallant's narrators tell. Because of this emphasis upon the modes through which memory makes meaning, the stories also invite readers to discern characters as frames or forms, as manners or idioms of perception. The narrators of *My Heart Is Broken* invite us to look carefully at the well-formed, neatly framed "tableaux" they present to us with such measured but matter-of-fact precision;[1] they also invite us to consider the silences surrounding their declarations of "heartbreak," declarations which often go unheard.

The form of these stories instructs readers most directly through the manners in which characters remember or forget. In *My Heart Is Broken,* the recurring concern with returns to the past, or with banishment from the past, calls attention to both the act and the art of remembering, which is a central theme in the short novel "Its Image on the Mirror" and in the closely linked story, "The Cost of Living."[2] Both first-person narrators learn that the "ghost" of self can be banished or evoked—within a relationship, within a family, within history— depending upon the forms through which memory records, reorders, or remakes the past. Whether this "ghost" emerges or recedes is also determined by the kinds of impasses which arise when characters' voices are greeted with silence: first-person cries of "heartbreak," like Jeannie's at the end of the title story, often go unheard in a society of deaf, would-be auditors. These breaks in dialogue make *My Heart Is Broken* a bleaker assembly of stories than those of

The Other Paris because there are fewer resolutions, ironic or otherwise, to characters' dilemmas. These characters are not allowed, as Carol Frazier is allowed, to take refuge in comfortably private fictions, seemingly free from history. Instead, the characters of *My Heart Is Broken* are painfully conscious and self-conscious, so that the only change possible in these stories is a change, rarely realized, in characters' manners of perception—a change in form.

In her introduction to *Home Truths,* Gallant writes that "fiction, like painting, consists of entirely more than meets the eye; otherwise it is not worth a second's consideration."[3] What meets the eye in "Its Image on the Mirror," the short novel published for the first time in *My Heart Is Broken,* is a series of framed portraits. Jean Price, the first-person narrator, presents readers with mirror images of characters and scenes, flat portraits which she transcribes with scrupulous objectivity, as if she were transcribing from memory.[4] But in the course of telling her story, Jean learns to explore what she mimetically represents; she remembers in precise, vivid detail, but at the same time she begins to announce and explore memory's distortions. In this process, she becomes, like her memories, "more than meets the eye," evolving from an objective reporter into a subjective explorer as her distanced, ghostless images resolve into more immediate, more ghostly figures.

One dimension of this opposition between mimetic, objective representation (an act of reporting) and subjective, engaged exploration (an art of recreating) is suggested in the verse fragment from a Yeats drama which prefaces the novel and gives it its title:

> What is love itself,
> Even though it be the lightest of light love,
> But dreams that hurry from beyond the world
> To make low laughter more than meat and drink,
> Though it but set us sighing? Fellow wanderer,
> Could we but mix ourselves into a dream
> Not in its image on the mirror![5]

For Jean, as for many Gallant characters, love is a secret kept by other people, a secret hinted at in the timbre of a voice, in the "sound of low laughter." Longing with Yeats's speaker to "mix herself" into a substantial dream rather than simply to stare at its reflection, Jean seeks to evoke the "ghostly" human imagination pervading (or announced as absent from) her flat mirror images. The figures Gallant opens her stories with often watch themselves, as does Jean, and see selfless reflections in mirrors, just as they "watch" their memories, seeing framed tableaus.[6] Because Jean separates subjects from objects, ghosts from images, her private memories from social history, form from content, first from third person, she is forced to seek out love as if it were hidden, a secret, to look everywhere for a reality hiding behind an appearance. But the relation between appearance and reality, Jean finds, is not so simple an opposition. Like Puss, the first-person narrator of "The Cost of Living," Jean remembers portraits in order to begin articulating herself to herself. She discovers that she must live with ghosts *and* mirrors, subjects *and* objects, within memory *and* history.

"Its Image on the Mirror," however, does not simply trace the paths of Jean's introspective progress. Jean's memories, like those of many Gallant characters, become a reflection of the broader image of recent Western history as wartime Montreal dramatically breaks in on Jean's reflections while she waits for the return of her husband Tom, who is overseas, and then learns of her brother Frank's death. Jean's final account of herself is of one who has "survived," awoken from a private dream, waiting for the war to end, finishing the story of her memories as if she had become a realist wakened from her own romance.

"Its Image on the Mirror" is both a report and a confession. Jean reports her memories as confessions: through changes in the way she calls up the past, changes which we see reflected in the changing patterns of her memories, she comes to a fuller way of making sense of herself and of history, by assimilating memory as experience rather than reporting on it as if its meanings resided within a frame. Jean is tantalized by her younger and more attractive sister Isobel, who, Jean imagines, possesses the secret of love. On one level, Jean's story is a report on her attempts to gain entrance into her sister's world. She succeeds at last, but only to discover that her representations of her sister, her portraits and reports, do not describe the figure she finally encounters. Jean is the eldest of three children, the one who falls most under the influence of her parents; the prevailing structural image of her family is the reassuring reflection of one generation in the mirror of another generation's conduct. As Jean reports on various family portraits, pictures she remembers vividly and transcribes exactly, she begins to change her language to render the changing significance of her memories; she adopts a different grammar, one that allows her to show her transformation from reporter into "survivor."

Jean's memories are arranged diachronically to show their relative importance as she begins deconstructing them in order to reconstruct her life.[7] She remembers her own and her siblings' childhoods and adolescences in Allenton, a town in Quebec near the Vermont border, and she recalls Isobel's and her own departure to take wartime jobs in Montreal. She remembers her marriage to Tom Price, after Isobel turns him down; Isobel's marriage at eighteen to her first husband, the "bumptious, the unspeakable" Davy Sullivan, and her wartime affair in Montreal with Alec Campbell, a failed poet turned schoolmaster (61); she recalls Isobel nearly dying of a kidney disease and then tricking the family by recovering. She reports on her sister's clandestine second marriage to Alfredo, a Venezuelan doctor; on her brother Frank's enlisting and going overseas, and his marriage to Enid; and on his death in England in an accident. Finally, she records the impact of Frank's death on the family, remembering her return with Isobel from Montreal to Allenton. Remembering their encounter in the family house, an encounter she records in the last of the novel's seven sections, Jean perceives for the first time the patterns of her life within the family and, beyond it, the larger, broken patterns of history, of life during the war. Jean interweaves these patterns of memory—of private life bound up in family life, of her life in wartime Montreal, arrested in its turn as she waits for death announcements from overseas—to form the structure of her story. But the structural coherence is suspect, depending as it does upon Jean's sense of memory as a camera eye.

Jean opens her dialogue with the past as a reporter, recording a "sight" she remembers in sharp detail. She begins her narration in the present tense, shifts to the past, and then to the "presence-of-the-past," enacting the dynamics of her moment of recollection, which intensifies *as* she remembers into the immediacy of a present, vivid memory. But at the beginning of Jean's narration, we see that memory is also fixed, frozen. Jean calls her memory a "tableau" which, like one of "those crowded religious paintings," tells a "story" (57). Jean reports at this point in her narration by transcribing a visual scene from memory into its static verbal equivalent, as if words will fix the memory and frame the picture she reports:

> My last sight of the house at Allenton is a tableau of gesticulating people stopped in their tracks, as in those crowded religious paintings that tell a story.... Our picture, in the afternoon of a July day in 1955, was this: my mother sat beside me in my car, the back of which was filled with sweaters and winter coats, the overflow of the moving. (57)

This picture from memory, arrested, dated, and framed to tell a story, continues for a few more paragraphs, always in the arrested sense of time created, paradoxically, by narration in the present tense. The effect of the present tense here is that individual gestures become stylized, hierophantic: "A tall priest in black points," a real estate agent "opens the door for a woman," a gardener "kneels before a row of stones, painting them white" (58). The gestures Jean records in this tableau take place not long from the narrative present: in the ensuing sections, Jean begins to circle further into the past in the "helical patterns" we find in many of Gallant's stories.[8] But Jean does not come full circle; the end of the novel leaves her immersed in a scene anterior to the one she records in her opening memory.

Following immediately on this report comes its denial: "My mother says I saw nothing of the kind," Jean recalls (58); this pattern of a carefully recorded memory, followed by a denial of its veracity, recurs as Jean recalls the same scene later in the novel (67). Her mother provides rational explanations for what she claims are pure products of her daughter's imagination, so that the precise details of a vividly remembered scene (and so, in Jean's mind's eye, a true one, even if the language she uses to describe the picture is suspect), are at once presented and then denied—at the beginning of a fiction formed as a series of well-framed portraits, well-formed memories. Jean's mother explains away what her daughter sees in memory: Jean's family, potential repository of vital memories, actually closes off these pathways to autonomy. And yet Jean models herself on her mother: she is "pleased to be like her. There is no-one [she] admire[s] more" (65).

Jean's other model within the family is Isobel; from childhood on, Jean remembers adopting Isobel's feelings as her own. When she remembers reading fairy tales and English schoolgirl stories supplied by their mother, for example, she also recalls herself appropriating Isobel's "credulousness" as her own:

> I was always putting myself in my sister's place, adopting her credulousness, and even her memories, I saw, could be made mine. It was Isobel I imagined as the eternal heroine—never myself. I substituted her feelings for my own, and her face for any face described. Whatever the author's intentions, the heroine was my sister. (84)

Here as elsewhere Jean is trapped within her family, caught between her admiration for her mother's propriety and self-control—qualities which she mirrors—and her pursuit of Isobel's apparently more romantic rebellions from propriety. But just as Jean, early in her account, reports on her tableaux from memory as if she were a witness, her habitual stance in pursuit of Isobel is as an observer. This attitude "silences" her sister: "Even when we were young I silenced her," Jean remembers. "She would catch my eye (*the hopeful, watching, censor's eye*) and become silent, 'behaving,' as our family called it, and nothing could bring her back except my departure" (85—emphasis mine). Jean's eye as a child, her "hopeful, watching censor's eye" continues to focus her narration, resolving it early in her story into distanced, discrete still-lifes.

Jean's pursuit of Isa is her guiding obsession throughout. In Montreal, the focus of her interest lies in Isa's affair with Alec Campbell; she recalls that "[N]o romantic story of my own (if ever I'd had one) tormented me as much as her story with Alec Campbell" (91). Jean follows her around Montreal, hoping to enter into Isa's life, which seems romantic, exotic, bohemian. Isobel becomes an image of Jean's creation, but Jean's mistake is to believe that her sister's life *is* that creation, to believe that Isobel *is* the figure in a painting by the sisters' only mutual friend, Suzanne Moreau, who paints Isobel as a "Personnage aux Plumes" (95). And when Jean catches up with Isa and Alec one winter night, she sees herself, again, as a witness reporting on a tableau:

Our breath hung between us in white clouds and there was something mar-
ble and monumental about the group we formed in our winter clothes on
the white street.... They were the lighted window; I was the watcher on
the street. (99)

In the closing section, when Jean finally enters Isobel's world, the "Personnage
aux Plumes" dissolves into an "ordinary" person (153), and the early encounter
with Isa and Alec echoes ironically through the reversals which govern Jean's
more engaged encounter with Isa in the "bright rooms" of Isa's life (149).

The distinction that Jean draws between images in mirrors and ghosts in the
rooms of the Allenton house is another of the dissociations of objective report
from subjective exploration which form the structure of Jean's story. Early in the
first section, Jean records: "Ghosts moved in the deserted rooms.... We never
saw the ghosts, but we knew they were there" (59). When she visits her parents
for a weekend, she looks at her image in the mirror, while ghosts look at her: "a
ghost in my old bedroom watched me watching myself in the glass. It was not
mischievous, but simply attentive, and its invisible prying seemed improper
rather than frightening" (60). These "ghosts" are Jean's figurative evocations of
the subjects she has suppressed behind her objective mirrors. "Improper" is an
important word in her mother's idiom, used to forbid any expression of an interior life, of emotion, intuition, dream, or unpleasant truth—expression of anything that might shatter the mirror of proper conduct. To exorcise the ghosts of
"poor Isa" and "poor Frank," as her mother calls them, Jean first remembers
and then thinks about how memories mean; one process is contained within the
other in the forms of her reports.

At the time of Jean's parents' move from Allenton to Montreal, recalled in
Jean's opening memory, no one has heard from Isobel in six years; she has been
living in Caracas with her second husband, Alfredo. Jean imagines that Isobel
has removed herself from the reassuring cycles of continuity in the family, and
Jean's mother imagines that Isa would naturally have been happier with a Canadian husband and children. The second section of the novel describes the whole
family's reunion at the parents' summer cottage: Jean, Tom, and their four children, Isobel, Alfredo, and their two children, and Poppy, Frank's child (Enid has
given Poppy to Jean's mother). Significantly, Jean remembers the whole day as a
series of patterns. She remembers that three of her children "sat in a ring with
the neighbour's children.... They were charming, there, in the porch, playing
jacks. The harmony wouldn't last an hour, but it made a pretty picture" (74).
Momentarily, she feels "the closest thing I have to happiness. It is a sensation of
contentment because everyone round me is doing the right thing. The pattern is
whole" (75). But the "whole pattern" breaks when she looks over at her sister's
family, sitting apart. She imagines Alfredo to be "daunted by our family like-

ness, our solidarity"; the separation she feels from Isobel sends her back to her earliest memories of the family, memories through which she tries to reconstruct the pattern of events leading up to this scene at the summer cottage.

Jean is defeated by her own separation of her life from her sister's, a separation reflected in Jean's witnessing of *herself* as she nears Isobel: "I was intensely conscious of my appearance as I advanced, composing in my mind's eye the picture they would have of me," she reports (76). She contrasts her own image of herself with her description of Isobel's family: the precision and conciseness of both descriptions in these well-formed, sharply detailed portraits reflect the work of a memory schooled in transcription. Jean visualizes surfaces keenly: she sees memories with a camera eye and frames them in verbal captions, captions which contain rather than relate. So, for example, the expression Jean sees in Isa's face at the summer cottage reminds her of how Isa had looked on her deathbed: "She summed me up. Her total tallied with mine, but failed to daunt her. My pride in my children was suddenly nothing. . . . I approached; we spoke" (77). Total, tallies, summings-up; Jean's language conveys the mathematical sterility of this kind of communication, and also suggests the artificiality of her distinction between herself and Isa. She has an acutely *visual* memory, but no language of her own. And when Isobel and her family leave shortly after this failed meeting, Jean recalls that everyone "seemed to have a private perplexity, to judge from our expressions" (77).

Jean's memories mean more to her as they evolve from framed reports into embodied reflections; history's messages also evolve in this novel, modulating from film-thin documentary images into a more contingent reality which directly affects Jean's life. Jean, Isobel, and Suzanne Moreau have husbands overseas whose absence creates an illusory stop in time for the women waiting in Montreal. They cannot imagine the reality of the places their husbands have gone to: their inability to fully understand where history—the war—is taking place coalesces with Jean's own inability to undertand how her memories mean. Jean establishes this connection between the ways in which memory and history are recorded when she recalls how Suzanne Moreau's husband "had been taken prisoner in Dieppe, in 1942, and vanished from her life":

I think she forgot him because she could not imagine where he was . . . her mind's eye could not reach the real place we had seen as a make-believe country in the films. She could not see the barracks of a prison camp because she had already seen them gray and white, with film stars suffering and escaping and looking like no-one she knew. Surely there was a true landscape. . . . We all received letters that were real enough, but the letters told us that everything we saw and read was a lie. Davy, Isobel's husband, saw a documentary film about Italy and even though it was a truthful film, and he saw himself, a glimpse of himself, he wrote that it was a lie. . . . It was Suzanne's husband's bad luck to have disappeared into a sham landscape. The men we knew dissolved in a foreign rain. (128)

Like Jean's framed pictures from memory, documentary films are true but not fictionally true, documentary but necessarily revelatory. Her images of the past, like the film of Italy, are "truthful"; like Davy Sullivan, she sees a "glimpse" of herself and her family in them, but these glimpses do not communicate significance. The "true" landscape of Jean's past eludes her, as does the landscape into which the men have vanished. Her documentary snapshots and tableaux do not announce meaning, nor do documentary films tell the same kinds of truths as the personal letters the women receive. Thus the "truth" conveyed by Jean's tableaux from memory becomes a private analogue to the public "truth" told by the documentary films. The form of Jean's memories (an eye but no voice, a picture with no language), like the form of the documentary films (images without enough context) fails to convey history, private or public.

In the last section of the novel, Jean finally enters into Isobel's "real" life, and so more fully into her own. This change in Jean is a change in her manner of narration. The opening of the last section contrasts radically with the opening of the first one: the contrast is all the more significant because it must be a result of Jean's process of remembering, since the events recalled in the last section take place *before* the Allenton tableau.

Jean and Isobel have returned to Allenton to mourn Frank's death. The form of Jean's memory, its "frame," has altered dramatically:

> Our period of family mourning continued for three days. One night *I saw, or thought I saw, or may have dreamed,* that my father sat on the stairs weeping. Our mother stood a few steps behind him so that their faces were nearly level. She was in a flannel dressing gown, a plait of gray hair undone and over one shoulder. Patient, waiting, she held a glass of water to his lips as if control could be taken like a pill. Everything in that scene, *which I must have dreamed, spoke of the terror of pity.* "The girls are home," she said, for fear that we wake and see him and join him in grieving aloud. (147—emphasis mine)

The first difference between this and Jean's opening "sight" is her own doubt about the nature of her perception of the event—her inability to declare whether she saw, or thought she saw, or might have dreamed the event—in contrast to the crisp detail of her crowded religious painting, which tells a story, and which she reports on with an emphatic, uncontestable "this": (57). Now it is unclear—even if she concludes (in deference, perhaps, to the improbability of her father ever showing emotion openly) that she "must have dreamed"—whether memory, dream, or imagination has conjured the image. Here, too, the image of Jean's mother consoling her father "as if control could be taken like a pill" is *part* of the memory. The mother's censoring reserve, which *follows* and *denies* the "truth" of Jean's opening memory, has now been assimilated *in* memory. The fact that Jean can now use figurative language to suggest the quality of her mother's control indicates her own fuller insight into the nature of this control, and tells of her liberation from her mother's stifling separation of expression from propriety. The scene now has a language, a significance it can "speak" to Jean—"the terror of pity." Jean's tableaux are now more fully integrated with their significance. The impersonal, "gesticulating" figures in the novel's opening image are "stopped in their tracks," held prisoner in the deceptive immediacy of the simple present tense; the figures in the later image are less constricted, their individual gestures more fluid, and their significance more figuratively conveyed. In both memories, formal structure conveys meaning, and we learn to read their significance by distinguishing between unqualified assertion in the first tableau (followed by unqualified counter-assertion) and hesitant conjecture, qualified by figurative language, in the second scene. Throughout the novel, we read discrepancies between Jean's confident observations and what we learn about what she observes. These differences become more explicit as the novel develops, until in the scene preceding this last section, Jean herself begins to recognize her own unreliability, confessing that she "had never known Frank," for all of her portraits of him (145). Recognizing that the forms of her portraits have up to this point precluded her knowing them, Jean begins to allow her memories to speak less pictorially, less objectively.

In this last section we can also recognize Jean's adaptation of language to conform with her changing intuitions of the relations between images and experience. When Isobel confesses to Jean that she is pregnant by Alec and needs her help, Jean realizes—in part, because she has retold Isobel's report, and so understands it and her sister more fully—that Isobel's story had a "flaw" (152). Remembering Isobel's appearance, she muses: "Someone who has lost his language wears that look, that despair. Fear, despair: despair is too loud for the quiet night. Remove the word, leave Isobel with cheek on hand, eyes gone yellow in the light of the lamp" (152). Jean is now writing fiction, finding her own language and voice, so that her images can speak; they need no framing captions. She is turning a report into a story, inviting readers to attend to the manner in which she allows her memories to be, freeing them into silence, beyond the frames of words used as a means of distancing: "'Afraid' is too loud, too. There remains Isobel, then; cheek on hand, a little tired. . . . Forget despair, fear. We were very ordinary. Leave us there . . . my sister and I at the opposite ends of the bed, with our childhoods between us going on to the horizon without a break" (152–53).

Jean begins with pictures and framed reports and ends with images she com-

mands and then allows herself to leave alone. She begins with a smug understanding of life's patterns as fixed and "immutable" and ends by waking up
from her patterned dreams into mutability. Her perfectly framed pictures blur
with significance, and images on mirrors become fuller figures. So Jean can now
see that Isobel is "ordinary" and not a "personnage aux plumes": "Looking
back and down from reality," Jean can "correct the story about plumes: Isobel
was considered attractive, though not a perfect beauty, and she was not lavish,
and not golden, and not a bird. Those were fancies" (148).

Free of her captions and frames, Jean can now respond, if only for a moment,
to Isobel's need for her "whole attention." Jean reaches out to touch her sister,
but, like other such meetings in Gallant's fiction, this encounter is very brief.
The sisters bridge their separation for a moment but then part:

> I moved forward, kneeling, in the most clumsy movement possible. It was
> dragging oneself through water against the swiftest current, in the fastest
> river in the world; I knelt on the bed near my sister and took her thin
> relaxed hand in mine. We met in a corner of the landscape and she glanced
> at me, then slid her hand out of mine and said, "Oh, don't." (153)

This moment of identification is a moment for metaphor, for water, swift currents, rivers, and landscapes; and metaphors in the language of Gallant's fiction
are as rare as is this kind of encounter between characters.

Jean closes her reflections with a beautiful lament, a meditation on winter
sleep and spring, the season which, like Eliot's April, "warns that death is returning after all" (154). She is writing a letter to Tom, pondering whether or
not to tell him the news about his first love; she decides that "the story could
wait" (154). Jean closes her story with a poetic farewell to her dreams and
memories, waking up from romance into history, reversing the direction taken
by Carol Frazier at the end of "The Other Paris." The ending is the most evocative passage in the novel, suggesting Jean's reach toward unifying private with
public, personal with social, and timeless with historical experience:

> I suspected, then, sitting in Frank's unhaunted room, that all of us, save my
> brother, were obliged to survive. We had slipped into our winter as
> trustingly as every night we fell asleep. We woke from dreams of love re-
> membered, a house recovered and lost, a climate imagined, a journey never
> made; we woke dreaming our mothers had died in childbirth and heard
> ourselves saying, "Then there is no one left but me!" We would waken
> thinking the earth must stop, now, so that we could be shed from it like
> snow. I knew, that night, we would not be shed, but would remain, because
> that was the way it was. We would survive, and waking—because there was
> no help for it—forget our dreams and return to life. (155)

The Frank Jean realizes she has never known has disappeared, so that Frank's room is unhaunted, unoccupied by image (Frank as a soldier, for example, as if he were "born to be photographed, in uniform, for the *Montreal Star*" [139]) or ghost. Winter has always been a season of waiting for Jean, a season she "knew [she] would not survive" (113). Although Jean reflects during her winter's wait that "at any moment [she] might become Tom's widow," it is *Frank* who dies. Jean wakes up from "dreams of love remembered"—such as her dream of Isa's and Alec's romance, the issue of which is a real pregnancy. Remembering dreams is the process which wakes her up to the world, the historical world in which Tom is absent because he is somewhere Jean cannot imagine. The anxiety Jean feels at living an adult life, beyond the family enclave, is suggested in her waking dream; if her mother is dead in childbirth, Jean will be left completely alone (and left responsible for her mother's death as well). Waking alone, she imagines, might mean wintry suspension, out of seasonal and family cycles. But the flat finality of her recognition that "that was the way it was" suggests that she understands that survivors must wake up to history, must return to the present tense, progressing from the past tense with which the passage opens and moving through a subjunctive blending of past dreams with their present significance.

Jean pursues meaning by framing her memories, distinguishing their features in an attempt to separate out their content. But what she finds in her frames and forms is not "content," but more forms. In this sense, Jean approaches her memories in a manner similar to the way in which readers approach fiction. Roland Barthes suggests that a text should not be thought of as "a species of fruit with a kernel . . . the flesh being the form and the pit the content," but as an "onion": the text, writes Barthes, is a "construction of layers (or levels, or systems) whose body contains, finally, no heart, no kernel, no secret, no irreducible principle, nothing except the infinity of its own envelopes—which envelop nothing other than the unity of its own surfaces."[9] Jean learns that Isobel's life is not a species of fruit, hiding the secret of love like a kernel within; she learns that appearance does not "hide" reality, form does not "hide" content. When Jean leaves images alone for a moment, they speak a language; they are free of her self-conscious attempts to fix absolute meaning. With this language, Jean can imagine a fiction rather than recall a documentary piece.

"The Cost of Living" (1962) is in several senses a minor-key inversion of "Its Image on the Mirror."[10] "Puss," another first-person narrator who calls attention to the tyranny, the "cost" of memory understood as objective truth, is the younger of two Australian sisters. She has run away from Melbourne late, at twenty-seven, and come to Paris, teaching music to eke out a living. Louise has stayed in Melbourne to nurse their invalid mother; now, both parents dead, she comes to Paris "wisely, calmly, with plenty of money for travel" (158). Puss, like Isobel, has been away from home for six years; Louise, like Jean, "was making a serious effort to know" her sister (158). Puss reports on Louise much as Isobel would on Jean. In fact, the sisters in these stories seem almost twinned, as if Gallant were splitting a character into two aspects in order to explore their relation to each other. She creates two complementary characters and voices and has each tell a similar story, but from an opposed perspective. Jean's voice in "Its Image on the Mirror" could be Louise's in "The Cost of Living," plain, proper, and "blunt"; Puss's voice in "The Cost of Living" could be Isa's, the rebel's voice, the romantic, the bohemian who at heart distrusts bohemia. One of the characters in each story stays home, tied to the family, while the other breaks away toward ostensible freedom; but finally the pairs of sisters are more similar than they are different.

Louise, like Jean, is careful, frugal, loyal; she nurses Puss through a bout of flu much as Jean does for Isa in Montreal. Like Isa and Jean, the Australian sisters are attached to the same man. Like Tom Price, he goes away to war: Louise, thirty-eight, was married at nineteen to Collie Tate, who went to Malaya with his regiment, was taken prisoner, and died "before she'd had very many letters from him" (165–6). The pairs of sisters share similarly genteel middle-class backgrounds, recalled as both narrators describe early family portraits. Both younger daughters have been disinherited by their families for running away, Puss literally, Isa figuratively. Both narrators call attention to the process of remembering, now doubting, now affirming the truth and clarity of memory's images, scenes, and dialogues, and both draw portraits and transcribe from memory as if they were witnesses in court; yet their police court exactitude obscures their most important revelations.

On one level, both stories are about the possibilities of relationship, and about love frustrated, denied, and concealed, love unannounced, or hoarded, or grudgingly apportioned. But more importantly, both stories enact the consequences of memory's language misunderstood. The tyranny of form—of snapshots, portraits, pictures, tableaux, framed still lifes—dictates its reports to both women, reports which Jean is more successful than Puss in transforming into the language of fiction. Both stories are about languages and images, vocabularies and grammars, and also about formal truths and fictional truths, just as much as they are about two sisters—in this case, two Australians in Paris, coming up against all of the jarring dislocations, the cultural confusions and contretemps Gallant's foreigners always encounter on alien ground. These cultural dislocations, instructive in themselves, also invite us to read expatriation, exile, and transience in the context of estrangement from language itself. Exile from language is implied more clearly with Puss, for whom expatriation is just as much a matter of a loss of idiom as of place. The language of Puss's narration, as the story's title suggests and Puss's vocabulary confirms, documents Puss's misconstruction of the economies, debits, and credits of relationship, and both her accounts of character and her manner of telling stories cost Puss more than

Louise's actual expenditures. Puss's straitened means link up figuratively with her straitened means of telling, so that her story becomes "telling" in at least three senses—narrating, (re)counting, and revealing.

Puss is jealous of her sister's inheritance, bitter at her own poverty; she is a parsimonious narrator, hoarding facts, circumscribing character more than reading or writing it. She tells her story after the other three important figures, Louise, Patrick, and Sylvie, have left the hotel and she has gathered up the objective, documentary evidence they leave behind—Louise's ledgers, Sylvie's diary, and Patrick's love letter to Sylvie, which Puss intercepts. Puss describes her sister's record of expenses, entered in two columns which Louise, like her father, has labelled "Necessary" and "Unnecessary," crossing out the customary "Paid" and "Received." These diaries are intimate documents, because Louise records amounts spent for love under "Necessary," along with the cost of more mundane purchases, such as aspirin for Puss. Louise's accounts reveal her "blunt, plain" attempts to express concern and affection for Sylvie by giving her gifts. "Blunt and straightforward," Louise had "merged 'Necessary' and 'Unnecessary' into a single column," Puss reports; "When I added what she had paid out it came to a great deal. She must be living thinly now" (193). Here as elsewhere, it is not clear that Puss always perceives that her language consistently figures as it tells.

Just as Puss's language is telling on several levels, the structure of her account reveals to her readers the connections in her narration between reminiscence and formed story. Just as Puss's tone seems to be lighter, more anecdotal, and more comic than Jean's, she also seems to arrange her memories more haphazardly than Jean does, as if she were telling her story as unpremeditated, formless reminiscence. But as we read her story we discern that its shape is instructive because it returns, like many Gallant stories, to one moment. Puss recalls this moment in recurring set pieces: Sylvie Laval asks Louise for money on the hotel stairway. The scene is crucial because it announces a moment of communication between Sylvie and Louise, the moment in which Sylvie makes her demand for recognition, and in which a foreigner acknowledges her. Puss opens the story by recalling this meeting: "Louise, my sister, talked to Sylvie Laval for the first time on the stairs of our hotel on a winter afternoon" (157). Although she returns to this scene twice (161, 168), Puss artlessly denies that her account is a story, a fiction with a pattern and a structure. She also interjects explanatory remarks when starting on a fresh tack, as if her account were spontaneous; when Patrick leaves, she makes an effort to distinguish her telling from that of a shaped fiction's narration: "In a book or a film one of us would have gone with him as far as the station" (183). The story instructs readers through its structure; Puss wants to deny her fiction its shape, her story its significance—a denial that is part of her cost of living.

As we read Puss's portraits of Sylvie, Patrick, and Louise, we learn another version of the lesson Jean Price teaches herself about the meanings of forms. Sylvie Laval is an aspiring screenplay writer and diarist. Showing a careful concern for how texts should be transmitted, Puss transcribes *verbatim,* including omissions and erasures, a description of Louise which Sylvie has written for an intended screenplay (160). But her own memories of Sylvie are less objective. Puss underlines Sylvie's shallowness, her insincerity and duplicity, her promiscuity, her penchant for gossip, and her greed. To Puss, Sylvie and Patrick are fake artists, fake bohemians, fake persons. She recognizes Sylvie's energy and vitality, but these qualities become expressions of insolence and aggression in Puss's renditions of Sylvie. Her attempt to imagine Sylvie as a drawing, a painting, recalls Jean's image of Isobel and Suzanne Moreau's "Personnage aux Plumes":

> Passing her, as she hung over the banister calling to someone below, you saw the tensed muscle of an arm or leg, the young neck, the impertinent head. Someone ought to have drawn her—but somebody has: Sylvie was the coarse and grubby Degas dancer, the girl with the shoulder thrown back and the insolent chin. For two pins, or fewer, that girl staring out of flat canvas would stick out her tongue or spit in your face. (162–3)

In contrast, when Puss reports what *Louise* has told her about Sylvie, she recalls that Sylvie "communicated" to Louise "with an intense vitality that was like a third presence on the stairs. Her warmth and her energy communicated so easily that there was almost too much, and some fell away and had its own existence" (169).

Patrick, like Sylvie, is an aspiring artist, an actor, a disembodied voice practising elocution all day in his hotel room. Puss is drawn to Patrick, her namesake, but only alludes to her attraction indirectly. As she does when she describes Sylvie, Puss reports what Louise tells her about meeting Patrick, an encounter between a consummate actor (and a native Parisian, graced in the art of smooth conversation) and a plain-speaking, "blunt" foreigner, resulting, Puss believes, in an affair. But Louise's relationships with Patrick and Sylvie go beyond her ledger accounts, while Puss remains isolated in a mode of recollection.

Puss mistakenly believes that she understands Louise completely, just as Jean Price believes she understands Frank. But when Puss condemns Louise for her "failure" to remember Collie Tate, we can understand her denial of implication as a comment on her terribly costly fidelity to her own sense of memory: "Patrick and Collie had merged into one occasion, where someone failed. The failure was Louise's; the infidelity of memory, the easy defeat were hers. It had nothing to do with me" (189).

Puss can only allude to her interior life through reference to her practical "incompetence" (a defect she shares with Patrick). Her revelations emerge from fragments of verse she remembers after waking up from a dream, and from another story, her fevered account of an incident in Hector Berlioz's life. She cannot explain why she tells the Berlioz story. She remembers that she saw Patrick and Sylvie together; then, returning from a music lesson, she goes to Patrick's room and tells the other story—in English, which Sylvie does not understand.

The structure of the end of "The Cost of Living" recalls the closing of "Its Image on the Mirror." When Patrick leaves, Puss becomes "dream-haunted," watching Louise look for Patrick. She dreams of "labyrinths, of search, of missed chances, of people standing on opposite shores" (188). She remembers a averse from a German poem which she had tried to set to music when she was "Patrick's age":

Es warent zwei Königskinder
Die hatten einander so lief
Sie konnten zusammen nicht kommen
Das Wasser, es war zu tief. (188)

(There were two royal children
Who were very fond of each other
They could not come together
The water, it was too deep.)

First Puss thinks that she and Louise must be the royal children; then she decides that they must be Patrick and Sylvie. Another probable pair would be Patrick and Patricia. But Puss is left at the end of her story, like Jean Price at the beginning of hers, with "winter ghosts" (191). The last word in the story is Sylvie's: when she returns the necklace Louise has bought her, she says to Puss: "I'd have been as well off without it. Everything I've done I've had to do. It never brought me *bonheur*" (193). Puss apologizes for not translating the French word: "*bonheur* is ambiguous. It means what you think it does, but sometimes it just stands for luck; *the meaning depends on the sense of things*" (193—emphasis mine). Puss's sense of things has not allowed for the ambiguity so nicely captured in Sylvie's last word. The cost of living for Puss has been love unannounced, while Louise, Puss tells us, pays the price for love too bluntly declared.

Both Jean and Puss make sense through indirection and reversals. Their objective reports communicate meaning through form; through form, these narrators teach us how to compose a figure, a "ghost" who never quite meets the eye. We compose Jean and Puss by studying their reports on Isobel and Louise; the more attention we pay to the shapes of these narrators' "whole patterns," the more fully we can read the narrators themselves.

The remaining seven stories in *My Heart Is Broken* are narrated in the third person. Although they are not as closely linked as "Its Image on the Mirror" is with "The Cost of Living," they also measure the distances between stilled lives and living moments, between characters who are framed, arrested in over-articulate manners and idioms, and silenced or inarticulate characters fumbling for words with which to declare their bafflement. In this book of stories, these are moments of defeat, of failures to bridge separations or complete dialogues. "The Moabitess" closes with a defeat imagined as a triumphs as Miss Horeham, remembering her secret attachment to her father, declares to herself: "Oh, how they would all die if they knew! Oh, how they would all of them die."[11] "Acceptance of Their Ways" closes with a tableau: Lily Littel and Mrs. Freeport talk at each other in Mrs. Freeport's "bare wintry garden," both dreading a loss of company.[12] Mrs. Freeport fears that Lily will eventually leave her for her (imaginary) sister in Nice, but Lily reassures her by straightening out the water lily in Mrs. Freeport's hat. Lily cannot leave, because she is still learning Mrs. Freeport's gentlewomanly manners, her "ways." In "Bernadette," readers are left with Bernadette's inverted hope for her unborn child, her "angel"—that when it dies, as she believes it must, it will pray for her in eternity. Appropriately, Bernadette is watching a film in the closing scene, just as she is a spectator watching her own "dark... personal fear."[13] When Bernadette feels her baby moving inside her for the first time, that crucial moment, announcing the possibilities of a new life, is immediately transfigured into a moment announcing another death. Bernadette's society of deaf auditors, Robbie and Nora, are Knights in name only, trapped in liberal posturing and a frozen marriage. Bernadette's spectacle goes unseen, just as Jeannie's declaration in the title story goes unheard.

The powerful title story is this book's finest evocation of the failure on one character's part to listen to another's declaration of heartbreak. "My Heart Is Broken" calls attention to the interruptions, silences, and misunderstandings that separate Jeannie from Mrs. Thompson, referring readers to the text of the society which speaks through these silences. The story opens with Mrs. Thompson speaking to Jeannie and closes with Mrs. Thompson's reflections on her past, even though it is Jeannie who has been raped, her heart that has been broken. The first allusion to the rape comes only after the story has been half completed; much of the discussion of the rape is indirect, at several removes; the camp's reactions are reported to Jeannie by Mrs. Thompson, who overhears the boss, Mr. Sherman, talking to Vern, Jeannie's husband. And most of what Mrs. Thompson reports focusses on the social consequences of the rape—the job it will cost Vern, the trouble it creates in the camp.

Mrs. Thompson is the conduit for a depersonalized social response to Jeannie's rape. The story opens with Mrs. Thompson's recollection of the day she read of Jean Harlow's death: she remembers that she had recently married, that "all the men were unemployed in those days," and that she read the news in an American newspaper while riding a streetcar in Montreal. She interrupts herself briefly to remind Jeannie (diminutive Jean) that *she* "wasn't even on earth" when Harlow died, and she concludes by calling Harlow's death her own biggest heartbreak: "You can believe me or not, just as you want to, but that was the most terrible shock I ever had in my life. I never got over it."[14] Mrs. Thompson's nostalgia for one of Hollywood's most famous sex symbols opens a story about sexual violence in the present; she thinks of Jeannie's rape in terms of her own "terrible shock" at reading of a film star's death, so that her vicarious bereavement is ironically opposed to Jeannie's experience. For Mrs. Thompson, Jeannie is an impersonator, asking for trouble by looking and dressing like a film star.

Mrs. Thompson's opening recollection is greeted with silence; throughout, Jeannie's responses signal the gaps in communication between the two women. She looks "uncomprehending" at Mrs. Thompson, or frowns "absently," or she "might not have been listening." The narration itself further separates the two women by describing Jeannie through a terse, bare style, contrasting sharply with the loose discursiveness of Mrs. Thompson's opening memory. Most of the sentences in the story's second paragraph, for example, simply declare Jeannie's appearance as a series of hard, bare facts, mutely opposed to Mrs. Thompson's chatty description of her reaction to Jean Harlow's death. We begin to read Jeannie's character in a series of spare assertions, their rhythm and structure unvarying:

> Jeannie had nothing to say to that. She lay flat on her back across the bed, with her head toward Mrs. Thompson and her heels just touching the crate that did as a bedside table. Balanced on her flat stomach was an open bottle of coral-pink Cutex nail polish. She held her hands up over her head and with some difficulty applied the brush to the nails of her right hand. Her legs were brown and thin. She wore nothing but shorts and one of her husband's shirts. Her feet were bare. (195)

The taut sentences recall Hemingway's terse prose style: Gallant's tightly compressed idiom evokes Jeannie's absence and abstraction as she pays more attention to nails and nail polish than to Mrs. Thompson until she is ready to speak.

Just as the story's governing style, idiom, and point of view are Mrs. Thompson's, so is the governing assessment of Jeannie's proper (third-person) place in camp society. In Mrs. Thompson's eyes, Jeannie has misunderstood her role as a wife: she should have realized that if her husband liked jobs in the bush, *her* job would be to make a cabin a home, as Mrs. Thompson has become so expert in doing. As long as the men "like the life," the women should be satisfied; since Vern "likes it better than anything"—except for the army—Jeannie should have been content (199). Both Mr. Sherman and Mrs. Thompson see Vern as the victim, Jeannie as the guilty party: Vern "ought to have thrashed *you*," Mrs. Thompson tells her (202).

Through this account of a woman's place in camp life, Gallant confronts Jeannie with a society organized around men at work, with their women out of sight. Both Vern and Pops Thompson miss the army, the best of all possible men's worlds; both have chosen the closest substitute, a raw, uncivilized camp in the bush. Women can be sexy on film, in Hollywood, but not in a road construction camp, not in northern Quebec. Harlow's death is "heartbreaking," but Jeannie's rape is her punishment for flaunting herself; it is all the more reprehensible of Jeannie to have dressed up and gone out because it has cost Vern his job.

The "dialogue" between the two women opens twice, first as Mrs. Thompson begins with her memory of Harlow's death, and then again as Jeannie tells her the story of trying to learn about sexuality and childbirth from a Lana Turner movie. Jeannie goes to the movie six times, but "in the end [she] never knew any more" (201). This confession follows directly upon Jeannie's description of the rape, which she says she would "have to see . . . happening to know what happened" (201). Like the Lana Turner movie, the rape teaches her nothing. It is inexplicable to her, a brutal event with no meaning, counterpointing the movie version of birth, which presents Turner with her twins as a *fait accompli*. Mrs. Thompson's responses to Jeannie's confessions, here and throughout, parallel Jeannie's absent responses to Mrs. Thompson: Mrs. Thompson "sat quite still, trying to make sense" of Jeannie's account of the Lana Turner movie (201).

The closest that Mrs. Thompson can come to imagining Jeannie's rape is to look out the "dark window" of the cabin and think of soldiers raping civilians: "'I wonder what it must be like. . . . I mean, think of Berlin and them Russians and all. Think of some disgusting fellow you don't know. Never said hello to, even. Some girls ask for it, though. You can't always blame the man. The man loses his job, his wife if he's got one, everything, all because of a silly girl'" (200).

Mrs. Thompson's own experience, as evidenced by her cabin's plastic furnishings, the dolls she pushes around camp in her pram, and the records she and Pops listen to (these "dated back to the year one") is all ersatz, second-hand, third-person; thus her most terrible shock has been vicarious—reading about a film-star's death. She can only transmit to Jeannie the codes of conduct which have emptied out her own life, making her little more than a mouthpiece. "A woman can always defend what's precious, even if she's attacked," she tells Jeannie, but she herself has not been able to "defend" any sense of her own autonomy, so that she cannot speak in her own voice (200). She can only "observe" that "taking advantage of a woman is a criminal offense"; but she immediately follows this observation with a report on what she has overheard Mr. Sherman say to Vern about bringing lawyers around, "acting" the overheard dialogue to Jeannie "with spirit" (201). Half-wishfully, Mrs. Thompson imagines that Jeannie will be scarred forever, haunted by a "terrible, terrible memory"; but Jeannie tells her that she "already can't remember it" (200).

The separation between first and third-person experience widens with Mrs. Thompson's response to Jeannie's last declaration, and we must read the story with attention to this irony. Throughout, Jeannie has been trying to tell Mrs. Thompson about loneliness and isolation, about innocence enforced by film-thin versions of experience. Mrs. Thompson, intently passing on her received notions of Jeannie's guilt, cannot see or hear her, save as an incarnation of Jean Harlow. Jeannie's final cry is an expression of desolation at not being *liked*: "'He could at least have liked me,' said Jeannie. 'He wasn't even friendly. It's the first time in my life somebody hasn't liked me. My heart is broken, Mrs. Thompson. My heart is just broken'" (202).

Mrs. Thompson's response is silence. She rocks in her chair, trying "to remember how she'd felt about things when she was twenty, wondering if her heart had ever been broken, too" (202). Mrs. Thompson has not passed through any initiation, violent or otherwise; she has lived in a perpetual, childish haze, confusing movies with life, dolls with babies, self-righteousness with selfhood. She cannot quite distinguish between Jean and Jeannie, an image and a person. Yet she is also the woman who has cheerfully adapted to the demands of camp life; the price she has paid for this accommodation is evidently the loss of an interior life.

Jeannie's final declaration of "heartbreak" must go unheard, just as Jeannie herself cannot formulate a substantial, autonomous response to her rape. Similarly, Veronica Baines' cry goes unacknowledged at the end of "Sunday Afternoon" (1962).[15] Like "Señor Pinedo," this story anticipates the stories in *The Pegnitz Junction*, Gallant's most overtly political book of stories. The story opens on a double exposure: first, Veronica watches a "scene" from her Paris apartment window; she is completely removed from the silent movie she observes, a historical episode with meanings she cannot fathom, since she "seldom read[s] the boring part of newspapers" (204). The scene is presented in the first instance by an observer recording time and place from a completely detached perspective: "On a wet February afternoon in the eighth winter of the Algerian war, two young Algerians sat at the window table of a cafe behind Montparnasse station" (203). The third in the tableau is a European girl much like Veronica, "an innocent from an inland place" who turns a "gentle, stupid face to each of the men in turn, trying to find a common language" (204). The scene dissolves, and we discover that Veronica has been watching these figures for most of the afternoon.

The story explores Veronica's interior life, a life ignored by the two men sitting in the apartment discussing politics—Jim, her American lover, and Ahmed, a Tunisian medical student. Jim believes that "life only began after it was prepared," while Veronica thinks "it had to start with a miracle"; both of these gimcrack ideologies are more artificial (and more foreign to French life) than Ahmed's attitudes, which were "not acquired, like Jim's. They were as much part of him as his ears" (213). Ahmed briefly and coolly considers making a play for Veronica, but dismisses the idea, and the men carry on their political discussion while Veronica imagines herself asking them whether she is "any better than the girl" she observed earlier in the café (215). The story closes on her cry for recognition; she can only gain the men's attention by alluding to the danger of discussing politics behind an open window:

> "You both think you're so clever".... "You haven't even enough sense to draw the curtains." While they were still listening, she said, "It's not my fault if you don't like me. Both of you. I can't help it if you wish I was something else. Why don't you take better care of me?" (217)

The historical world, which enacts silent tableaux Veronica watches from her window, has little relevance to her. Her political innocence counterpoints Jeannie's sexual innocence; both women cry out for the only kind of recognition they can fathom—to be "liked"—and both cries go unanswered.

In all of the stories of *My Heart Is Broken,* the interior life of the individual is a subject more alluded to than proclaimed—incoherently articulated in dreams, in feverish accounts of romantic episodes, in misinterpreted folksong fragments. When it is announced, as in "My Heart Is Broken," or in Angelo's pleas in "An Unmarried Man's Summer," or in Veronica's cry in "Sunday Afternoon," it goes unacknowledged or is misunderstood. Characters like Angelo therefore go unacknowledged by characters like Walter Henderson, who composes his life as if it were an arrested frieze, a "mosaic" picture stopped in time, replacing the "broken patterns" of less well-formed, more figurative lives. The narration frames Gallant's characters in *My Heart Is Broken,* distancing their images in reports like the opening description of Jeannie, or Puss's description of Sylvie Laval, or Jean Price's portraits of Isobel, Frank, and her mother, or the description of Walter Henderson's "mosaic." Gallant makes the dialogues in these stories interrupt as much as they communicate: in many stories, dialogues between characters are cut short, or cut off. But ranged alongside these objective reports and framed portraits are subjective ghosts, and the broken dialogues are potentially completed by sudden cries from the heart. The distances between subjects and objects, ghosts and images, Jeannie's cry and Mrs. Thompson's overheard reports, alternately widen and narrow as Gallant explores the reaches of memory. Memory in these stories reports, reflects, frames, and recreates the past; memory transcribes the past, and when its images on the mirror are allowed to speak, evokes and explores it as well. In Gallant's next book, her novel *A Fairly Good Time* (1970), images on mirrors will reflect in a wider social frame, and identity will become a creation and an essence more comically composed of the foreign and the familiar.

3

Green Water, Green Sky and
A Fairly Good Time
Madness, Memory, and the
Comedies of Identity

The short story has proven itself to be Gallant's major form, and for good reason. First, Gallant's characters, who are often figures on the verge of perceptions they cannot quite accommodate, or stranded beyond the end of one era, before the beginning of another, are rendered most effectively in sharp glimpses, not in the fuller, more rounded portraits traditionally associated with the narrative and temporal amplitudes of the novel. Often, as many of Gallant's readers have noted, they are characters on a margin; and in this sense they provide strong contemporary confirmation of Frank O'Connor's central suggestion, in his admirable study, *The Lonely Voice,* that the short story is most often populated by characters on the fringes of society.[1] Gallant's characters typically come alive through a quick succession of sharp insights which gain in intensity because they are embedded in patterns of tightly controlled, subtly varied repetitions. Within these structures, images often seem to call and recall each other as figures of finely discriminated changes in perception.

Second, the conceptions of time which function on so many levels as important formal elements in Gallant's fiction—either time past as it is recreated or recollected, or the present, converging in moments sparked and quick with illumination—also gain in intensity and effect in the more concentrated field of the short story form, where the play of Gallant's narration can reverberate more closely amidst its own echoes. Third, and closely related to Gallant's rendering of time, is the distinctive rhythm of Gallant's language. One of Gallant's major stylistic strengths is her genius for alternating between spare, lean assertions—often ironically framed as unequivocal, univocal declarations of bare fact—and the contrapuntal music of expanding, reflective, contemplative structures, in which perspectives seem to enlarge as the sentence grows, so that breadth of description seems to become increasingly significant in proportion to its opposition to the taut rhythms of the shorter structures. These alternations, too, work to more powerful effect within a form often noted for its foregrounding of style, rhythm, and pattern.

Finally, there is the quality—and the vitality—of description in Gallant's fiction. The intense, self-contained glance at a scene, a gesture, a phrase, in which reported details become so sharp as to seem overdetermined, to signify more than they could, or should, is another of Gallant's major formal signatures. These glances, so sharp that they must penetrate deeply or not at all, function most effectively within the highly wrought frameworks of Gallant's stories, in which details can signify so quickly and yet so much, and less effectively in her novels.

In Gallant's case, however, a genius for the short story form has not precluded significant accomplishments in the novel. There are no other Canadian writers with whom to compare Gallant in this regard: to name three obviously different cases, Margaret Laurence's and Margaret Atwood's novels represent their most powerful fictional achievements, although both have written fine books of short stories; and Alice Munro's career best exemplifies the development of a pure short story writer (excluding the contentious debate over the form of *Lives of Girls and Women*). Gallant's two novels to date, *Green Water, Green Sky* (1959) and *A Fairly Good Time* (1970) reward consideration both for their divergent treatments of one of Gallant's major themes—the consequences for individuals of the preservation, reinvention, or annihilation of the past—and for their alternately tragic and comic depictions of individual identities on trial within the social structures of marriages, families, and cultures.[2]

Green Water, Green Sky is the less successful of the two novels, in part because most of this novel was originally published in *The New Yorker* in the summer of 1959 as three separate, although closely related short stories: "Green Water, Green Sky," "August," and "Travellers Must Be Content."[3] At different times throughout her career, Gallant has written series of linked stories: these three comprise one of the first of these series and are among the most closely linked stories.[4] This is also the only series of linked stories that Gallant has developed into a novel, with only slight revision and with the addition of a short fourth section, structured as parts one through four.[5] It is worth noting that *A Fairly Good Time*, too, finds its genesis in a short story—"The Accident" (1967)—although in *A Fairly Good Time*, Gallant goes much further beyond the original short story to develop more fully her exploration of Shirley Perrigny.

In *Green Water, Green Sky*, the forms of the short stories remain to govern the structure of the novel, and sometimes this tends to isolate passages of description which do not stand out in quite as stark a manner in their original contexts. Often, the narration will seem to stop abruptly and the point of view to shift as a personality, an attitude, a street corner is described in sharp, almost static detail; these arrested and arresting passages of description disrupt the narrative less successfully in the novel than in the short stories, where the effects of disruptions are heightened and strengthened because the more highly elaborated structure of the separate short stories accommodates them more fluently. But many of the novel's strengths also result from its origins in three short stories; in particular, the shifts and disruptions in chronological time which figure so importantly in the development of character are most clearly signalled by the order of the novel's four parts.

Green Water, Green Sky develops through the mirroring effects of a perspective which reflects, deflects, and refracts the past in characters' memories. This mirroring effect is first suggested in the novel's title and then reflected throughout the novel's development. The structure of the novel functions as both the framework for and a formal explication of Gallant's major purpose, the study of Flor's descent into madness.

The novel presents Flor's development and deterioration in three related, but not chronological sequences—the three original short stories—and concludes with three other characters' reflections on Flor, who has by then been confined in a rest home in Paris. In Part One, Flor is an American teenager in Venice with her mother, Bonnie. They have been living a transient and isolated existence in Europe since Bonnie's husband caught her in an affair and divorced her. Bonnie's decision to uproot herself and her daughter, to cut them off from the Fairlie family, constitutes their first major rupture with the past, and sets in motion the fatally claustrophobic relationship between mother and daughter, both of them trapped within the confines of Bonnie's obsession with her own reputation and her deluded aspirations for her daughter. The unnatural, destructive bond created between mother and daughter becomes a force which gathers strength as Flor reaches adolescence, and which ever more clearly and inevitably precipitates Flor's deterioration. Nowhere in Gallant's fiction—and this is the central strength of *Green Water, Green Sky*—is there a more complete or more compelling study of the smothering of an identity, or a more harrowing presentation of madness, both from within the character's consciousness and from surrounding points of view. And nowhere in Gallant's earlier fiction is the power of the family—here, the Fairlie clan—anatomized more closely as a necessary prison, a structure which both confers and confines identity.

Counterpointing Bonnie's and Flor's severance from the extended family, Part One frames Flor's developing tragedy within the apparently less devastating abandonment of George, Flor's younger first cousin (George's father and Bonnie are Fairlie siblings), who has been tricked into spending the day with Bonnie and Flor while his parents sneak off for some time alone in Venice. But like other such abandonments in Gallant's fiction—most notably in "An Autobiography" (1964), in which stories about parents deserting children form the structure of the narrator's confession—this one is deeply traumatic for the child, although it becomes only an amusing memory in the Fairlie family annals. Readers interested in Gallant's own views about children being tricked or abandoned by their parents might recall Gallant's remarks in a 1982 interview:

> Three weeks after my fourth birthday I was put in a very, very severe institution. Dressed in black. I don't remember the first night, but I do know that my mother said, "Sit there, and I'll be right back." And she never came back. And that I remember vividly.... I remember very well sitting on a varnished chair and my mother having said that incredibly stupid thing to say to a child, "Now, you sit there like a good girl, and I'll be right back." And as far as I am concerned never returned.[6]

The structure of Part One, like the structure of many of Gallant's short stories, forms around two related scenes, one near the beginning and one at the conclusion of this opening section. The first scene takes place a few pages from the beginning of the novel: as George, Bonnie, and Flor return from the beach, Flor buys a cheap glass necklace which breaks as she tries to pull it over her head; then, in a gesture which in several ways signals her later deterioration, she flings its glass beads in the air, sending George scurrying after them. The scene is representative in its rendering of Flor and George in their relationship at this early stage, when Flor is an object of both dread and fascination for George, both alluring and menacing, capable, he thinks, of murder, but also beautiful—and also his cousin:

> The necklace breaking, the hotly blowing wind excited Flor. She unstrung the beads still in her hands and flung them after the others, making a wild upward movement with her palms. "Oh, stop it," her mother cried, for people were looking, and Flor did appear rather mad, with her hair flying and her dress blowing so that anybody could see the starched petticoat underneath, and the sunburned thighs. And poor little George, suddenly anxious about what strangers might think—this new, frantic little George ran here and there, picking up large lozenge-shaped beads from under people's feet. When he straightened up, hands full of treasure, he saw that Florence was angry, and enjoying herself, all at once. Her hands were still out, as if she wanted to give just anyone a push. But perhaps he imagined that, for she walked quietly beside him, back to the hotel, and told him, kindly, that he could keep all the beads.[7]

George cherishes one glass bead as a talisman, a good luck charm which he keeps for years after this incident. The bead also becomes an artifact through which George can preserve a record of this crucial incident in his and Flor's past: "It was a powerful charm; a piece of a day; a reminder that someone had wished him dead but that he was still alive" (5–6). As well, George will later superimpose this memory on another, earlier memory, and here one of the meanings of the relation between "water" and "sky" first alluded to in the novel's title begins to define itself. First, George remembers leaning over a railing with Flor on that day in Venice, watching a boat loading, and meeting Flor's eyes, "green as water, bright with dislike," as she tells him that it would be easy for her to push him into the water. He also remembers "the heavy green water closing out the sky and the weight of clouds" (6). What George sees, but cannot quite apprehend, is the quality of "bright dislike" in his cousin's eyes—in her precocious but distorted "adult" consciousness, which becomes a state of mind and a form of identity rendered as "water," connected through Flor's eyes with an interior, submerged, and menacing awareness, in which George might drown, into which Flor might push him. To fall into this awareness, to be drawn into the imprisoning complex of "love and resentment" which has entrapped Flor in her deadly relationship with her mother, would drown out "sky" for George, inverting his reality as Flor's has been inverted.

But George's identity will grow within different confines, in which memory, although always subject to distortion and to its own reversals, to its own superimposition of "water" over "sky," will provide him with a tenuous purchase on his past and with an identity, problematic as it might be, as a Fairlie. We are shown early that George's memory does not preserve a "true" past when he superimposes the memory of Flor looking at him on an earlier memory, "glass over glass." As a child he had fallen into his Fairlie grandmother's pond: "The most oppressive part of the memory was that he had lain there, passive, with the mossy water over his mouth. He must have been on his back; there was a memory of sky. The gardener fished him out and he was perfectly fine; not on his back at all, but on his face, splashing and floundering" (6–7).

George's memory is unreliable as to his position in "water" and "sky," his immersion in interior states of mind or his emergence into an external world; indeed, what characterizes all the Fairlies (save for Bonnie and Flor) is their group identity as a clan, a collective whose members look and behave like each other, possessors of an assemblage of traits rather than separable and autonomous individuals. But beyond that enclave lies a world in which Bonnie and Flor cannot survive; and George regards and remembers Flor's interior world—signalled most luminously through her green eyes, bright with dislike—with awe and fear. In her consciousness, George would drown, as she eventually will. Flor, Bonnie's centre of attention with no centre of her own, has pledged herself to care for her mother, abandoned by the Fairlies; she tells George in this opening sequence that "[Y]ou stinking Fairlies weren't loyal. You see him [Bonnie's first husband, Flor's father] all the time"; George remembers Flor crying at this point "[S]he'll never do anything anymore. I'll always keep her with me" (11). But

Flor will never gain the insight into her own motivation necessary for her to establish an identity apart from her mother, as the narrator makes clear in describing Flor's declaration: "She meant these words, they weren't intended for George. It was a solemn promise, a cry of despair, love and resentment so woven together that even Flor couldn't tell them apart" (11).

The first part of the novel closes with Flor's marriage to Bob Harris in New York. Harris is unfit for a Fairlie in two senses: he's Jewish, and he's a businessman comfortably immersed in the commerce of that larger middle-class world which amuses the Fairlies from a distance, but which cannot presume to share their social vocabulary or their position. George has only seen his cousin a few brief times in the intervening ten years; now he attempts to return the bead to her, but she refuses it. She remembers the day in Venice only in undifferentiated colour: "'Do you remember how green it was all the time?' Flor said to him. 'Everything was so clear and green, green water, even the sky looked green to me'" (17). George does remember it, he thinks, after looking "inadvertently" into Flor's eyes, "dark-lashed, green as the lagoon had been"; as he did earlier, George remembers the quality of the day emanating first from Flor, from what he sees, and saw, in her eyes. But when George now tries to return to Flor *his* talisman, representing what he has preserved of that day, she refuses the bead and disclaims the memory. She denies having bought the necklace, or having broken it on purpose:

> "It's just that I'm not a person who breaks things," Flor said. "Of course, if you say it happened, it's true. I haven't much memory."
> "I thought you sort of broke it on purpose," he said.
> "Oh, George," said Flor, shaking her head, "now I know it can't be real. That just isn't me. It didn't happen." (19)

Here, at the crucial point when Flor refuses this facet of her past proferred to her by George, the connection between Flor's destructively entwined emotions and George's fascination with her is established within the same controlling image of water and sky reflecting, one within the other: "Sometimes it was as though Flor had never left his thoughts, even when he didn't think of her at all. Because of her, the twin pictures, love and resentment, were always there, one reflecting the other, water under sky" (19). And bound up in Flor's refusal is her fatal rejection of the possibility of insight or of any connection with the Fairlies. For George, that day's abandonment in Venice becomes an exception which proves the rule; for Flor, abandonment in a wider sense shapes her lack of a firm identity, moulds her relationship with her mother, and, perhaps, spurs her to break the necklace and scatter its beads.

The second part of the novel—originally, this section was published as "August"—is set in Paris, where Flor has begun to deteriorate psychologically.

She is in analysis, but breaks off her therapy; indeed, psychoanalysis and any explication of consciousness through reference to the unconscious are treated
quite ironically at the surface level throughout this novel, as if to warn readers
that glib Freudian interpretation will not go far towards understanding Flor's
and her mother's relationship. Gallant has remarked in an interview that at one
point in her life she "went through a great period of Freud" and that his ideas
were "gospel" for her, "almost like a code."[8] But in *Green Water, Green Sky,*
Freudian doctrine, at least as it appears in diluted form in the consciousness of
characters without any real understanding of its significance, is treated quite
ironically, as in the following cutting description of Doris Fischer, a young
American woman in Paris who fastens onto Flor for a time:

> Doris was proud of her education—a bundle of notions she trundled before
> her like a pram containing twins. She could not have told you that the
> shortest distance between two points was a straight line, but she did know
> that "hostility" was the key word in human relations, and that a man with
> an abscessed tooth was only punishing himself. (58)

Bonnie, who is living with Flor and Bob in his apartment, is reluctant to leave
Flor alone for August, when Bob will be away on business and Bonnie is to visit
friends in Deauville. But Flor is left alone finally, and sinks into a torpor,
wandering through the apartment, hoping to dream—to "achieve the dreams
she desired" (81). But her dreams elude her, as does any sane entrance into her
own interior life. And finally, driven out of the apartment into the city to try and
fill a prescription for sleeping pills, she comes upon a staged scene in reality
which reawakens her to her lifelong terrors, which have now begun to over-
whelm her. In a café, she witnesses "a laughing couple," who are "pretending to
give their child away to a policeman": "The policeman played his role well,
swinging his cape, pretending to be fierce. 'She is very naughty,' said the mother,
when she could stop laughing enough to speak, 'and I think prison is the best
solution.' All the people in the café laughed, except for Flor" (82).

The child is terrified, but no one notices until the child "suddenly went white
and stiff in the policeman's grasp" (82); Flor, talking to herself, says that "It's
because of things like that . . . I'm not afraid of bombs" (82). This real-life stag-
ing of the threat of abandonment, which perhaps recalls to Flor her lost father,
drives her back to the apartment, where she reads a long and incoherent letter
from Doris, whom Flor has locked out of the apartment. All of the characters
surrounding Flor have their own deeply flawed perceptions of themselves, and
Doris is among the most pathetic in her fumbling insecurity and her struggles to
understand her own failing marriage; but it is Doris's letter that makes a central
point about children's treatment of their parents:

Florence, another thing. Everybody makes someone else pay for something, I don't know why. If you are as awful to your mother as she says you are, you are making her pay, but then, Florence, your mother could turn around and say, "Yes, but look at my parents," and they could have done and said the same thing, so you see how pointless it is to fix any blame. . . . We all pay and pay for someone else's troubles. All children eventually make their parents pay, and pay, and pay. (84)

This is the last "insight" we see Flor reading before her final hallucinatory regression into a perfect childhood reunion with her long-departed father. Because she cannot have children—a biological metaphor, perhaps, for her inability to separate herself from her mother and become an autonomous woman, capable of being a real mother herself, rather than a trapped "mother" to Bonnie—Flor will not be able to test Doris's glib suggestion that she may change her mind about this theory when she has her own children. This scene closes Part Two, and it is, chronologically, the latest and the last we see of Flor.

The short story which comprises the third part of the novel was originally entitled "Travellers Must Be Content," a line from *As You Like It* and the last clause of Touchstone the clown's speech in Act II, Scene iv, which Gallant has taken for the novel's epigraph: "Ay, now am I in Arden; the more fool I; when I was at home, I was in a better place: but travellers must be content." This is a fitting epigraph for a novel in which various kinds of departures from "home" motivate and ultimately shape all of the major characters' identities, and it is an epigraph which comments incisively on the character of Wishart, the figure at the centre of this part of the novel. In her devastating portrait of Wishart—whose name is emblematic of his developing a totally fabricated identity, a totally invented persona, an "art" created out of a wish—Gallant presents a character who is the antithesis of any essentialist conception of a "genuine" or authentic identity and who has gone several steps further than any other character in totally denying his real past. In reality, Wishart is the child of English working-class parents, escaped from a slum; in the fantasy he has created, he has invented a squire for a father and made himself over into a cultured Englishman in America, summer companion of various hostesses in Europe. He is a cultured mountebank, putting his fabricated Old World sophistication on display in America (reversing the direction and the course of development many of Gallant's North American characters take on their travels to postwar Europe), parlaying a faked aristocratic mien into a passport valid on both sides of the Atlantic.

In his veneer of sophistication, his invented past, his personality created *ex nihilo*, Wishart makes a perfect companion for Bonnie—and worse, her ideal choice of a husband for her daughter. It is fitting that Bonnie should be duped by Wishart, but tragic that she should imagine him a desirable match for Flor. If Wishart represents an ideal husband for Flor in Bonnie's mind, we can only infer that Bonnie's aspirations for Flor have been delusory from the beginning, hopelessly enmeshed in her misconceptions of her own life's course.

Because we read this section after Part Two, Flor's breakdown, vividly depicted but not completely apprehended in Part Two, now begins to seem to have been as inevitable as it is inexorable. Flor's madness becomes inseparable from Bonnie's delusions, and Wishart becomes a sinister personification of Bonnie's essentially deluded aspirations for her daughter and herself. Flor's meeting Bob Harris on this vacation thus becomes a repudiation of her mother's wishes and a rejection of Wishart, but this repudiation cannot save her from sinking into the lost childhood which engulfs her at the end of the novel's second section.

Having followed Flor's disintegration to its apparent end in the Paris apartment, and having then doubled back to encounter Wishart in his failure to satisfy the wishes of either mother or daughter, we are brought to the fourth and concluding section, which is the only part of the novel not to appear originally as a separate short story. Nevertheless, this part of the novel could almost have stood alone, as the narrator recapitulates the plot of the previous three parts. Chronologically, the events in this concluding section take place two years after the marriage at the end of Part One; George, then seventeen, is now nineteen and has arrived for his long projected visit to Paris. But instead of meeting Flor and Bob, he has dinner with Bob and Bonnie. Flor, the absent centre of the evening, of this section, and of the whole novel, has been taken to a rest home, and the conclusion is imbued with the hollow and distracted sadness in Bob Harris which Flor's absence has created and which Bonnie, increasingly manic and shrill, attempts to deny. Flor's early vivaciousness, so much the centre of her mother's nervous and charged vitality, has been replaced by Bob's gentle distraction and George's bewilderment. In a perverse but fitting reversal, Bonnie has completed the cycle of destruction she began when she sequestered her daughter with her in her European exile; now she has, in one sense, taken Flor's place with Bob, and her annihilation of Flor is complete.

All of Bonnie's poses, all of her arts, her melodramatic turns of phrase, her genuine fits of distraction, and her petty cruelties, are concentrated in the dinner scene and in the long walk back to the apartment. George—the prototypical Fairlie, armoured in received notions of conduct—nevertheless has a notorious habit of blurting out the truth before he can stop himself, and he does so now, responding unwittingly to Bonnie's malicious or simply unintentionally monstrous remarks. This unlooked-for spontaneity culminates in a revelatory insight for George, and in an insight for readers into his own impetus to escape from the Fairlie cage, and to rid himself of his obsessive memory of Flor and their day in Venice:

"I wouldn't have wanted a son," Aunt Bonnie said. "Your daughter's your daughter all your life. You know what *your* mother wrote me last spring, Georgie? She wrote, 'It's hard to understand it but soon he'll be finished with us.' And you were what, eighteen? Why, Flor at eighteen was like a little baby. She was never finished with me."

George thought, She is now.

Of course, he had said it. This time his reaction over the blunder was against the others. He was sick of his mistakes. He was sick of Aunt Bonnie and sick of Flor. If he had still owned the bead he would have got rid of it now. (147–48)

As we witness this impossibly awkward trio manoeuvre through the evening, we see Flor's madness refracted through their memories as the three of them manufacture a past they can live with. Bonnie, who must remember a beautiful and innocent daughter whom she had to nurture and protect on her own, is finally and fully revealed as a smothering and possessive victim of her own delusions; here as in her creation of Wishart, Gallant is unsparing, and among all of Gallant's family victims and victimizers, Bonnie is singular in the extent of her damaging influence on her daughter. The unredeemed starkness of the portraits of Wishart and Bonnie contribute much to the hard clarity and severity of the whole novel; there is little relief from the taut presentation of Flor's disintegration, and the sharp ironies which in other Gallant fictions modulate into cutting and comic observations rarely function to this end in this most sombre of Gallant's early meditations on parents and children trapped within mutually destructive relationships.

The final scene opens with George's failed attempt to give Flor back to Bob Harris. Bob invites George to visit Flor, thinking Flor might recognize her cousin, and asking George whether he hadn't been "pretty close" to Flor (154). George, a consummate Fairlie in this crucial moment, says "the most considerate thing he could think of. . . . 'To tell the truth, I hardly knew her. I think in my whole life I only saw my cousin six times'" (154).

The last paragraph leaves us with George's failure, with everyone's failure to connect with Flor, and presents us with a final composite image of Flor's indeterminate identity, of her several guises in George's mind and memory, revealed in the only appropriate form, now that she has become a chimera. He and Bob have taken a taxi back to Bob's car, which they had left near the restaurant to indulge Bonnie's whim to walk her home. On the walk, George had seen a girl emerge "in the most poetic way imaginable, out of the Paris night," and saw in her an incarnation of his readiness for "something to happen"; but Bonnie had squelched his image by identifying her as a Scandinavian nursemaid who is in France to learn French. Now, in the taxi, the novel closes with George's "authentic hallucination":

He saw Bonnie and Aunt Flor and the girl on the Quai Anatole France as one person. She was a changeable person, now menacing, now dear; a minute later behaving like a queen in exile, plaintive and haughty, eccentric by birth, unaware, or not caring, that the others were laughing behind their hands. (154)

Here are fragments of "Flor," in George's mind, in a true hallucination, among the guises in which she persists in his memory. Superimposed over remnants of Flor's "dear and menacing" figure, glass on glass, green water under and over green sky, we can also catch glimpses of Bonnie's various guises; and Bonnie, and through her, Flor, by nature could not care, or had to be unaware, that others—the other Fairlies?—were laughing behind their hands. But the image is just that—an "authentic hallucination." Flor is really not there.

Green Water, Green Sky depicts the tragedy of a young woman who ultimately falls out of the social structure, whose only route to what she perceives as her true "self" lies through the essentially private, interiorized mythology of her own madness. *A Fairly Good Time* focusses on Shirley Perrigny's jousts with identity from a different, almost opposed perspective, through a series of social lenses. Gallant's longest work of fiction and her finest novel to date, *A Fairly Good Time* (1970) is a sustained, comic, but deadly serious exploration of a naive young North American woman's quest, impelled by social expectations she only dimly apprehends, for a life less encumbered by the inscrutable demands of her French husband, of various idiosyncratic families, and of her own terribly persistent need for self-explanation. Through the course of her baffled but persistent adventure towards self-recognition, Shirley becomes one of the most successful of Gallant's women in achieving a measure of equilibrium and independence for more than a brief moment, for more time than the flash of an isolated insight. On this level, *A Fairly Good Time* is a comedy of manners which shows Shirley trying to navigate the turbid crosscurrents of French sexual, marital, familial, and cultural norms. French institutions present themselves to Shirley as mysteries; appearance and behaviour—her own included—become codes to be deciphered, riddles to be solved. Her routes to insight take Shirley careening through a maze of social strata, through labyrinths of conduct from which she finally emerges with a measure of equanimity. At the novel's end, Shirley will finally be able to have the "fairly good time" promised in the title and its epigraph, which Gallant has taken from Edith Wharton's story "The Last Asset."

Shirley's trajectory takes the shape of the traditional comic voyage, but with some ironic and decidedly modern twists. She achieves the traditional goal of comedy—reintegration—but not via the traditional marriage scene; rather, she achieves her own reintegration by successfully completing her separation from her husband Philippe. In another ironic variation on the traditional comic goal of discovery or recognition following disguise or concealment, Shirley's various masks are shown to have concealed her not so much from others as from herself. Gallant shows us Shirley's difficulties in recognizing herself in various ways—most comically, at the height of Shirley's disorientation, when she walks towards a young woman she sees in a restaurant, only to realize at the last possible instant that she is about to walk into her own image in a mirror. (In this novel as in all of Gallant's fiction, the richly suggestive properties of the mirror as a "looking glass," with all of its implications for an identity reflected in a reverse image of itself, for a "mimetic" reflection of self often desperately sought and yet just as often misperceived or misinterpreted, are developed to powerful effect.) The novel's most impressive achievement of tone and mood is the unerring, delicate balance it maintains along the sharp and serious edge of its comedy; one false step, and Shirley would topple over into either bathos or tragedy.

This novel, like *Green Water, Green Sky,* finds one of its origins in a short story, but *A Fairly Good Time* goes much further beyond the form, structure, language, or content of the story than does *Green Water, Green Sky* in relation to its antecedents. "The Accident"—which is about the death of Pete, Shirley's Canadian first husband, in Italy on their honeymoon—becomes part of a long flashback in the novel. Shirley imagines herself explaining to Philippe her reasons for coming to France after Pete's death, so that the episode provides Shirley, and readers, with a firmer background against which to measure her protracted separation from Philippe. Another short story, "In Transit" (1965) follows Philippe beyond *A Fairly Good Time* with his second wife, but Gallant has remarked that this story "was part of it [the novel] too, but I didn't want it and I rewrote it as a story. That is, I rewrote the whole novel and it didn't belong any more."[9]

The first remarkable quality of *A Fairly Good Time* is its rhetoric. The novel opens with a chapter-long letter to Shirley from her mother in Canada, a letter which serves as a model of the essentially oblique or indirect communication which is the novel's major formal (and comic) reflection of the mystifications that isolate Shirley from other characters. Ostensibly, the letter is about everything Shirley's mother can tell her about bluebells; late in the novel, we discover that Shirley had picked bluebells on a walk with Philippe, his soldier friend Hervé from the Algerian war, and Hervé's wife, and sent a flower in a letter to her mother. But in reality the original letter from Shirley had obviously also been about her troubled marriage, and her mother's response only alludes to Shirley's problems in the most indirect way. Like other letters in the novel, this one corroborates an early observation about Shirley, but one which for many readers might resonate across most, if not all of the family relationships in Gallant's fiction: "Shirley never failed to expect her mother's letters to contain magical solutions, and never failed to be disappointed. The correspondence between mother and daughter, Montreal and Paris, was an uninterrupted dialogue of the deaf."[10]

Shirley's mother's letters serve as comical exemplars of this uninterrupted dialogue, deafening precisely in proportion to its persistence, but also revelatory in its establishment of Shirley's relationship with her mother, an eccentric who instructs her daughter with the conviction born of a lifetime of stalwart idiosyncrasy in Western Canada. Perhaps the most significant quality of Shirley's deaf dialogue with her parents is her childhood memory of her father's response to her dreams; she had to pay her father at a prescribed rate if he was to have to listen to them. (An important episode recounting the forbidding of children's telling parents their dreams forms the conclusion of an early Gallant story, "Jorinda and Jorindel," in which fairy tales and adult conduct are deftly and suggestively juxtaposed.)[11] Throughout Gallant's fiction, dreams figure as longed for, dimly apprehended, urgent communications from the unconscious; most often, they are either denied, mistrusted, misinterpreted, or simply reported without comment. In this novel, the suppression of dreams figures as one aspect of the blockading of Shirley's interior life, and the dream she narrates in a letter to Philippe—a letter which, we discover, she begins on paper, but, in another layer of rhetorical distortion further emphasizing Shirley's short-circuited attempts at communication, she completes in her head—vividly evokes Shirley's fears as a woman in a world of inarticulate male animals:

> My only nightmare (if you hate dreams just skip this) has to do with normal people turning into animals. I am with one, two, three, men. All at once I notice a change in their expressions; their eyes are like dogs', then wolves'. I think that if I go on speaking I can force them to be normal again, but my words are incoherent to them and they take my voice to be a threat. They can't understand what I am saying. They can't listen or reason. They are unpredictable and cruel. They can't help it. They can only hide or attack. In the dream I am not attacked. Are you surprised? I am the rescuer. I am the rescue party. Yes, I save someone, anyone, even you sometimes. . . . This dream is not worth a cent, and my father would not have heard about it for under a thousand dollars. (217)

Letters, imagined letters, notes, and telephone messages serve as the chief means of communication from Shirley to Philippe; and balancing this line of dialogue at a remove, Philippe "speaks" to Shirley chiefly through what she reads in the various kinds of writing that Philippe leaves on his desk in their apartment. These essentially "written" means of communication reflect what is referred to as the "white silence" in which they conduct their marriage (125). Rarely do we see Shirley and Philippe speaking face to face—and when we do, the scene usually takes place in Shirley's memory—although the major frame for what stands in place of a conventional plot is Philippe's leaving Shirley, an action which is finally completed by Shirley's emancipation from Philippe. And in a further, incrementally ironic comment on the original reason for their separation, we learn that Philippe has silently left Shirley because she has gone to help Renata, a friend whose melodramatic threat of suicide represents a barely comic personification of one of Shirley's options.

Superimposed upon these forms of indirection or secondhand communication are the obliquities created by two languages and two cultures. Not only does French rendered into English repeatedly figure as another screen of translation interposed between Shirley and her experience (aptly, Shirley works in a large department store as a translator for tourists), but Shirley's "Canadian" directness constantly bangs up against Philippe's and other French characters' native circumspection. In their relationship, the typical Gallant revelation of North American conduct in its contretemps with European codes of behaviour becomes both a concentrated comedy and a concise anatomy of a young, foreign wife's acutely vulnerable position in her marriage to a French husband. In this regard, *A Fairly Good Time* is Gallant's most complete and most condemnatory dissection in fiction—parallelled most closely in her essays by her detailed account of French women's social and legal positions in "The Gabrielle Russier Affair"—of women's subservient positions in virtually all French institutions. The widows, wives, daughters and single women in this novel all orbit around tyrannical males, besotted with their institutionally sanctioned positions of power. Dead or alive, the male characters exert a pervasive and oppressive control; their portraits range from caricatures to images of menacing, if melodramatic bestiality, from comic images of the melodramatically perverse—like the sketch of the minor figure of Karel, Renata's neo-Nazi boyfriend—to fuller evocations of the genuinely incestuous—like the figure of the more important "Papa" Maurel, father of Claudie Maurel, Shirley's most comical foil, and probably also the father of Claudie's child. Ludicrous though many of these figures may appear, the general image of the influence of the male figures in this novel remains quite threatening, and readers might well find *A Fairly Good Time* to be the most profound reflection in Gallant's fiction of women's subservient positions in contemporary French society.

The social frame that Gallant presents in *A Fairly Good Time* forms a dense and baffling foreground for Shirley's trials. Gallant's evocation of Paris in this novel is the most complete in her fiction until the various depictions of Paris which are so essential to the "stories of Paris" collected in *Overhead in A Balloon* (1985).[12] In *A Fairly Good Time,* we read the typically detailed, tangible descriptions of place—parks, city blocks, the interiors of apartment buildings, the flat gray feel of anonymous suburbs, the atmosphere filtered through the shades of light in cafés—but we also find a social French milieu which seems alternately provincial, impervious, or caught in a twenty-year time warp in its attitudes to the world beyond its borders. The fallout from the Algerian crisis lingers in many characters' consciousnesses (the novel is set in the sixties);

ominously, French soldiers in Algeria are most often associated with torture and rape, as if one strand of French right-wing sentiment were particularized in violence and brutality against women. This is a connection which comes close to home for Shirley: Philippe and his friend Hervé, Shirley recalls at one point in her long, imagined letter to Philippe "were in Algeria, and you know something you will never say" (247). In a café, Shirley watches Germans being recruited to play officers in war films—a scene which recurs in various contexts in several of Gallant's "German stories"—and commits one of her infamous gaffes when she asks Helmut, a character who is going to bring a camera back from Germany for Philippe, to bring her a flag for a friend who "collects all that sort of thing" (128).[13] And the French attitude towards Americans, which borders on the xenophobic, provides an interesting comment on stock French postwar political perceptions, counterpointing the French attitudes towards "American" women which Shirley must contend with. The conversation at a party in Shirley's apartment building is representative: after Shirley tells a ludicrous story about an American officer who, after the Liberation, allegedly caused terrible and permanent liver disease by feeding Philippe's sister Colette too much milk, the talk turns to contemporary American incursions:

> The women listened seriously now. One or two men had joined them—a brother-in-law, and a man who had owned a cork factory in Algeria and had been dispossessed. America was to blame, said the brother-in-law. Of course, for the officer had been an American. The hypocritical milk trick was held up, a mirror in which they saw reflected Americans shipping arms to Algerian rebels, Americans interfering with the weather. (114)

The most significant among the novel's myriad reflections of French social institutions, however, is the Maurel family—Claudie, her son Alain, her parents, Madame and "Papa" Maurel, and her sister, Marie-Thérèse. It is fitting that the Maurels should provide the focus for the novel's most important two-way mirror, reflecting both an absurdly distorted (and yet also representative) image of the French family, and, in Claudie Maurel, a reverse image of one of Shirley's possible fates. Shirley is thrown together with Claudie in a restaurant when Claudie manipulates her into paying her bill; from there, Shirley is drawn into an excruciating relationship with the whole Maurel family, through which she is exposed to all of the crippling power structures which entrap this family in a web of interlocking neuroses. Shirley's perceived status as a hopelessly naive foreigner is thrown into sharp relief in her various encounters with the Maurels; ironically we see her entrance into their apartment and her increasingly intimate involvement in their lives in directly inverse proportion to her growing separation from Philippe and his family. In comic contrast to the way in which Shirley is dragged by Claudie to her first visit to the Maurel apartment (from which

Shirley flees in disarray), when Shirley tries to visit Philippe at his widowed mother's apartment, his mother rebuffs her at the door. The transformations of Shirley's role in the Maurel family—from a hapless foreigner, Claudie's exotic find, to Claudie's surrogate elder sister and potential saviour—help us to trace the emerging contours of Shirley's developing identity.

The character of Papa Maurel, exemplar of the all-powerful French father, provides a fine example of how Gallant's comedy operates on several levels at once. On the surface, Papa Maurel is simply an ill-tempered, intelligent, tyranni- cal clown when Shirley meets him at her first Sunday lunch with the Maurels. His rule over the family is unquestioned, his foul temper indulged at every turn. The scene at the dinner table is a hilarious, hysterical dance of attendance on his every whim; on this level, the Maurels might be seen simply as a delightfully bizarre reflection of a certain class of French family, dominated by a clownish tyrant, and we can appreciate Gallant's superb handling of the family's rituals of obeisance at the dinner table. But the comedy has a more serious and more menacing purpose, as Papa Maurel's reign extends beyond these relatively in- nocuous borders to smother and cripple the women in his domain.

At first, Claudie's penchant for acting the part of the perpetual adolescent, perpetually on stage, might seem just another facet of the family comedy; but gradually we learn with Shirley that Papa's power has expressed itself more directly and literally than Shirley had originally perceived. Alain, Claudie's hopelessly neurotic, pampered, and psychologically undeveloped son, is in all probability Papa's child. This incestuous relationship, which figures as the psychosexual extension of Papa's socially sanctioned, institutionalized tyranny, casts a darker shadow over the comedy of this family's internecine wars, and makes Claudie a victim of more than her own shallow pretensions. Papa's power over Claudie and the rest of the family is further confirmed when he defeats Shirley's attempt to rescue Alain from the family for a six-week stay in the country with her friends; and Shirley's own privileged position in the Maurel family is confirmed when she is enlisted by Marie-Thérèse to return Claudie to the family fold when Claudie tries to move out with a boyfriend.

For Shirley, the Maurel family provides a crash education, both by precept and concept, in the positions of women in the French family institution. Not only is she confronted with Claudie, an object lesson in perpetual subjugation, but she also learns from Madame Maurel, whose story of her marriage provides Shirley with eloquent and firsthand testimony about the pervasive influence of Papa. When Claudie is returned once and for all to the prison of her relationship with her father, Shirley is catalyzed to move in the opposite direction; watching Papa and Claudie together in Claudie's hotel room—Papa has come to get his daughter, and Shirley is "embarrassed to be here with Papa while Claudie fin- ished putting her clothes on"—Shirley reflects, contemplating the price of a sur- render like Claudie's: "All right, then. . . . Settle my problems. Run my life. How much would it cost me? She gave up wondering. Claudie would know soon" (295).

At this point Gallant provides us with a nine-month hiatus, time to allow for the changes in Shirley apparent when she returns to Paris at the end of the novel. She has gone to Greece to visit her lover, James, who lived in the apartment upstairs from hers, and whom she knew before Philippe, and she has been to Canada for her mother's funeral. Neither James nor any further instruction from or connection with her mother has deflected her intention to complete her separation from Philippe, and fittingly, her emancipation is counterpointed by Claudie's further regression. On a final visit to the Maurels, Shirley sees a "silhouette . . . and then a girl of about fifteen came into the room" (302). It is Claudie, of course, and she reminds Shirley of her last sight of her mother:

> There was something so passive in her waxen young face that Shirley felt she was again seeing a picture of the rouged and powdered dead. It seemed to her she had seen traces of this effigy from the beginning. Yes, in the taxi, that first day. She remembered Claudie's face, and she recalled a drowned pigeon in the current of the Seine.
>
> "My girl," her mother called her now, as if Claudie had found a relationship but lost her own name. (302)

In contrast, Shirley has found hers—her first married name, Higgins—because Philippe has divorced her for desertion. But the divorce has finally freed her to find her own way again, now that she has emerged from her bafflement at the images she has been seeing of herself in others' mirrors.

If the Maurel family provide Shirley with a social lens through which to focus her failing marriage, the more private centre of Shirley's conflict with Philippe can best be defined through one of the many strands of opposition the novel proposes between them, which is their opposed views of what is mysterious and what is plain in human conduct. Their disagreement, never openly voiced, extends beyond their conflict to at least partially illuminate Shirley's internal conflicts. Early in the novel, the narrator draws a telling distinction: "The quest for mystery in ideas seemed to Philippe to eliminate certain problems of behaviour, while the mystery of behaviour seemed to Shirley the only riddle worth a mention" (17). Clearly, both beliefs are being presented here in a reductive and ironically simplistic formulation, and this observation need not be seized on as the key to unlock Shirley's and Philippe's "locked situation," to borrow Gallant's phrase. But the distinction does help to make sense of Shirley's preoccupation with the maddening riddles of behaviour which she must either decode or reformulate in order to come to terms with herself; and the comedy of the novel moves her towards the liberating perception that behaviour need not be understood exclusively either as a mirror or as a mystery, either as a completely learned social, and socializing set of responses, or as a completely private individual expression of a separate, uniquely separable self.

In its most comical incarnation, Philippe's obsession with the "mystery of ideas" is reflected in his madcap determination to interpret the underlying cosmic relevance of "Goosey Gander." Philippe's close friend and confidante, the neurasthenic writer Geneviève, is composing an interminable and appalling novel, from which we read excerpts over Shirley's shoulder. Gallant's caricature of Geneviève is only the first of the novel's sparkling send-ups of women—Renata's portrait is another—each representing a parodied aspect of Shirley's personality, a route to a spurious identity which is manifestly shown to be a dead end. As a child Geneviève had an English governess who "had maintained that Goosey Gander held a universal key. Life, love, politics, art, death, explanations of the past and insight into the dreadful future were there for the reading...." (17). Fittingly, the nursery rhyme's fascination for Geneviève and through her for Philippe rests on a mistranslation which has rendered the original "Whither shalt thou wander" into "Witha Waltha"—the cryptic, pregnant phrase which preoccupies Philippe throughout the novel despite Shirley's attempts to explain the mistake.

This vignette can be read on several levels: simply as a comic deflation, a puncturing of the balloon of the interpretative mode itself as a means to insight; as a comical creation intended to suggest the intuitive discomfort with ideas (or with a literary work which does not cunningly and cryptically conceal profundity) which might compose the underlay beneath Philippe's (French?) conception of behaviour as identity; or, perhaps, as merely the most absurd reflection of Philippe's (French?) obsession with hermeneutical operations, to be performed on any and all verbal artifacts—particularly on English ones. On the novel's final page, in one of the funniest of the concluding signals of her newfound (and hard-won) autonomy, Shirley cheerfully gives up on trying to convince Philippe that he's on a very wild goose chase; her final note to him, written at the bottom of one of his latest interpretations of the lines, reflects her emancipation from his obsession: "Darling Philippe, I have finally come round to your way of thinking. G. Gander is without doubt concerned with loyalty, fidelity, passing the buck and the situation in Berlin" (308).

But Philippe is also a successful journalist and television personality whose investigative pieces, jazz columns, and interviews are serious fare for the French middle-class intelligentsia, and here Gallant's critique of Philippe acquires a wider social dimension. Philippe's drearily repetitive and shallow pieces of reportage, with their comically banal, drearily repetitive titles, regardless of the subject at hand, constitute an indictment of the veneer of the pseudo-activist, pseudo-psychoanalytical, pseudo-intellectual commitment to analyzing or improving French social conditions. From the very beginning of the novel, because we spy with Shirley on Philippe in his protracted absence from their apartment, we see that his personal conduct and history belie his public image. Philippe thus becomes a faintly damning, faintly damned representative of his generation and gender, his class and their convictions. His absence for most of the novel becomes a further indictment: Philippe is one of the novel's central images of the abstract and yet very tangible power of the male in his position in French life. Because he remains a figure defined most clearly through others' reactions—principally, Shirley's—to his absence, his shadow becomes comically distorted in its thin, cartoon-like aura of menace; but his power over Shirley, despite the comedy of its portrayal, is very real.

Shirley's measure of success in attaining the self-composure conducive to having a "fairly good time" stands in dramatic contrast to the presentation in Gallant's first novel of Flor's stark passage into madness. But both novels, each in its own form, style, and structure, chart the territory explored by so many of Gallant's women in their adventures towards and away from identity. Both novels—particularly *A Fairly Good Time*—locate these quests in a powerfully imagined, meticulously conceived social ambience, always subject to the purchase of the larger culture's memory on its collective past. When the individual's identity is severed from its connections with its past, the resulting displacement can end in the obliteration of any social frame of reference; and when the individual's identity is refracted, deflected, and mistranslated into the social images which form the language of another culture, it takes the energy and persistence of a determined, if naive character like Shirley Perrigny/Higgins to arrive at any measure of coherence or autonomy. But in both tragic and comic frames, these two works demonstrate convincingly that although the short story may be Gallant's chosen form, it is certainly not because she cannot write a novel. And in the title novella of her next published book—*The Pegnitz Junction* (1973)—we find that the "short novel" form she first worked with in "Its Image on the Mirror" has undergone a transformation into the most problematic, most allusive, and most resonant work—her own favourite among all of her works of fiction—that Gallant has produced to date.

4

The Pegnitz Junction
The "Corruption of Memory," the "Interference" of History

The implications of the "German stories" of *The Pegnitz Junction* extend beyond their German characters to resonate across the whole range of Gallant's canon. These stories constitute Gallant's most sustained study of the forms in which recent history has haunted the West. In *My Heart Is Broken,* suppressed selves haunt individuals watching images in memory's mirrors; in *The Pegnitz Junction,* history's ghosts haunt a whole culture's image, and mirrors onto the past set off moments of conflagration which burn holes in the present tense. Reading the German stories, we arrive at ironic moments of "junction" between history forgotten and history too clearly remembered. And like Christine, Herbert, and Little Bert in the title novella, we are left looking for a way to read ourselves home.

We should note Gallant's choice of epithets when she tells Geoff Hancock that in writing the German stories she was trying to discover Fascism's (not Nazism's) "small possibilities in people."[1] The stories *are* a series of painfully acute probes into postwar German culture, and they *do* articulate a specifically German psychology of inertia and bewilderment, enacting postwar German culture's dazed introspection into its own recent history. But the "Fascism" Gallant recreates in these stories is both more generally Western and more particularly human than a specifically German political, cultural, or emotional aberration. These are not fictions which indict Germany by exonerating the rest of Western culture; in fact, another of Gallant's impulses to write the German stories sprang from what she perceived as Canadian (and Western) misreading of the German concentration camps. Gallant was a reporter for the *Standard* in 1945 when the first pictures of the concentration camps arrived. Asked to write captions for them, she chose a more restrained idiom than that deployed in much Canadian (and Allied) reporting towards the end of the war. Judging from the articles published in the *Standard* in 1945, the typical Canadian reaction to news of German atrocities was shrilly hysterical and self-righteous; in retrospect, the tone of these pieces also seems sanctimonious, given what we now know (and it was not a state secret then) about Canadian immigration policies during and after the war. Gallant's reaction to the pictures was to search for a language with which to articulate a more objective, more documentary response, a language which would not frame the pictures, defending readers from responding more directly to the images themselves.

During the forties Gallant was also, in effect, taking notes for what she describes as her "personal research" into the collapse of German culture. Discussing *The Pegnitz Junction* in her interview with Hancock, Gallant tells the story of the book's origins:

> I wrote the German stories because I was trying to explain something to myself. They were a kind of personal research. . . .
>
> One thing you truly cannot imagine was what the first concentration camp pictures were for someone my age. . . . When the first pictures arrived in Canada I was twenty-two, working on a newspaper. . . . You can't imagine the first time seeing them. I kept saying, "We're dreaming. This isn't real. We're in a nightmare." You couldn't believe it. . . .
>
> Now, imagine being twenty-two, being the intensely left-wing political romantic I was, passionately anti-fascist, having believed that a new civilization was going to grow out of the ruins of the war—out of victory over fascism—and having to write *the explanation* of something I did not myself understand. I thought, "There must be no descriptive words in this, no adjectives. Nothing like 'horror,' 'horrifying' because what the pictures are saying is stronger and louder. It must be kept simple." . . .
>
> What I wrote and thought at twenty-two I think and believe now. I wrote, then, that the victims, the survivors that is, could tell us what happened *to them,* but not *why.* The *why* was desperately important to people like myself who were twenty-two and had to live with this shambles.
>
> . . . I never lost interest in what had happened, the *why* of it, I mean. Nothing I ever read satisfied me. . . . I had the feeling that in everyday living I would find the origin of the worm—the worm that had destroyed the structure. The stories in *Pegnitz Junction* are, to me, intensely political for that reason. It is not a book about Fascism, but a book about where Fascism came from. That is why I like it better than anything else. Because I finally answered my own question. Not the historical causes of Fascism— just its small possibilities in people.[2]

The captions Gallant wrote for the pictures were turned down, and in the copy that was run, Gallant recalls, "all [she] could see were the adverbs and adjectives smothering the real issue, and the covering article, which was short, was a prototype for all the clichés we've been bludgeoned with ever since."[3] The covering article appeared in *The Standard* (Rotogravure section), 19 May 1945, p. 26. The whole seven-page section is prefaced by a warning on a covering page:

"Special Section on the Atrocities in German Concentration Camps"

These important news pictures have been printed in a special section so that readers with children may remove them if they wish. It is suggested that they be kept for future reference. In time to come it may be a necessary antidote to pleas by sentimentalists and pro-Nazis that Germany is suffering hardship as a result of her defeat. Though Germans will have to work hard to rebuild their shattered cities, may well go hungry till after the rest of Europe is fed, their lot will be paradise compared with the hell they inflicted on others.

The captioned photographs are prefaced by the following covering piece:

"This is FASCISM: From Mussolini's Italy It Spread to Germany—And It Is Still a Threat"

Over a hundred photos of German concentration camps have come to The Standard from various picture services. They were taken by Canadian, British and American photographers. We are publishing only a few and not by any means the worst. But we believe it important for Canadians far from the terrors of war, to see and understand the nature of the enemy. This could have happened here. Our soldiers died to save us from it.

It would be tragedy indeed if they had died in vain. It is up to us, the living, to make sure that the Nazi-Fascist spirit which stifles free speech, incites race hatred, encourages intolerance and cruelty, despises humanity and peace, glorifies tyranny and war, is finally eradicated. These ideas are not yet dead in Germany, still live in every land. Till they too are defeated everywhere there can be no lasting peace.

Look at the photos. Thousands of Canadian soldiers have seen these things. The British have seen them; the Americans have seen them. General Patton forced German civilians to go and see what their army had done. Eisenhower went himself to look. He wired to Prime Minister Churchill suggesting that members of the British Parliament should come and see. U.S. Congressmen flew across the ocean to look as did a delegation of American newspapermen. All agreed that no word or picture could ever convey the full horror of the reality.

Here in Canada we can see all around us the peace and freedom we are fighting for. These photos show what we are fighting against.

In *The Pegnitz Junction,* Gallant avoids the various clichéd responses to a subject which, since the forties, has been treated in every mode from the luridly docudramatic to the luridly sensational. In the foreground of Gallant's stories, a culture's breakdown intrudes everywhere, always particularized through what Gallant has called "short circuits" in communication between individuals.[4] Gallant's questions about a culture's collapse form the fissures that riddle the surfaces of these stories, fissures which open up as a culture tries to span the chasm in its history created by the war.

Reading these stories—particularly the title novella—we discover their unity precisely in the fragmentation of time that they enact. *The Pegnitz Junction* is in this limited sense the most unified of Gallant's books, in that its stories, unlike those assembled in *The Other Paris* and *My Heart Is Broken,* focus on one time and one theme. The characters are native exiles who feel most displaced at home. They are bewildered by the fragmentation of time they perceive; the "junction" these stories close with is not a destination but a stopping point, a moment in history from which there may or may not be further "progress." Recent history is a nightmare from which the characters cannot awaken; their lives are paralyzed by time rather than lived in time. They find recent history's significance menacing, and the connections between wartime and peacetime more numerous than the distinctions. The result is a series of stories in which ambivalent attitudes towards history erode the forms through which memory might recover whole selves, a whole culture, or a whole past.

Memory in *The Pegnitz Junction* is atrophied, withered, and characters are more apt to forget or falsify the past than to remember or clarify it. Many of these stories enact an indeterminate, precarious present moment through the sense of arrest and suspension in time Gallant creates by using the simple present tense. But even though individuals, families, and cultures attempt to sever the present from the past, to suspend themselves out of the flux of history, the past continually manifests itself, psychologically, socially, in private and public life. The ordinary distends in *The Pegnitz Junction* because characters are unable to make plausible connections between past and present; they cannot establish sufficient continuity to communicate a firm enough sense of self to ground them in time and place.

The ironies which form the fractured unity of this book begin with the title of the book's first story. In "The Old Friends" (1969), Helena, a famous West German television actress, and an unnamed police commissioner are not "old" friends, even though the commissioner believes he has known her "forever";[5]

nor are they friends in any but a deeply ironic sense. Like several of the other stories in *The Pegnitz Junction,* "The Old Friends" is narrated in the simple present tense, effectively enacting this friendship's suspension out of time and beyond historical implications. The relations between past and present in this story are radically discontinuous, and they cannot be strengthened either by individual memory or by collective historical sense. Helena and the commissioner talk at each other in an atemporal, ahistorical vacuum, an ambience whose ironic significance is suggested by the story's setting in an Edenic garden in a luxurious Frankfurt suburb, where Helena allows the commissioner to take her and her mysteriously acquired son to tea. The story's structure is fairly straightforward: the narrative present follows the course of their seemingly innocuous afternoon dalliance over champagne. But Helena consciously ruptures their conversation and the banality of the present moment, "orphaning" the commissioner, by casually referring to her Jewish grandmother, killed in Silesia during the war. The narrator broadens and deepens the significance of this fissure in the relationship until it becomes apparent that the "friendship" is a tissue-thin transparency laid over the interlocking tensions between historical victim and victimizer. The point of view—and this is typical of point of view in Gallant's fiction after *My Heart Is Broken*—becomes elusive: the voice and perspective shift and shift again, modulating now into a tone implying the commissioner's perspective, now to one implying Helena's angle of vision, then again to "our" perspective on Helena as a kind of cultural prize, a noteworthy representative of the "0.4" percent of West Germany's postwar population that is Jewish. Helena is "popular, much loved, and greatly solicited. She is the pet, the kitten—*ours*" (94). One of the effects of this shifting point of view is to draw both reader and culture into the relationship, to dissolve this "friendship" into a diffuse representation of "our" difficulties in reading the connections between victims and victimizers, particularly when the roles are reversed.

We hear of Helena's waste of time earlier that day, when she is interviewed by a "gaunt female reporter" (an Englishwoman), who asks her about her childhood experience in the prison camps. Like Peter Dobay in "An Autobiography," Helena as a child had been saved by chance from transport to a death camp; now the reporter wants to know if "the child . . . in these camps . . . [was] . . . sexually? . . . molested?" (95) Helena's response ("it was forbidden" [95]) really tells the reporter nothing, just as the commissioner learns nothing when she repeats her response to him in the garden, at the end of the story. But we learn to draw the distinction Helena has learned to draw—between her firsthand experience of "destruction" and the public, postwar, peacetime conception of her experience, which seeks to locate her suffering in a domestic and civilized context, one in which rape—a physical violation with devastating psychological consequences—is the worst possible violation of individuality. But Helena's own context is more radical: the psychological obliteration she has experienced in the camps has made the mere brutality of rape seem insignificant. The shifts in point of view in the passage below convey the movement from personal to public responsibility and bewilderment, making the reporter's response, like the commissioner's, representative rather than idiosyncratic:

> Rape is so important to these people, Helena has learned; it is the worst humiliation, the most hideous ordeal the Englishwoman can imagine. She is thinking of maniacs in parks, little children attacked on their way to the swimming pool. "Destruction" is meaningless, and in any case Helena is here, alive, with her hair brushed, and blue on her eyelids—not destroyed. But if the child was sexually molested, then we all know where we are. We will know that a camp was a terrible place to be, and that there are things Helena can never bring herself to tell. (95)

But "we" (the reporter, the commissioner, the reader) do not know where we are any more than does Helena, for whom "reality was confounded long ago. She even invents her dreams. When she says she dreams of a camp exactly reproduced, no one ever says, 'Are you sure?'" (96). Thus Helena's view may be fabricated as well; her "exactly reproduced" version of the past is too precise, too mimetic to be believable.

Before returning to the garden scene, the narrator telescopes time to focus on Helena's original meeting with the commissioner on a train; this encounter is presented from a point of view looking over Helena's shoulder, so that when we return to the garden, which has become less Edenic, the commissioner's bewilderment has clearer origins. Helena closes the rupture she had opened a moment before—when she told him she could imitate her grandmother's Yiddish accent, because she must have heard it before her grandmother was killed—assuring the commissioner that rape was forbidden in the camps. Finally the point of view shifts again as we see the commissioner's relief at their reunion and his satisfaction that the friendship will continue—even as we realize that he has failed once again to confront the underlying tensions which always threaten the relationship. Gallant traces the complex motives behind this transparently superficial alliance, showing how Helena and the commissioner are bound to each other by their passage through history, which has cast them in a symbiotic relationship between parent and child, teacher and student, guard and prisoner. As peacetime erodes the distinction between uniformed prisoners and uniformed officialdom, the civilians' roles become more clearly interdependent and interchangeable. Helena cannot stop "teaching" the commissioner, needling him with sharp, wounding observations and jokes which thrust up in his face the destruction of identity she has experienced, while the commissioner cannot allay his professional anxiety over the official "errors" and "mistakes" which must surely, he believes, have been the causes of Helena's suffering. The commissioner "knows only one meaning for each word"; his strictly denotative model of language determines in turn his interpretation of experience, which can have only one meaning, one dimension (90). All of the commissioner's categories of perception would depersonalize Helena's experience; he can only conceive of her past in terms of an imaginary dossier, "typed . . . on cheap brownish wartime paper, in a folder tied with ribbon tape" (94).

The faultlines running through the relationship also represent a larger cultural fragmentation. The commissioner's apparently random references to German history and culture begin, ironically, to cohere, suggesting a whole culture's ambivalence towards its past. The story's critique of the commissioner's sense of history begins with his glib assurance that he has known Helena "forever," that he "cannot remember when or how they met," but he has "*always* known her"—that this "*must* be true" (89–90). *As types,* he and Helena have indeed "always" known each other, as is demonstrated by the relevance to *their* particular relationship of the joke Helena tells him about a Prussian officer and an old Jew on the train.

The commissioner's certainties are confounded as the narrator gives readers the details of Helena's first meeting with him; more importantly, readers learn that the commissioner's most significant "failing, as a friend, is his memory" (96). This failing extends to his sense of history, to his understanding of Helena's experience and, by extension, to his understanding of their shared past. So, for example, the commissioner, waxing incoherent as he enthuses over the beauty of the lit up swimming pools in the suburban gardens at night, tells Helena of seeing them from a helicopter: " . . . it looked . . . it was . . . it should have been photographed . . . or painted . . . described by *Goethe,* he cries, it could not have been more . . . " (90). In his inarticulate rapture, he summons up Goethe, a hilariously inappropriate appropriation in this context, but one which begins to make ironic sense in light of the commissioner's other references to German history and culture. Meeting Helena for the first time on the train, he propositions her with another quantum leap backwards—*over* the recent war, into a past more safely out of reach, with less perplexing resonances: "In the daytime," he suggests to Helena, "you could go to a museum . . . where you can see ancient boats made out of hide, and you can see the oars. There are guided tours . . . The guide is excellent!" (97). But the commissioner himself is a less than excellent guide in his tour of the recent past, Helena's as well as his own. Again, mistaking her on the train for a refined lady, he stammers: "I apologize. You seem . . . a woman like you . . . so educated, so delicate . . . so refined, like a . . . *Holbein*" (98).

For her part, although she uses her gifts as an actress and mimic to entertain the commissioner, Helena's performances always have a potential "sting," symbolized best by the wasps which invade the commissioner's garden retreat, attracted by the bittersweet nasturtiums on the table (91). Although her stories wound the commissioner, Helena is both unable and unwilling to press the point home and sting him into self-knowledge. So, when she tells him the story of the Prussian officer and the old Jew, he looks at her "so bewildered," "so perplexed," that she can only *imagine* explaining the joke's application to him. And the commissioner's response, she imagines, would be typically unambiguous, depersonalized, stripped of connotation: "But he would only know that another injustice had been committed; another terrible mistake" (99). Helena's broken dialogue with the commissioner takes place against a *shared* reluctance to interpret that past; their delicately balanced "friendship" can be toppled over into a void by a single word from Helena, and a single word can rescue it. The volatility of what is left unarticulated threatens to crack the commissioner's veneer of affable and professional solicitude and to upset Helena's cruel passivity, but the story closes with the "old friends" reunited in the garden, and with Helena allowing a wasp to escape from the glass the commissioner had trapped it in (99).

In many stories, Gallant will repeat a word or phrase, or draw attention to the same detail in jarringly different contexts to bring a point home. The significance of the references to German history and culture in "The Old Friends" emerges most clearly through the juxtaposition of a real with an imagined reaction. First, Helena recites Schiller's "The Glove" to the commissioner in a range of accents. When she gets to the line, *"Und wie er winkt mit dem finger"*—significantly, declaiming the words in the commissioner's own Hessian accent, in a speech which conveys the arrogance, the imperiousness of the king's impersonal, totalitarian gesture of authority (a gesture made in deference to the fair Cunigonde's imperious demands) as he signals with his forefinger—the commissioner laughs so hard that he "has a pain" (92). His laughter is edged with the pain of recognition, a pain "like pleurisy, like a heart attack, like indigestion," he would like to tell her. But she interrupts him with her wounding reference to her grandmother's exterminated Yiddish accent. The full significance of his painful laughter—painful because charged with stinging insight into self and history—emerges later in the story when the narrator tells us that "only her friend, the commissioner, accepts at once that it [Helena's experience in the camps] was beyond his imagination, and that the knowledge can produce nothing more than a pain like the suffering of laughter—like pleurisy, like indigestion" (95). The commissioner cannot recognize his complicity in Helena's experience, and Helena cannot articulate her experience less enigmatically, so that both she and the commissioner (and the "gaunt" reporter, another survivor) might understand fascism's small possibilities in people. The frequent ellipses in the commissioner's comments (and in the reporter's questions) seem almost an enactment of an elliptical view of history. These gaps might become vectors into the past, but only the reader is illuminated, and then only ironically. Neither character can do more than act out a public role, remaining an old friend in name only. Gallant prescribes no solutions to the impasses or to the ironic junction which Helena and the commissioner have arrived at, sitting in the garden. The story simply presents this moment, this particular "locked situation," as a comment on a culture's condition.

The pattern established in "The Old Friends," of characters and their relationships presented as particular reflections of cultural standoffs, continues in a more radical sense in Gallant's stories about ex-soldiers, ex-P.O.W.'s, and ex-Legionnaires. "Ernst in Civilian Clothes" (1963) heads a group of stories about ex-soldiers returning to Germany, or living marginal lives in Paris. Willi, Ernst's fellow ex-P.O.W. in Paris, figures centrally in two other uncollected stories, "Willi" (1963) and "A Report" (1966); Ernst reappears in a minor role in "Willi." "The Latehomecomer" (1974) (which Gallant thinks "might have been the best" of the German stories), is the confession of a young soldier who returns to Germany after spending years in France as a labourer and P.O.W.[6] Significantly, the same suspension in time which works so effectively in "The Old Friends" recurs in "Ernst in Civilian Clothes," "Willi," and "A Report," all three of which are set in an unstable present, detached from and so all the more subject to the past.

Ernst and Willi were taken prisoner by the Americans and handed over to the French at the end of the war; arriving in France, Ernst joined the French Foreign Legion because he saw that they were being served better food than the P.O.W.'s. Now Ernst, ex-soldier, ex-P.O.W., ex-Legionnaire, feels alien and vulnerable in civilian clothes on the eve of his return to Germany. He and Willi are members of a marginal German community stranded in postwar Paris, where, like Willi, they have all just barely found "a way of living, not quite a life."[7] Conditions in Paris in 1963 are grimmer than the "disappointments" Carol Frazier found, and they have wider, more explicitly political significance. The winter is the coldest since 1880; the Algerian crisis is barely resolved; civilians rush home from the jobs as if they were escaping from prison. In spite of the semblance of organization and authority provided by policemen and traffic lights, the alienation and disorientation Ernst feels are shared by the general public: "every person and every thing is submerged by the dark and the cold and the torrent of motorcars and a fear like a fear of lions" (137).

Gallant's portraits of Ernst and Willi are studies in dislocation. Ernst's uniforms—Hitler Youth, werewolf, German soldier, French Legionnaire—"have not been lucky. He has always been part of a defeated army. He has fought for Germany and for France and, according to what he has been told each time, for civilization" (135). Willi is "not displeased" that life in Paris is "like wartime. He might enjoy the privations of another war, without the killing" (140). Ernst has learned that all armies are alike, and the soldier's condition is his image of the human condition; Willi, a compulsive collector of documentary "evidence," newspaper clippings about the war, cannot arrive at an interpretation of the past which will include "all the evil he has been told was there" (143). Ernst, like so many of the characters in these stories, has fewer problems with interpreting the past because of his "life-saving powers of forget-fulness" (143). Gallant suggests in her comments on the German stories that survivors might be able to describe what had happened to them, but not *why*; neither Ernst nor Willi can adduce reasons for their war experience because they do not conceive of their actions as having any particular historical significance. For Willi, the Hitler Youth movement was simply another moment in German cultural history: "'What was wrong with the Hitler Youth?' says Willi. What was wrong with being told about Goethe Rilke Wagner Schiller Beethoven?" (143) In the title novella of this collection, another list is reeled off by the "cultural group leader" as he tries to comfort his opera party stranded at the Pegnitz junction—a list of "perhaps one hundred familiar names" which termi-nates abruptly with his mention of "the Adolf-time. . . . " (69–70)

In civilian clothes, Ernst feels "disguised," a "marked man." His uniforms have identified him for so long that he no longer knows which set of "facts" about his origins is true. He is either thirty-four or thirty-six, either an ex-Legionnaire or the shadowy figure he dreams of—a figure in a flooded cellar, calling out for "Mutti" (144). But at the end of the war, when he discarded his werewolf uniform and tried to return to his parents' home, his mother turned him away from the door while his father burned his SS uniform in the basement. There can be no return to family or childhood for him. The "stamped and for-mally attested facts" win out; like the commissioner in "The Old Friends," Ernst learns to assign one meaning to every experience. So he tells people "without remembering why" that he was born in Mainz, the German town he passed through as one of a trainload of German P.O.W.'s en route to France. When the train stops in Mainz, another young soldier tells Ernst that "Mainz is finished. There's nothing left. . . . My father says this is the Apocalypse" (134).

Ernst's dream about the figure in the flooded cellar, searching for his mother, signals his own arrested development and his continuing search for someone (or some institution) to obey, or to love. But the ironies of Ernst's condition, a con-dition resulting from his recruitment at the age of seven out of the family and into the Hitler Jugend, are echoed in the domestic melodrama he hears and ob-serves across Willi's courtyard, where a French mother chases her child around the apartment and beats him; the child, crying out for help, calls "Maman." The lesson for Ernst is clear:

> His [the child's] true mother will surely arrive and take him away from his mother transformed. Who else can he appeal to? It makes sense. Ernst has heard grown men call for their mothers. He knows about submission and punishment and justice and power. He knows what the child does not know

—that the screaming will stop, that everything ends. He did not learn a
trade in the French Foreign Legion, but he did learn to obey. (139)

Not only is civilian life like a wartime experience—as seen in the image of troops
of civil servants rushing from their offices—but the family life is another
battlefield, where the child screams for help or for love from the very person he
is trying to escape.

The story closes with Ernst deciding that dreams are of no use to him in the
daylight world. He puts on a face that "no superior officer, no prisoner, and no
infatuated girl has ever seen. He will believe only what *he* knows" (147). But the
only feeling he can summon up for Germany is a thin haze of sentimentality
manufactured by gazing at the posters of German scenery that Willi has on his
walls. The final line of the story signals Ernst's continuing paralysis; even
though he has decided that "life begins with facts: he is Ernst Zimmerman, ex-
Legionnaire," the last cry is the French child's calling for help to his mother
while she beats him. From beginning to end, Ernst's story is about paralysis in
time: the story opens with repeated suggestions of immobility and stasis, and
closes with Ernst making his decision, "stiff with the cold of a forgotten dream"
(147). Ernst's resolution to suppress his dreams and "invent his own truths"
leaves him, like "the old friends," stranded at a junction from which there appears to be no possibility of direction.

"A Report" (1966) and "Willi" (1963), neither of which is included in *The
Pegnitz Junction,* can be read as minor-key variations on "Ernst in Civilian
Clothes." Just as "The Cost of Living" tells the story of "Its Image on the Mirror" in the voice of an "Isobel" figure, so "A Report" and "Willi" focus more
sharply on Willi, who is a minor figure in "Ernst in Civilian Clothes."

"A Report" is actually several reports: Madame Monnerot's detectives report
to her on her husband's activities, while Gallant reports on two opposed, ex-
tremist French attitudes to Hitler and the war, and on Willi's ambivalent attitudes to recent history. Gallant presents the two French perspectives through
Monnerot and the Laurent family. Monnerot collects war memorabilia—Nazi
uniforms, boots, flags, swords, and portraits—and apes Himmler and Heydrich.
Willi procures these mementos for him, sometimes substituting fake articles for
real ones. Monnerot worships the power that Germany represented: he
"despises Germany for having been defeated."[8] The Laurent family has a
seventeen-year-old servant, Bobbie Bauer; she is a perfect symbol of postwar
displacement, "born of a French corporal with the Army of Occupation and a
seventeen-year-old German bilingual stenographer, in Coblenz, May 5, 1947"
(63). The Laurents, intent on accusing *her* of war atrocities, invite her to watch
a television documentary on the war. But Bobbie is "extremely puzzled and
depressed" by the film, "which had no action whatever, but showed ugly, un-

kempt, naked women standing in a field of tall grass, in a disorderly queue. . . . Presently the image changed to an abstract design of white faintly striated in gray which, when the picture became sharper, was seen to be a pile of bodies" (63). Bobbie thinks the film is about "some lost tribe in the jungle, perhaps in South America"; the Laurents tell her "'*You* did this. . . . If it wasn't you, it was your father'" (64). Both perspectives, Bobbie's and the Laurents', fail to place the past or to explain fascism's "small possibilities in people"; the irony is compounded, since Bobbie's father is in fact a French corporal. Bobbie flees from the Laurents' apartment, only to run into Monnerot, who of course has another distorted perspective on the past.

Beyond these reports on French postwar attitudes, there remains Gallant's study of Willi. He is emotionally indifferent to the spectacle of Monnerot posing in uniform; only his sense of correctness is disturbed by Monnerot's absurd collection of medals. Willi survives by refusing to interpret; he will not comment on the past or on Monnerot's infidelity to his wife. So Mme Monnerot thinks Willi "the very bastion of common sense. He may be ready to sacrifice his principles, but no one can say what his principles are" (65). He remains closemouthed, like the brothers in "One Aspect of a Rainy Day": this story opens with Gunther, the elder, swearing a silent oath of allegiance to Hitler, and so—in his younger brother's eyes, at any rate—committing himself even if he does not speak the words out loud:

> He had seen his older brother, Gunther, swear personal allegiance to Hitler when Gunther was fifteen and he, Stefan, only six. Actually Gunther promised nothing aloud, but stood with his lips tight.[9]

Like the commissioner, like a soldier or a guard, Willi "sticks to the information in the report. He speaks like a rational machine" (65). But when Mme Monnerot asks him why he is doing favours for her husband, Willi's third reason stops him short: he thinks that he "must be expecting something" (65). He considers the war trophies he has procured, and feels "bewildered, as if he had been given permission to laugh" (65). Like the commissioner, he arrives at a "junction," a moment delicately balanced between laughter and fears. Laughing and weeping at the same time, he tells Mme Monnerot to advise her husband that he will keep looking for the boots to complete Monnerot's uniform. The pain of this momentary insight, the nature of which is never clear, is so acute, and so bewilders him, that he cannot stop laughing or crying; it is as if he recognizes an ironic equivalence between the fake war memorabilia and his own principles.

In "Willi," Gallant looks at his past from another angle, again suggesting the distinctions between faked and genuine allegiance. The story's most powerful moment poses the question which bedevils many of the characters in *The Pegnitz Junction*: in what sense do individuals bear responsibility for their actions in uniform? Willi is eking out a living in Paris, this time by training young French students to march and sing in war films; in one film, he manages to get his friend Ernst a bit part. But Ernst, for all his experience in armies, cannot act the part of an SS man in the film: "Ernst wouldn't hurt a fly. Somebody must have hurt a fly once, or they wouldn't keep on making these movies. But it wasn't Willi or Ernst."[10]

"The Latehomecomer" dramatizes the condition of native exile more powerfully than any of *The Pegnitz Junction* stories because the first-person narrator's sense of his own fragmented life forms the story's centre. The central irony here is that at twenty-one, coming into manhood, the latehomecomer returns home with a lifetime of memory, hoping that his mother will have remained as he left her; the story closes on his wish that he were "a few hours younger" and that he had not discovered the past eradicated and his mother in her new identity, married to a stranger.

The theme which threads through all of the German stories is most clearly articulated in "The Latehomecomer" by a character sitting in on the latehomecomer's muted welcome at his stepfather's table. Willi Wehler, who is the father of Gisele, the girl whom the narrator will marry years later, gives him "advice that would be useful to [him] as a latehomecomer": "'Forget everything" he said. "Forget, forget. That was what I said to my good neighbour Herr Silber when I bought his wife's topaz brooch and earrings before he emigrated to Palestine. I said, 'Dear Herr Silber, look forward, never back, and forget, forget, forget'."[11]

But the latehomecomer remembers, compulsively, his prison camp life, his time in postwar France, his childhood before the war. As he remembers, he also tells the characters sitting around the table the story of his taking an American airman prisoner—the "longest story [he] had ever told in [his] life"—without knowing why (132). He remembers his botched affair with a young French girl (like Willi, he is an innocent), and, looking back on this homecoming scene, recalls that this was the first time he had ever seen Gisele; she is the only character "without guilt" (127). She is a member of a generation immune to the past, because her father's generation has carefully erased all connections. The narrator reflects that Willi "would have called any daughter something neutral and pretty," since the "pagan, Old Germanic names" are in disrepute (133). But in erasing the past, the civilians who were passed over by the war have erased the latehomecomer as well, so that his most powerful feeling is of exclusion; he recalls that this first day of his freedom in Berlin is "one day after old Adolf's birthday," but no one else makes any mention of the fact. Finally, all that he can express is bewilderment at his return: "Why am I in this place? Who sent me here? Is it a form of justice or injustice? How long does it last?" (137 His questions form the story's central moment, a moment in which a character comes home to a sense of displacement, remembering a past which everyone else is trying to forget. Because his memories are the most powerfully described of all the recollections in these stories, he becomes the most displaced character, the one who feels the severence of past from present most acutely.

Balanced with the third-person stories about isolated, displaced ex-soldiers are three women's first-person accounts of isolation. Taken together, "An Autobiography" (1964), "O Lasting Peace" (1972), and "An Alien Flower" (1972) provide a private and domestic perspective which complements the public, "attested" identities the soldiers have thrust upon them; at the same time, the women also reflect on the same sense of a suppressed or vanished past. Their voices are confessional and, on first reading, the structures of their stories seem deceptively causal. Hilde, the narrator of "O Lasting Peace," ends her story by adding, following her most revelatory statement, "I've forgotten why I wanted to mention this";[12] Erika, the narrator of "An Autobiography," prefaces sections of her story with comments like "What I wanted to comment on was children" or "but what I have wanted to say from the beginning is, do not confide your children to strangers";[13] Helga, who narrates "An Alien Flower," interjects the same kinds of informal, colloquial pointers. As is the case with "The Cost of Living," however, the structures of these stories are actually tightly controlled patterns of revelation, through which the women's self-assured declarations modulate into tentative, resigned insights into their conditon.

Hilde works in a travel agency to support her mother, her aunt, and her Uncle Theo; she is a martinet at work and at home, declaring that the others would be lost without her. The story turns on the opposition between Hilde's condemnation of her family's private, "secret" lives, which she thinks are childish and insignificant, and her Uncle Theo's pleas for a more charitable and Christian view of her charges. To Hilde, her mother, aunt, and uncle are "aged children who can't keep their own histories straight. They have no money, no property, no recorded past, nothing but secrets" (163). She sees herself as their "inspector": "A lifetime won't be enough to come to the end of their lies and their mysteries. I am the inspector, the governess, the one they tell stories to" (151). The story takes its title from a hymn Theo has composed; Hilde thinks it "sounds preachy, even when sung in a lively way" (155).

The story is set on Christmas eve, which becomes an ironic comment on Hilde's uncharitable perspective. She denounces the East German refugees living in the apartment next door as boors, threatening them with legal action for the noise they make; she refuses to cash an out-of-town customer's traveller's cheque because of trivial discrepancies in his signatures; she refuses Theo's request that she take the family to an opera on Christmas day, or that she send money to her father, who has left her mother after a fifteen-year affair with another woman. Hilde looks at her family with an unforgiving eye, scorning Theo's shady wartime manoeuvres to survive. Theo, in revealing contrast to Ernst, erased his public, "attested" identity by disappearing from a recruitment office with his official file. He served as a camp guard on the Eastern front, but was friendly enough to his Russian prisoners that when they broke out, they tied him to a tree, teaching him a phrase to repeat phonetically if the Russian army got there before the Americans. (Ironically, the only phrase that Theo can say in a foreign language is "Pro domo sua"—the title of one of Cicero's orations, meaning "In Defence of His Home." Cicero was seeking damages for his house, which was destroyed by enemies after he went into exile.)

Theo's final act of mercy is to advertise for a husband for Hilde. Signalling her lack of insight into her own "secret life," Hilde mentions this episode as an afterthought, a final grievance: "One last thing: without my consent, without even asking me, Uncle Theo advertised for a husband for me" (165). She finds the prospective suitor unsuitable, "a peasant who sits with one foot on the other"; her final declaration completes her drama of self-revelation as she berates her family:

> "You are so anxious to have this apartment to yourselves.... You have made yourselves cheap over a peasant.... How would you pay the rent here without me? Don't you understand that I can't leave you?" At the same time, I wanted to run out on the balcony screaming "Come back!" But I was afraid of knocking the flowerpots over. (166)

As is often the case in Gallant's stories, larger patterns of meaning emerge from juxtaposed details. Hilde's fear that she will knock over the flowerpots recalls an earlier scene on Christmas Eve, when her mother, distressed that her "own little knife and fork," all she has saved of her past (the rest was firebombed) is missing from the table, locks herself in the apartment. The family is forced to ask the East German refugees next door for help. Hilde instructs the little boy: "'Break the panes.... Use a flowerpot. Be careful not to cut yourself.' I was thinking of blood on the parquet floor" (160). In both cases Hilde wants to compartmentalize, to separate, to maintain class distinctions, to avoid messy relationships. It takes the family a year after this incident, she recalls, to re-establish the correct distance between themselves and the East Germans.

Erika, the narrator of "An Autobiography," teaches botany in a girls' school in Switzerland—neutral territory. Her story, like the others in *The Pegnitz Junction,* focuses on abandonment, dislocation, and disinheritance. Erika repeatedly tries to keep her narration on track, reminding herself as she reminds us that she wants to "talk about the children"—children abandoned in Swiss finishing schools, a baby abandoned for a day by its parents, a little girl abandoned for a Swiss summer holiday. In each case, what Erika refers to as the "corruption of memory" transforms abandonment into something more acceptable to parent, child, or lover; these private accommodations are linked to the general suppression of the recent past which is endemic among the schoolchildren's parents:

"They [the children] are ignorant and new. Everything they see and touch at home is new. Home is built on the top layer of Ur. It is no good excavating; the fragments would be without meaning. Everything within the walls was inlaid or woven or cast or put together fifteen years ago at the very earliest."[14]

But finally, Erika's story focusses most closely on her own sense of abandonment, her own dislocation. An aunt, her only surviving relative, summons her to Paris to disinherit her because Erika is too much like her father, a professor of medieval German who had moved the family from Munich to Debrecen in 1937, not because of impending danger, but because "[H]is objection to Munich was to its prevailing church, and the amount of noise in its streets" (104). Ironically, he is later shot in Hungary by a Russian soldier. Cut off from her own past, Erika returns from Paris to bump into an abandoned lover, Peter Dobay, with his new wife. These two are an absurd pair, affectedly calling each other "Poodlie." Dobay has invented his own version of his affair with Erika, so that she feels as if she were caught up in someone else's private mythology. But she cannot tell Peter the truth, even though she resolves: "I shall write about everything, all of the truth" (128). The letter she intends to write to Peter remains a blank sheet: she closes her story with the admission that she has "wasted the sheet of paper. There has been such a waste of everything; such a waste" (129). The "waste" has been the uses of the past: suppressed, transformed, invented, mythologized. Erika casts herself in the role of one who would "interpret between generations, between the mute and the deaf, so to speak" but her final commentary suggests only continuing "waste," isolation, and entrapment in her own condition as much as in her own form of narration.

More than any other work in Gallant's canon, "The Pegnitz Junction" experiments instructively with mixed modes, with polyphonic narration, with literary parody, caricature, and extended metaphor. "The Pegnitz Junction" enacts all of the separate individual and cultural dislocations recreated in the constellation of stories which comprises this book; it transfigures the displacements of postwar culture—historical, political, social, literary—and of postwar native exiles, postwar soldiers, civilians, lovers, and children—into an errant train ride which takes readers towards the whole book's destination without end, the stammering moment in which Christine's, Herbert's, and little Bert's train stops them out of time at the Pegnitz Junction.

"The Pegnitz Junction" explores the strained relationships between Christine, twenty-one, her older lover, Herbert, and his son, little Bert. These three have gone to Paris for a week's holiday, which was meant to be an "emancipation" for Christine but has proved a debacle. They are returning to Germany because a strike has closed the Paris airport—one of the first of the story's many signals of social breakdown. The train's meandering course across France and into Germany seems to epitomize the general aimlessness of contemporary German culture, an aimlessness which has, perhaps, subverted Germany's determination to carry on with its "economic miracle"; the journey's end at the Pegnitz Junction is less a homecoming than the fullest development of Gallant's theme of paralyzed bewilderment, a theme which has surfaced in all of the German stories. Images from the past, specifically of the war, intrude everywhere into the present. Aboard one of the trains, the feeling is of "glossed-over poverty"; Christine thinks that the trains "sounded sad, as if they were used to ferry poor and weary passengers—refugees perhaps."[15] The trains are running off-schedule, with scant services aboard, and the uniformed figures of authority, like the customs man, are loutish (16).

Christine, poised uncertainly between Herbert, the progressive, liberal, "pacifist, anti-state" (and yet also ominously passive, "sleepwalking, dreaming") engineer, and her fiancé, an unnamed theology student, can never bring herself to choose between the two men or to direct her life. Her failures to act reflect a general cultural inertia, most fully realized in the story's crucial moment at the Pegnitz Junction. Christine is also eerily sensitive: she both picks up and creates "information," stories and scenes "transmitted" to her by other passengers, or suggested to her by scenes and people she gazes at from the train window. She constructs a story about a German family picnicking by an old family castle they mistake for a museum; she constructs another fiction about a man she spots walking near the East German border at one of their many stops. She also "tunes in" to a letter from one American soldier to another, as a pregnant woman, abandoned by one of the soldiers, mulls over its contents. As she receives and transmits this "information," the oppressive aimlessness and confusion of the train ride heighten; the landscape (it is "baked and blind"; this is the hottest July since 1873 [21]) becomes surreal, intensely suggestive to Christine. But Gallant's point is not that Christine is mentally unbalanced. Gallant comments:

> She [Christine] is not inventing or making up stories. Everything that the young woman sees when she looks out the train window, she really does see. A kind of magic, if you like. To my mind, a short circuit. She really does know all these stories. She really does know what has happened to everyone. Someone wondered if she was schizophrenic. No. There is a German expression, "I can hear him thinking." I've always liked that. I could hear him thinking. Because one does very often.[16]

Gallant tells Geoff Hancock that "a great deal of conversation in it ["The Pegnitz Junction"] is cut off, short-circuited."[17] Christine's "short circuits" bypass her few exchanges with Herbert, so that the story consists largely of a series of monologues transmitted through Christine.

The novella opens with an expository passage which does not describe Christine, even though she will be the most important figure; "she" is not even named for over a page. Instead, the opening locates her birthplace, a city destroyed in the war: "She was a bony slow-moving girl from a small bombed baroque German city, where all that was worthwhile keeping had been rebuilt and which now looked as pink and golden as a pretty child and as new as morning" (3). This description sets in motion the pervasive tensions between the suppression of wartime destruction (by superficial, cosmetic restoration) and the continual emergence, in memory and in other, more tangible forms, of reminders of the war. Seen from a contemporary perspective, the town can only be ironically "baroque," bombed into antiquity, quaintly historical. Its restoration has made it innocent, "pink and golden," but its freshness, that of a "pretty child," must be suspect. Gallant's use of "pretty" here recalls its use in "The Other Paris" and elsewhere to suggest superficial attractiveness; the city can only appear "as new as morning" if the destruction of (night-time) bombing has been erased from sight, and so from memory.

Christine herself has a "striking density of expression in photographs, though she seemed unchanging and passive in life, and had caught sight of her own face looking totally empty-minded when, in fact, her thoughts and feelings were pushing her in some wild direction" (4). This early description anticipates Christine's unnoticed mental activity on the train; because the narrator locates her "at one of those turnings in a young life where no one can lead, but where someone for the sake of love might follow," we anticipate her "turning" to reach a new point of departure. When she does not seem to decide anything, when instead she ends up in the nightmarish confusion which pervades the Pegnitz Junction, this early commentary becomes another indication of the general cultural failure to decide, or to "turn."

Before setting the train journey proper in motion, the narrator draws a telling distinction between Herbert and the theology student:

> Unlike the student of theology, he [Herbert] had not put up barriers such as too much talk, self-analysis, or second thoughts. In fact, he tended to limit the number of subjects he would discuss. He had no hold on her mind, and no interest in gaining one. . . . He often said he thought he could not live without her, but a few minutes after making such a declaration he seemed unable to remember what he had just said, or to imagine how his voice must have sounded to her. (4)

Herbert's inability to remember, his dislike of barriers such as introspection or too much talk, effectively estranges him from his own past. He cannot "think" anything personal: he can only *say* he *thinks* he cannot live without Christine, and then forget what he has just said. Yet Christine admires "Herbert-the-amiable" for his smooth, pleasant manner of living on the surface, untroubled by the past. The story, however, explores the ways in which Herbert's amiable nature masks unresolved ambiguities; indeed, Herbert is so "pleasant," so ambiguous, that he often confounds the people he speaks to.

The events of "The Pegnitz Junction" begin in Paris where Christine, Herbert, and Little Bert are staying in an old hotel. The view announces the toppling of religious and natural orders alike as the contemporary secular age advances: "The view from every window was of a church covered with scaffolding from top to bottom, the statue of a cardinal lying on its side, and a chestnut tree sawed in pieces" (5). A new car park is to be built under the church, and the chestnut tree is to be "replaced by something more suited to the gassy air of cities" (5).

From the beginning, Herbert tries to shield Little Bert from history—particularly from anything to do with soldiers or war—and from Christine's sexuality. But every night in Paris, Bert creeps into their room and carefully inspects Christine's body, after which he tells his father that he is afraid of the dark. While Christine is dressing on the last morning, Herbert turns Little Bert's head away, but by this time Bert "had certainly seen all he wanted to night after night" (9). Herbert also turns Little Bert's head away from the plaque at the Paris railway station commemorating "a time of ancient misery"—the last war—"so ancient that two of the three travellers had not been born then, and Herbert, the eldest, had been about the age of Little Bert" (11). Throughout, this disparity between the date of the relatively recent war and its perception as an "ancient" historical event distorts the connections between the present and the past and heightens our perception of the train ride's metaphorical dimensions, particularly as the train appears to travel over a landscape which eerily integrates fragments of the past into the present.

The stay at the Paris hotel is the scene of the first of a series of confrontations with authority, confrontations which reveal the sharp differences between Herbert's and Christine's reactions to displays of power, to threats, orders, and fascism's "small possibilities in people." When the French night porter bursts into the bathroom and screams at Christine for drawing a bath so early, Herbert's response is passive, "extraordinarily calm"; "without standing his ground for a second," Herbert reacts "as if he were under arrest, or as though the porter's old pajama top masked his badge of office, his secret credentials. The look on Herbert's face was abstract and soft, as if he has already lived this, or had always thought that he might" (7). Herbert's docility seems to be a habitual response to displays of authority; his quiescence is that of one acculturated to totalitarian posturing. But Christine, born after the war, has inherited a different attitude, and her own reaction, ineffective though it may be, is both articulate and vehement; she tells the porter he is a "filthy little swine of a dog of a bully" (7). Little Bert "look[s] up at their dazed, wild faces" and adopts a large bath sponge, christened Bruno, which will be his imaginary friend for the rest of their journey (7). By setting all of these developments in motion in France, before the trio boards the train, Gallant comments not only on Germany's relationship with its own past, but also on French perspectives on the war and on the "Dirty Boches," as the porter calls them. Christine's hallucinatory sensitivity surfaces for the first time here, too: she reacts to the porter's parting shot by crying at the window, where she "sees" "larches pressing against the frame" (8). But although she reports on them in detail, they belong to a private landscape from the past:

> Through tears she did not wish the child to observe, Christine stared at larches pressing against the frame of the window. They had the look they often have, of seeming to be wringing wet. She noticed every detail of their bedraggled branches and red cones. They sky behind them was too bright for comfort. She took a step nearer and the larches were not there. They belonged to her schooldays and to mountain holidays with a score of little girls—a long time ago now. (8)

The larches and the schoolgirls recur: at one of the stations, Christine's carriage is "overrun by a horde of fierce little girls who had been lined up in squads on a station platform" (20). The horde is a "commando," taking over Christine's compartment, leaning out windows and trailing streamers "past miles of larches with bedraggled branches, past a landscape baked and blind" (21). Here and at other points, Christine's apparently innocent, schoolgirl past merges with a more ambiguous present. The girls are no longer schoolgirls, but more warlike, more military, and they are also curiously adult, so that Herbert "appraise[s]" the "bossy blonde" who leads them "as though she were twenty" (21). When the horde gets off the train, Christine watches the bossy blonde's toughness dissolve as she is absorbed into her family's theatrics, a melodrama similar to that of the family in "About Geneva." For Christine, everything signifies; every event evokes a memory or a story, so that her own past and the culture's history blend in tableaux such as the scene with the "fierce little girls."

As the train travels across France and crosses the Rhine into Germany, reminders and suggestions of the war and the past multiply. There are "shell-pocked grey hangars" across the Rhine (16); at a stop very near the East German border, Christine sees barbed wire and soldiers at observation posts. The conductor issues orders on every possible occasion; when he warns Christine to keep the train windows closed because of brush-fires, she imagines "the holocaust they might become" (36); past and present merge again when the narrator comments, following Christine's plea to the conductor to let her open the window: "It was true that there were no signs of trouble except for burned-out patches of grass. Not even a trace of ash remained on the sky, not even a cinder" (36). Straggling troops of soldiers appear at crossings; at one "unknown station," the train as if it had a mind of its own, pauses long enough for them to view one of these detachments, as if this display were one version, one incarnation of the past, one possible station toward the future:

> Their train slowed at an unknown station, then changed its mind and picked up speed, but not before they'd been given a chance to see a detachment of conscripts of the army of the Federal Republic in their crumpled uniforms and dusty boots and with their long hair hanging in strings. She saw them as she imagined Herbert must be seeing them: small, round-shouldered, rather dark. Blond, blue-eyed genes were on the wane in Europe. (50)

Christine registers Herbert's ambivalence towards the past as she watches him "brooding" over the spectacle of these "untidy soldiers," even though he is a pacifist (51).

At the stop before Pegnitz, portents of disorder begin to mount. Christine listens to a "cultural group leader" placating his assembly of theatre-goers, stranded at the station, by listing a series of great German political figures. Significantly, the cultural leader is linked with the buffoonish (but also loutish) figure of the conductor: he sits "not quite ... [like] a cultured person, more the way a train conductor might sit between rounds" (69). After lulling his group by listing about "one hundred familiar names," the leader "suddenly said, 'The Adolf-time ... '" [sic] (69–70). Christine picks up the group's sudden "creaking thoughts": "Oh, God, where is this kind of talk taking us?" (70) All of these allusions, direct and indirect, to the "Adolf time" form an increasingly ominous background for the train ride, which ends in Pegnitz in a flurry of soldiers, of posturing authority and terrified passengers.

Herbert and Christine continue to respond differently to authority, even though they (like the horde of little girls) recognize that the conductor is a mere caricature of power. Herbert's response is to compose a mental letter of complaint to the proper authorities; he imagines mailing it to a range of media outlets, "but not to any part of the opposition press. He wanted to throw rocks at official bungling, but the same rocks must not strike the elected government" (55). Again we realize that Herbert's style is to conform amiably, to maintain the status quo no matter how severely provoked; when all of the passengers in the compartment are suffocating in the heat, he sits "'as calm as an incarnation of Buddha,'" even though he is suffering as much as anyone else (27). Yet the figures in power are consistently presented as clownish impostors, acting their roles out; in fact, Herbert himself is an expert mimic. Christine thinks that the conductor's voice is very much like Herbert's, imitating a "celebrated Bavarian politician addressing a crowd of peasants" (20). Herbert's amiable passivity constitutes an invitation for authority to impose itself. The conductor, however, repeats his orders "quite hopelessly," "for who could possibly be afraid of such a jolly little person?" (21) The question proves rhetorical, as we see during the course of the train ride; the conductor, like the French porter, like the group cultural leader, is both comically harmless and a potentially terrifying figure. The empty posturing of authority—the "small possibility" of fascism in individuals—appears sufficient to inspire obedience, "sleepwalking," and terror.

The divisions between Herbert and Christine run deeper than their different responses to these posturings from figures of authority. When Herbert explains his work to the Norwegian who is sharing their compartment, we learn that Herbert is "scrupulous about providing correct information but did not feel obliged to answer for pictures raised in the imagination" (23). He is another in the line of "commissioner" figures in these stories, allowing only one meaning for every word; even in his conversations with Little Bert, he carefully slants his information, speaking like the modern technocrat that he is. The narrator is careful to point out this quality in Herbert's language: describing Herbert's explanation to Bert about the train ride, the narrator transcribes Herbert's language word for word: "because the German train would not have a restaurant car, Herbert went on calmly. His actual words were, 'Because there will be no facilities for eating on the second transport'" (9). In both cases, Christine distinguishes between her view of "information" and Herbert's: "Christine thought that she knew what 'information' truly was, and had known for some time. She could see it plainly, in fact; it consisted of fine silver crystals forming a pattern, dancing, separating, dissolving in a glittering trail along the window" (23). But because Herbert cannot (or will not) respond to Christine's suggestions that events signify, that their individual discomforts are linked, perhaps, to a more general disorientation, communication between them is, as Gallant puts it, "short circuited." The gap between Herbert and Christine is clearest when Christine speaks figuratively, violating Herbert's categories of acceptable discourse. When she tries, for example, to extend the significance of their individual discomfort, to make it into a reflection of a more general condition, Herbert refuses to respond:

> "But sometimes . . . one feels more. More than just one's irritation, I mean. Everything opens, like a pomegranate. More things have gone wrong than one imagined. You begin to see that too."
> "Little Bert has never seen a pomegranate," said Herbert. There were forms of conversation he simply refused to accept. (26)

Following on this, her first intimation of a general breakdown of order, Christine begins to receive the first, and longest of the stories she "picks up"—this one from the old woman sharing their compartment. Christine's "information" functions on several levels: she calls it "interference" because it distracts her from her own problems with Herbert and Little Bert, but it also provides her with insight (often comic, often banal) into individuals' wartime experience.

The two characters who share their compartment bring with them the two things Herbert dislikes most while travelling—the smell of food, and singing. The old woman's story is of her forty-seven-year sojourn in America, one of a quartet of first cousins who paired off and married. Her tale is a comical, never-ending list of the food she cooked for all of them; she is now a diabetic, munching endlessly on an assortment of candy and fruit. Interspersed among her list of dishes is the story of the families' isolation in America, particularly during the war, and the story of the next generation's assimilation. She has come back to tend her husband's grave in Germany so that she can inherit his money. Her reminiscences "interfere" sporadically with Christine's own musings, while her compulsive eating nauseates her fellow passengers. The other passenger is a Norwegian "as tall as Herbert, wearing a blond beard" (16); he has come to Germany to teach a summer course on his special use of yoga in singing. Egged on by Christine, who is annoyed at Herbert's infatuation with a little girl she sees at a crossing, the Norwegian fills the compartment with his singing, adding to everyone's discomfort. More importantly, he serves as a foil for Herbert's pleasant ironies on the issue of Germany's payment of war reparations. Both Herbert and the Norwegian (both are "amiable") profess to be open-minded on the subject; each is anxious not to offend the other. Herbert's tone is so pleasant, so neutral that it is "impossible for the two strangers to tell if [he] was glad or sorry" at the fact that beneficiaries, according to actuarial studies, died earlier than normal. Herbert's refusal to be held accountable for these debts—and the Norwegian's belief that he should be accountable—are conveyed politely:

> "It is only right that you pay," said the Norwegian, though not aggressively.
> "Of course it is right," said Herbert, smiling. "However, I object to your use of 'you'." (49)

Herbert's attitude to the past is more sharply ambivalent than his politeness conveys. His ambivalence centres on his family's wartime experience. Herbert has had "bad luck with women": his wife ran off, and his mother was put in a prison camp when he was three for holding to her religious convictions. Her camp experience erodes all of her former faith in people and God. She leaves Herbert twice, "once under arrest and once to die" (14–15). Herbert's ambivalent attitudes combine his mother's warped vision of humanity with his own seemingly enlightened, amiable veneer of liberalism. His mother's life and death "gave him such mixed feelings, made him so sad and uncomfortable, that he would say nothing except 'Oh, a Christian sermon?' when something reminded him of it" (14).

Like many other couples in Gallant's fiction, Christine and Herbert *do* come together for a very brief moment; this contact crystallizes many of the tensions and contradictions that have emerged on the train journey. Herbert takes Christine to an empty compartment and draws the curtains closed; the first thing he must know is why Christine is reading Dietrich Bonhoeffer's essays. Bonhoeffer was martyred by the Nazis for his resistance; his *Letters and Papers from Prison* are exhortations to individuals to assume responsibility for their actions, to take courage in their Christian faith. When Christine explains to Herbert that she is reading the book for an examination, the theology student's test becomes hers, and Herbert's, and Germany's. And when Christine explains that his test is for those who have "failed their year," her comment resonates beyond the particular situation, extending to a general failure to pass Bonhoeffer's rigorous test. Herbert, typically, only understands Christine on one level. He responds: "'That accounts for the Bonhoeffer. Well. Our little Christian. What good does it do him if *you* read?'" Christine's response takes in more meanings than the literal: "'It may do me good, and what is good for me is good for both of you. Isn't that so?'" (45) Christine despairs at reconciling Bonhoeffer's claims for an ethical, moral response to life with Herbert's demands for a relationship liberated from the past. So she tells him that she loves him, but that there has been too much "interference"—too much information from sources like Bonhoeffer, sources which would ruffle Herbert's equanimity.

Herbert cannot understand Christine on this level, and Christine becomes annoyed with Herbert for "veering off into talk and analysis," like her fiancé; but talk and analysis are avenues of communication which might lead to a reconciliation between them and with their shared past (46). Suddenly Herbert begs her to marry him—"tomorrow, today" (46). But as the narrator has pointed out earlier, Herbert is incapable of remembering anything that he says about love or commitment: "Herbert did not hear what he was saying and his words did not come back to him, not even as an echo. He did not forget the promise, he had not heard it. Seconds later it was as if nothing had been said" (46). If Christine picks up "interference" and "information" from the atmosphere, then Herbert counterpoints her extraordinary sensitivity with his blank inscrutability: Christine picks up signals from strangers, but Herbert cannot remember what he says. Now Christine arrives at a perception which many Gallant figures share as they contemplate other characters: she realizes that she "knew nothing about him" (47). At the same time, she recognizes, again, Herbert's talents as a mimic, which do not square with her image of him as a "busy and practical man" (47). The point of this recognition is that Herbert's practicality stops short of a talent for communication. So, for Christine, "the landscape was hopeless" at the end of this interrogation (47); the only thing that Herbert is concerned about is "this train, which is running all over the map" (47).

The closing episode at Pegnitz brings together the motifs which have coloured the journey from its beginning. Past and present merge as the dialogue continually echoes beyond the literal level, recreating a wartime atmosphere charged with menace and confusion. So, for example, when little Bert asks Christine to take him to the bathroom, her exchange with Herbert is ominous: "'Is there time?' she asked Herbert. She saw him nod before a new wave of soldiers pushed him back" (78).

Throughout, little Bert has pestered Christine to read him stories about Bruno the sponge from the Bonhoeffer essay collection. But each time she begins to read, Herbert has cut her off, complaining that her inventions are too silly, too military, too imaginary, all potentially harmful to little Bert. Now little Bert has gravitated to Christine's sphere of influence. She reads a line of Bonhoeffer: "'Shame and remorse are generally mistaken for one another'"; she concludes that "'it's no good reading that'" (80). At this point Christine looks to little Bert for support and for human contact, looking as well to the future rather than only to the past. Here as elsewhere, Gallant reverses an earlier "tableau" to convey a character's transformation. Soon after they board the train, Christine opens Bonhoeffer to read, and "little Bert [is] beside her in a second. He [stands] leaning, breathing unpleasantly on her bare arm, commanding her to read about Bruno" (12). At Pegnitz, the roles are reversed. Now, after reading Bonhoeffer, Christine "leaned against the child and felt his comforting breath on her arm" (80). The reversal communicates little Bert's metamorphosis into a child from a "little (Herr)Bert" for Christine, and it also conveys Christine's need for human contact, for "comforting breath."

True to form, the conductor appears and performs a final characterization of authority. "Being something of a comedian," he does an "excellent imperson-ation of someone throwing a silent tantrum" (80), recalling, perhaps, Hitler's histrionics, or Chaplin's imitations of Hitler's histrionics. Little Bert can see that he is playing, but the women sitting in the waiting room, who resemble refugees ("grouped by nationality" [79]) are terrified. Christine is "surprised to feel the panic—stronger than mere disapproval—that the other women were signalling now" (80). Christine faces down the conductor, who immediately begins to plead his case to her, as if he were about to be put on trial for war crimes: "'But I was kind on the train. I let you keep the window open when we went through the fire zone. . . . You'll testify for me, then?'" (81). Like the unmasked con-ductor, the group cultural leader has also been stripped of his authority in the pandemonium: Christine spots him with his group in the middle of a crowd; he has "lost his spectacles and was barely recognizable without them. His eyes were small and blue, and he looked insane" (78).

As the confusion in the station mounts, Christine cleaves to little Bert, telling him that "'whatever happens . . . we must not become separated. We must never leave each other'" (79). Her own confusion is apparent; when little Bert asks her to read again, demanding "what happens?" she confesses, "'I don't know anymore'" (81). The story moves to its unresolved close in a commotion suggesting the imminent departure of prisoner transports, while Christine, characteristically, is "wondering and weighing, as reluctant as ever to make up her mind" (87). The other women in the waiting room respond to the "great stir" in the yards "as if they knew what this animation meant and had been waiting for it": "Lights blazed, voices bawled in dialect, a dog barked . . . the women picked up their parcels and filed out without haste and without looking back" (87). Christine, perhaps more confident at the new bond established between her and little Bert, "relaxe[s] her grip on the child, as if he were someone she loved but was not afraid of losing" (87). Her final response to his demand that she read is to start again on a story which Herbert had interrupted earlier, a tale about five brothers with the same name: "She had been hoping all day to have the last word, without interference. She held little Bert and said aloud, "Bruno had five brothers, all named Georg. But Georg was pronounced five different ways in the family, so there was no confusion. They were called the Goysh, the Yursh, the Shorsh . . . " [sic] (88).

At this point, Christine and little Bert have reached a momentary respite from the confusion surrounding them. Christine is not docile enough, not meek enough to file onto another train. Nor is it clear at the end of the story whether their next train is at the Pegnitz Junction; Christine hears Herbert in the distance, trying to get information, she imagines. She does confront the conductor when he tries to intimidate little Bert, and her appeals to the child are positive gestures towards relationship. Fittingly, the ending is the most ambiguous, the most open-ended of all in this book; nevertheless, the fact that Christine's last word is a story about brotherhood and community, told to a child, indicates at least the hope for a new direction, out of the destructive and repetitive cycles suggested throughout.

Gallant comments in an interview on the dilemma of German adolescents growing up in the "Hitler time":

> Try to put yourself in the place of an adolescent who had sworn personal allegiance to Hitler. The German drama, the drama of that generation, was of inner displacement. You can't tear up your personality and begin again, any more than you can tear up the history of your country. The lucky people are the thoughtless ones. They just slip through. As for guilt—who can assume guilt for a government? People are more apt to remember what was done to them rather than what was done in their name to others. To wrench your life and beliefs in a new direction you have to be a saint or a schizophrenic.[18]

One of her German stories, "One Aspect of a Rainy Day," specifically takes up this question of personal allegiance to Hitler; but "dramas of inner displacement" are in one way or another at the core of all the stories in The Pegnitz Junc-

tion. The title novella is only the most radical, the fullest treatment of this book's common theme—that recent history has swamped individual experience, distorting characters' sense of the present, because the past has been suppressed, misinterpreted, or "buried." The "inner displacement" results from the impasse characters arrive at when they try to realize the past. If they "tear up their personality" (as Ernst, for example, tries to do), they destroy any private sense of self out of uniform, in civilian clothes, aside from attested facts, stamped documents, official dossiers. If on the other hand a character tries to forget the history of his country (a history universally condemned, but one in which individuals who have lived through it cannot find the "stain of evil" the rest of the West perceives), then he suffers a cultural disinheritance. Inner displacement troubles most of the characters: Helena's identity has been obliterated by her experience in the camps, while the commissioner is a bewildered "orphan." Erika lives a "wasted" life in neutral territory, disinherited, telling stories of abandonment; Helga's past has been "purified, swept clean" of associations, so that she lives a displaced life in the house Julius has given her, telling Bibi's story, which is the story of another displaced person. Because experience is depersonalized, any private basis for identity is threatened; when memory tries to recreate a sense of the past, it confronts the destruction which is a part of everyone's history in these stories.

Having arrived at this moment of ironic "junction," where neither memory nor history can direct individuals or a culture on to the right track, we might well wonder where Gallant's fiction can go from here. From *The Other Paris* to *My Heart Is Broken* to *The Pegnitz Junction,* she has continually expanded and developed the implications of discontinuities between the self and the world in time, taking in larger areas of experience with each successive book. The distance between Carol Frazier and Christine or between Jeannie Thompson and Helena is the distance between individuals baffled by social and political forces, and individuals who themselves become expressions or manifestations of a cultural condition, submerged in history, so that readers are never sure where personal and social experience separate.[19] The stories of *The Pegnitz Junction* close with quiet signals of resignation, or disclaimers (Hilde's "I have forgotten why I wanted to mention this," for example, or ironic resolutions like Ernst's). In her next book, *From the Fifteenth District,* Gallant continues to write stories dramatizing sterile, melodramatic lives touched in moments with the illumination of a significant gesture, a telling insight, or with the "light of imagination," and she also continues to write stories which are "intensely political." But at the same time, she returns in the Linnet Muir stories to another kind of fiction, as "Proustian" as the Pegnitz stories are anti-Proustian—stories in which memory makes history into home.

5

From the Fifteenth District
History and Memory in the
"Light of Imagination"

In the seventies, Gallant's fiction developed in two related directions. Her fifth and, to date, her finest book of stories, *From the Fifteenth District,* appeared in 1979, while five of the linked Linnet Muir stories were published in *The New Yorker* between 1975 and 1977.[1] These five stories, along with a sixth Linnet Muir story and ten other stories, were collected in *Home Truths* (1981), which won the Governor-General's Award for fiction and which has an important place in the Gallant canon.[2] But *From the Fifteenth District* stands as Gallant's finest book both because of the superb quality of its individual stories and because of the ways in which several of the stories, taken together, evoke the gradual decline of the British presence and influence in postwar Europe. All of the stories in *From the Fifteenth District* reward close consideration;[3] but four stories in particular—"Potter," "The Remission," "The Four Seasons," and "The Moslem Wife"—represent Gallant's finest achievements in their respective domains.

In "Potter," Gallant sparks a succession of comic collisions between stock images of East and West, head and heart, age and youth, politics and passion as Piotr's Eastern European sensibility undergoes an education in the ambiguities of a younger "Western" love. "Potter" extends the typical Gallant comedy of North American encounters with postwar European realities in two directions. First, through the character of Piotr, Gallant provides her fullest exploration of the Eastern European postwar experience. Piotr—his Canadian lover Laurie cannot pronounce his name, rendering it alternately as "Peter, Prater, Potter, and Otter"—is an Eastern European intellectual, a Polish poet, translator, and university lecturer who was imprisoned in Poland after the war for allegedly subversive activities (he had translated some German poetry).[4] He meets Laurie Bennett on one of his working visits to Paris at a party given by his Polish émigré friend, Marek. Piotr's education, his profession, his politics, and his experience constitute a totally foreign, unreadable universe for Laurie, and the most comic level of the story shows us Laurie's profound illiteracy in these areas. Piotr is married with two children, but separated from his wife in Warsaw; because he met his wife in prison, where she brought him soup to save him from starvation, his relationship with Laurie seems all the more ethereal and depoliticized, taking place as it does in a "Western" realm apparently innocent of connections with history, with the war or with any postwar suffering. Laurie's "idea of history began with the Vietnam war; Genesis was her own Canadian childhood" (169). But Piotr's character is not created simply to dramatize Laurie's cultural, political, and historical naïveté; and in the second extension of Gallant's typical cross-cultural comedy we discover that Laurie's character, too, is finally more complex than those of other Gallant North American innocents abroad—descendants of that early and prototypical Gallant character, Carol Frazier.

By setting Piotr's affair with Laurie in Paris, Gallant is able to recreate both Piotr's Eastern and Laurie's Western fascination with and uses of the French cultural mystique. Piotr's Polish friends, Marek and Maria, provide telling counterpoints to Piotr's lovestruck experience in France. Marek survives on the margins of French society, cultivating a network of strategically placed acquaintances. He lives amidst the constant whisper of low-level intrigue, using political or business connections as tiny levers in his teetering progress up the French social ladder. In one of his short-lived triumphs, he secures an invitation for Piotr to a French dinner party, only to see Piotr violate all the rules of staged dinner talk by responding to queries about his past in a register sharply out of tune with his interlocutor's social muzak:

> The pregnant girl's social clockwork gave her Piotr along with the next course. "Is this your first visit to Paris?" she said. Her eyes danced, rolled almost. . . .
>
> "It is my third trip as an adult. I came once with my parents when I was a child." . . .
>
> "The rest of the time you were always in your pretty Poland?" The laugh that accompanied this was bewildering to him. "What could have been keeping you there all this time?" . . .
>
> "Well, at one time I was in prison," he said, "and sometimes translating books, and sometimes teaching at a university. Sometimes the progression goes in reverse, and your poet begins at the university and ends in jail." . . .
>
> "Have you ever had veal cooked this way before?" she said, after a quick glance to see if their hostess was ready to take on Piotr again. . . . Piotr was

still hers. "And where did you learn your good French and your charming.
manners?" . . . "In Poland?"

"The hardest thing to learn was not to spit on the table," said Piotr.
(191)

The other life imagined for Polish émigrés in Paris is equally marginal, although Piotr finds more solace in Maria's company than in Marek's. Maria is a
Polish sculptress who was once passionately political, but had been "arrested
casually" in Moscow and "released at random," and has lived in Paris since then
(188). Now, in the unrecognizable political landscape of the sixties and seventies, her previous militancy has become a faded romance; her present experience
is shaped amidst the more stable comforts of the novels she reads, which help
her to place Piotr and his affair with Laurie amidst the fictional characters who
populate her life. Gallant's portrait of Maria is more sympathetic than that of
Marek; through Maria, we gain insight into a life totally shaped for a time by
political and historical contingencies, but then left on the margins, never having
been afforded the chance to develop a private existence, so that her only sense of
love must be from her reading. She is "as virginal as her name," a "discreet, mistaken old woman" with whom Piotr "talked of nothing but politics and art"
(188). Indeed, "Potter" plays on several levels with the attempts of characters to
substitute fiction for life. When Piotr tries to write about his betrayed love for
Laurie, seeking relief, he fails miserably, producing "a long wail, something for
the ear, a babbling complaint" and decides "he would never write in that way
about his life again" (201). And yet if he knew how to read his account, perhaps
she would have found it prophetic, for it reveals two images of Laurie, both of
which will be confirmed in their relationship. He is familiar with the first image,
of an "unbreakably jaunty" girl, "lacking only in imagination"; but the second
one, of "a smaller young woman who was fragile and untruthful and who loved
out of fear," is unknown to him (201).

The central comedy of the story reflects Piotr's failures to conceive of his love
for Laurie in terms which he can accommodate without transforming himself.
At first he simply drifts through his infatuation with her, feeling rewarded in
ways he cannot comprehend, finding her inarticulate, misspelled letters to him
in Warsaw endearing confirmations of her essential innocence. But this first
stage collapses directly upon his return to Paris, after he has secured a long-
awaited visa to lecture in France on an exchange. Piotr suffers his first pangs of
jealousy and betrayal when, after a three-day idyll, Laurie suddenly announces
that she is going to Venice with an unnamed "friend." Utterly undone, Piotr
wanders around Paris, trying to understand his situation; in an image which
reveals just how foreign Piotr feels himself to be in this new-found identity, he
imagines himself almost literally disembodied:

His grief was so beyond jealousy that he seemed truly beside himself; there was a Piotr in a public park, trying hard to look like other people, and a Piotr divorced from that person. His work, his childhood, his imprisonment, his marriage, his still mysterious death were rolled in a compact ball, spinning along the grass, away from whatever was left of him. Then, just as it seemed about to disappear, the two Piotrs came together gain. The shock of the joining put him to sleep. (186)

But this image of the profound shock to Piotr's identity only foreshadows the eventual course of the relationship. Piotr develops a "stone" in his chest, a hoarse throat, and other attendant ailments—all psychosomatic, perhaps, but nevertheless real testimony to his grief and the depth of his feelings for Laurie. As he languishes in Paris, constructing and reconstructing his image of Laurie to accommodate his new perception of her in her betrayal, it seems as if Piotr might be able to avoid radically altering his identity—as if by renouncing Laurie, he might be able to escape the possibility that his love for her will transform him into someone quite different. But just as he appears to be on the verge of recovering from the lovesickness that Laurie has left him with, he gets a postcard from her, confessing that she loves only him and she is returning to Paris to be with him.

But in the interim, the delicate political balance of forces upon which Piotr depends for his foothold in Paris has intervened. In a comic but telling reversal of roles—and in an incisive comment on political posturing in the academy, East and West, on the parts of both faculty and students—the French scholar in Warsaw has breached acceptable doctrine by attempting to convert her Polish students, whom she finds too complacently bourgeois, to a more active Marxist view; for his part, Piotr in Paris is confronted at his lectures by "lowering" students who ask him if he is a fascist because their understanding is that only fascists are let out of Poland. The Poles have revoked the French teacher's visa, and so Piotr must also return.

Piotr is thus provided with an external force, a sociopolitical deus ex machina which will save him from further involvement with Laurie. But finally—and this is the story's central revelation—it is not these larger political, cultural, or historical forces which determine Piotr's course of action with Laurie. In a more conventional story, we might have been presented with Piotr's forced return as an exemplary, cautionary tale about the impossibly rigid, state-controlled, Eastern European ethos which enforces the abnegation of any personal life, making it impossible for a character like Piotr to form a relationship conceived of beyond the bounds of history and politics, national borders, and rifts between continents. But in this story, the larger social determinants function in a more subtle manner as avenues of escape for Piotr, so that he can free himself of what turns out to be Laurie's genuine need for him; and it is here that we discover the fuller implications of the reversal that Gallant has effected.

At first, our sympathies may lie with Piotr, the duped and doting older lover. Laurie has been carrying on several other relationships all the while; she is not as young as Piotr thought her to be, and has been in Paris, Marek tells him, for years. Her apparent youthfulness, Piotr concludes, may simply be the mark of her obliviousness to change, her lack of a memory—all evidence, from Piotr's point of view, of her essential betrayals. But now, when Laurie has discovered her genuine need for Piotr, it is Piotr who betrays her, and who also betrays what we have seen to be the depth of his feelings for her. He cannot bring himself to sever his connections with his past, oppressive as it has been; he cannot divorce his wife or abandon his children, even though he knows that there are no vital connections for him with his family. Therefore, he must resort to constructing the last of his fictions about the nature of his feelings for Laurie; after we have seen him suffering all the heartache so aptly suggested in his various physical ailments (and so aptly diagnosed as "bachelor's disease" by the predatory woman doctor he stays with, trapped in her own unhappy marriage) he comes to the convenient conclusion, in bed on his final night with Laurie, that for her he feels only a mild affection:

> No one but Piotr himself could have taken the measure of his disappointment as he said, So there really was nothing in it, was there? So this was all it ever was—only tenderness. An immense weight of blame crushed him, flattened him, and by so doing cleansed and absolved him. I was incapable of any more feeling than this. I never felt more than kindness. There was nothing in it from the beginning. It was only tenderness, after all. (212)

The palpable relief that filters through Piotr's measured assertions in the story's closing sentences attests to his real feeling of release from the bonds of a relationship that threatens to disrupt his categories of experience with the realities of human need: he has detected in Laurie traces of the disease that afflicted his wife—the need to be loved. The form in which Gallant presents Piotr's reflections upon this realization is a fine example of how irony riddles ostensibly "objective" insights in Gallant's fiction; the narrative point of view is balanced delicately along a continuum, at one end of which Piotr appears to be speaking for himself, but at the other end of which an ironic omniscience begins to gently mock Piotr's perceptions:

> Laurie, though fresh from a shower, had about her a slightly sour smell, the scent that shock and terror produce on the skin. . . . He remembered his wife and how her skin, then her voice, then her mind had become acid. . . . And so she became ugly, ill, haunted. It seemed to him that he saw the first trace of this change in the sleeping Laurie. She had lost her credentials, her

seal of aristocracy. She had dropped to a lower division inhabited by Piotr's wife and Piotr himself; they were inferiors, unable to command loyalty or fidelity or even consideration in exchange for passion. Her silvery world, which had reflected nothing but Piotr's desperate inventions, floated and sank in Venice. This is what people like Maria and me are up against, he thought—our inventions. We belong either in books or in prison, out of the way. Romantic people are a threat to civilization. (211)

The familiar Gallant play on "invention"—on romances which delude naive North Americans in Europe about the real nature of postwar experience—has been inverted here; it is the Eastern European sensibility which lives at a remove from personal need and from passion, safely ensconced in an elaborate social construction of identity which will protect Piotr from Laurie's needs. In "Potter," then, we have come a long way from the more straightforward comedy of Carol Frazier's romance in "The Other Paris"; Piotr's and Laurie's world suggests a more dense, more complex, far more ambiguous ground for relationships, and Gallant's depictions of Eastern and Western, male and female sensibilities are more sophisticated here than in earlier stories.

Impressive as "Potter" might be, the finest three stories in *From the Fifteenth District* are "The Four Seasons," "The Remission," and "The Moslem Wife." These stories, each in its own form and mood, recreate the mid-century decline of the English presence in continental Europe. All three stories are set in or alongside Liguria, a shifting borderland region on the Mediterranean coast of northern Italy which Gallant has appropriated as a fictional territory resonant with all of the historical, political, and cultural echoes of permanent transience. In Gallant's stories, Liguria's and southern France's foreign colonies—particularly the English colonies—become both reflections of their preserved but embattled traditions, and remnants of a vanishing way of life, swept out of existence by the massive transformations which permanently altered European reality in such a short span of time. "The Four Seasons" is set in the late thirties and early forties; "The Moslem Wife" spans the years from 1920 to the late forties; and "The Remission" is set in the early nineteen-fifties; through these three stories, we are provided with a comprehensive and powerfully evocative fictional representation of this period in recent Western history.

"The Four Seasons" is one of the few of her own stories which Gallant has discussed, and her remarks about its origins provide us with insight into one kind of source for her fiction:

> The story of the little servant girl had been told to me by the girl herself, by then a woman. She had been employed when she was eleven or twelve by an English family in the south of France. I set the story in Italy, for a number of reasons. The child was Italian. She had something the matter with one hip

and one shoulder all her life, as the result of carrying the children of this couple around when she herself was still quite small. They paid her very little at first, and then nothing at all. When the war broke out the family went back to England. They told her they had no money and would pay her after the war. She told me about how she had cried, and how her mother had beaten her because she did not believe this story. The family came back to their villa after the war and paid the girl in pre-war francs. Do you know what that meant? A few cents. And there they sat, in their charming villa, comfortable, respected. I used to look at them and think, "You bloody hypocrites."[5]

Although it is the Unwins' exploitation of Carmela, the servant girl, that forms the nucleus of the story, the story's setting in Italy provides Gallant with another opportunity to explore the rise of fascism and its "small possibilities in people"—one of the impulses behind *The Pegnitz Junction.* In "The Four Seasons," the Unwins' enthusiastic response to Mussolini's rise (in their view, he is bringing long-needed "order" to Italy) becomes a measure of their own totalitarian leanings, but it also establishes a connection between their treatment of Carmela and their view of Italy (and of their position in Italy as privileged, even patriarchal foreigners). The story of the Unwins and Carmela is so deeply embedded in a reflection of the English colony's response to Mussolini that finally the Unwins' exploitation of Carmela seems to merge with Italy's entrance into the war.

From the story's beginning, the British presence in Italy is depicted as a superimposed abstraction. Carmela's school in Castel Vittorio was built long before the thirties by a Dr. Barnes with "no better use for his money," and Carmela's education there leaves her with no lasting or practical knowledge about her own country. All she remembers from the school are the three portraits on the wall, none of which will provide her with the kind of knowledge she needs—one of Dr. Barnes, one of Mussolini, and one of the King bedecked with medals. Alongside these three, but suggestively "somewhat adrift," given what the story will reveal about human suffering and exploitation, is an image of the Sacred Heart (3).[6]

Carmela's voyage from her village to the coast to work for the Unwins becomes an innocent's descent into the fallen adult world, and the course of her education takes her through the hell of the Unwins' vision. But it is not only the English colony and the Unwins in particular who live in this foreign and fallen world; the story also presents subtle portraits of the Italians' involvement with the foreign colony and of their own responses to the approaching war. On Carmela's first errand for the Unwins, for example, she suddenly recognizes a man from Castel Vittorio, now a chauffeur to the "Marchesa," an American who lives alongside the Unwins. As befits his new station, the chauffeur makes

no sign that he recognizes Carmela (although when he sees her at the Unwins—
in her own connection with the colony—he grants her a "diffident nod" [6]).
This deception, she instantly realizes, has been her first lesson in the social
hierarchies which will order her "real" life: "Her real life was beginning now,
and she never doubted its meaning. Among the powerful and the strange she
would be mute and watchful. She would swim like a little fish, and learn to
breathe underwater" (5). More telling than this portrait of the sycophantic
chauffeur, however, are the depictions of Carmela's little brother and his Italian
boss. When the deportation of Jews from Italy starts, a lucrative traffic in smug-
gling them across the border into Monaco in fishing boats begins, and Lucio,
formerly a stonemason, buys an interest in a boat and takes "Carmela's brother
along" (28). Like Carmela, her brother is a child who is keenly perceptive about
the social strata in the colony, but only dimly aware of the causes or nature of
the larger changes he witnesses; and Lucio sees the new situation simply as a
chance to make a profit. Nor is Carmela's mother excluded from censure for her
lack of awareness or compassion: she sends Carmela a message to stay with the
Unwins as long as possible because the family will need the money, and she cannot rely on Carmela's brother, who was "perhaps earning something with the
boat traffic of Jews, but how long could it last? And what was the little boy's
share?" (29)

The story follows the course of Carmela's rapid and forced initiation into the
social organization of the colony. Unbeknownst to the Unwins, she quickly
learns English and so becomes adept at catching the drift of their conversations
or the gist of letters left lying around; more significantly, she becomes expert at
reading their moods and attitudes. This is revealed most effectively when
Carmela serves tea on the occasion of Mr. Dunn's, the new padre's, visit to the
Unwins. Mrs. Unwin is an agnostic who will eventually undermine the padre because she fears his efforts to effect any kind of change in the colony; on this first
visit, Carmela sees that the padre is missing all of the cues from the assembled
guests at the Unwins that it is serious business to suggest changes in the way the
church has tended its flock. Present at the Unwins for this confrontation are
Miss Barnes—descendant of the Dr. Barnes mentioned in the story's opening,
and therefore a contemporary representative of the longstanding tradition of a
"benevolent" British presence in Italy—and Miss Lewis, a "bolshie" young
Englishwoman from Miss Barnes' perspective, who infuriates Mrs. Unwin by
lecturing her about her verbal abuse of Carmela. The opposition to one of the
padre's proposed changes nicely captures the Unwins' and Miss Barnes' determined clinging to the past: when he mentions that the church clock is slow and
that he "might have the time put right," he is met with hysterical responses, cul-
minating in a screamed command from Mrs. Unwin to have "no involvement"
of any kind with "anything" (21). It is only at this point that Mr. Dunn realizes
that Mrs. Unwin and Miss Barnes are in dead earnest; nor is he to preach boring

sermons like his predecessor, Mr. Unwin warns him. It is inevitable, given Mrs. Unwin's stance, that the padre will make a vindictive enemy of her when he speaks out, however obliquely, against intolerance, or about courage and tyranny, and on an Easter Sunday he crosses the line forever when he mentions Hitler by name (27).

But the figure who finally most fully embodies charity, mercy, and compassion is another victim of the times, the Jewish Doctor Chaffee. He ministers to the Unwin children, both of whom have rickets, and also looks at Carmela, who is tiny for her age. He prescribes pills for Carmela, but she never takes them, although she preserves them for years as another talisman from the mysterious foreign and adult world she has been thrown into. For the Unwin children, he recommends a summer away from the coast and the heat, and so the Unwins take the children and Carmela into the mountains, where they leave Carmela alone and in charge. When they return, conditions have begun to deteriorate, and Jews have begun to be deported. Another vein of the Unwins' attitude is now bared; it is painful to have "to think of dear Dr. Chaffee as someone in trouble. . . . but it might not be desirable if all these good people were to go to England now" (26).

Carmela's last glimpse of Dr. Chaffee prefigures her vivid and revelatory memory of him at the end of the story. Carmela crosses the border into France every week to buy groceries; on one of her trips, she sees a group of refugees, Dr. Chaffee among them, being marched to the French frontier. The tragic misunderstandings and benedictions suggested through Carmela's silent exchange with Dr. Chaffee resonate throughout the story:

> She remembered how she had not taken the pills he had given her—had not so much as unscrewed the metal cap of the bottle. Wondering if he knew, she looked at him with shame and apology before turning her head away. As though he had seen on her face an expression he wanted, he halted, smiled, shook his head. He was saying "No" to something. Terrified, she peeped again, and this time he lifted his hand, palm outward, in a curious greeting that was not a salute. He was pushed on. She never saw him again. (26)

Carmela, without a larger context in which to understand the meaning of Dr. Chaffee's deportation, can only be ashamed that she did not take the medicine he prescribed; he is a doctor who was unable to minister to her both because he was "foreign" in her perception and because, on another level, he has no cure either for the larger disease which will sweep him away or for the exploitation of Carmela by the Unwins. Like Mr. Dunn, Dr. Chaffee is powerless to heal anyone. And for his part, Doctor Chaffee misunderstands Carmela's gesture as well; he thinks that her reaction is born out of shame at her guilt and complicity in his deportation, and so he pardons her in a greeting that also, perhaps, suggests his dim recognition that they are each in their way victims of forces beyond their control.

Like many of Gallant's finest stories, "The Four Seasons" turns on a series of repetitions in which early scenes and details are subtly altered later in the story, both to suggest the completion of a pattern and to suggest crucial changes within that pattern. Early in the story, Carmela, on her first walk from the Unwins' house to the marketplace, sees her surroundings as utterly foreign and fabulous—"a clinic with a windbreak of cypress trees and ochre walls and black licorice balconies," for example (4). Her most fairy-tale vision is of a café, from which she hears a woman—the Marchesa, Mrs. Unwin's mortal enemy—describing some ugly new houses under construction:

> "Hideous. I hope they fall down on top of the builder. Unwin put money in it, too, but he's bankrupt." The woman who made these remarks was sitting under the pale-blue awning of a café so splendid that Carmela felt bound to look the other way. She caught, like her flash of the sea, small round tables and colored ices in silver dishes. (4)

Throughout the story, Carmela has replied to Mrs. Unwin's baffling chatter with cryptic remarks of her own, such as "Every flower has its season" (4) or "Every creature has its moment" (13). Carmela's "moment" comes late in the story and attests to the general collapse of moral order around her. The Unwins, realizing their danger, are fleeing to England; Mr. Unwin has offered to drive Carmela to a bus stop to start her on her way home. On the way, he spots the padre at the café which was the scene of Carmela's earlier vision, and they join the padre for an ice cream. The approaching chaos has collapsed the social order; Carmela is now seated with her former employer and with the padre, and she is served one of the fabulous dishes of ice cream. While she eats the ice cream, too dazed to believe in her good fortune, the padre tries to tell Mr. Unwin that he will not be bullied, that he is going to stand firm in his convictions. But Mr. Unwin is too intent on unburdening his story of his miserable marriage to Mrs. Unwin to listen to the padre. Responding to Unwin's lament, the padre tells him to "[T]hink about the sacraments—whether you believe in them or not. You might arrive in a roundabout way. Do you see?" (32) But Unwin is too far sunk in his own unhappiness to believe in sacraments; and when the padre turns to Carmela, she responds: "I have just eaten my way into heaven" (34). On one level, we might be tempted to understand Carmela's reply as an innocent statement, and her reference to heaven as innocent vernacular, referring to the miraculous turn of events whereby she has found herself seated at this table, eating this ice cream; the distance she has come from the beginning of the story does seem miraculous. But the occasion of this moment is her departure from the Unwins, with no money to show her mother; the padre has been denounced by anonymous letters, almost certainly written by Mrs. Unwin; and "heaven" seems an abstraction powerless to invoke compassion or charity in any of the story's characters in the face of the war. Her reply, then, must in some measure be understood ironically as her recognition of the only realm in which "heaven" is likely to be possible at this time—in the momentary, miraculous, and ephemeral appeasement of her hunger. So, too, the padre's reply to Carmela—"Then I haven't entirely failed"—must be read as a rueful admission of his elemental failure to awaken in the Unwins or in anyone else a sense of their involvement or moral responsibility (34).

The closing paragraph of the story firmly establishes what will impress itself most vividly on Carmela's memory as she makes her way home from the coast to Castel Vittorio. She will not remember her experience in any chronological sequence, but only in terms of what will have the most lasting and powerful effect on her. In further confirmation of the impact of the "heavenly" experience of eating the ice cream, Carmela sees "towering clouds that seemed like cream piled on a glass plate" (34). Her earlier childhood memories, of "Dr. Barnes, Mussolini and the King in wooden frames," are "closer" than her memory of the padre and Unwin, who are "already the far past." But what Carmela keeps most vividly from her seasons on the coast is the earlier image of Dr. Chaffee: "[B]oth [the padre and Unwin] then were lost behind Dr. Chaffee in his dark suit stumbling up the hill. He lifted his hand. What she retained, for the present, was one smile, one gesture, one man's calm blessing" (35). Like Dr. Chaffee, Carmela has become a refugee and a victim, exploited in her childhood and then abandoned in her own country; the only lasting image of her experience with the Unwins will be Dr. Chaffee's "calm blessing," a gesture whose significance she can only imagine.

In the "Four Seasons," Gallant makes brilliant use of a child's exploitation to particularize a country's drift toward chaos; the Unwins' situation finally reflects both the English colony's precarious position at the outbreak of the war, and Italy's relatively passive acquiescence in the rise of fascism. "The Remission" explores the fading English presence abroad from a postwar perspective, in the early fifties on the French Riviera. "Remission" becomes an apt metaphor for the lingering, ultimately fatal illness suffered by a whole generation of Englishmen after the war—a generation which saw its cast of mind, its notions of civility, its entire worldview fade out of sight. Alec Webb, the dying Englishman who brings his family with him to the Riviera, typifies this generation, and the disease that is killing him incarnates a more widespread social malaise which has afflicted all the men of his background and experience:

He had been easy to subdue, being courteous by nature, diffident by choice. He had been a civil servant then a soldier; had expected the best, relied on good behaviour; had taken to prison camp thin books about Calabria and Greece; had been evasive, secretive, brave, unscrupulous only sometimes — had been English and middle class, in short.[7]

Alec's lingering illness, and by extension, the decline of his generation, is posed against the spectacle of Elizabeth's coronation; the story takes place "during the reign of the new Elizabeth" (75), and she, unlike the "old" Elizabeth, will be ruling over a declining empire, and burdened with the very recent memory of wartime suffering. So that the colony can watch the coronation ceremony, Alec's wife Barbara has a television installed at Lou Mas, the villa Barbara's brothers have leased for the Webbs. Alec has suffered a crisis the night before and should not attend, but appears in the doorway, impeccably dressed as always. His position as the last representative of an era is made painfully clear:

> He was the last, the very last, of a kind. Not British but English. Not Christian so much as Anglican. Not Anglican but giving the benefit of the doubt. His children would never feel what he had felt, suffer what he had suffered, relinquish what he had done without so that this sacrament could take place. The new Queen's voice flowed easily over the Alps — thin, bored, ironed flat by the weight of what she had to remember — and came as far as Alec, to whom she owed her crown. He did not think that, precisely, but what had pulled him to his feet, made him stand panting for life in the doorway, would not occur to James or Will or Molly, not then, or ever. (90)

Alec's decline, like the more general "remission" that it particularizes, is all the more final because of its effects on his three children. Left without a father, a tradition, or a country, the children are disinherited in several senses. Their displacement becomes even more acute when Alec is replaced in his house and his wife's bed by Eric Wilkinson, an Englishman who has made his living in the postwar era by playing bit parts in films, always as the stock British character who really only survives as a fiction. Wilkinson's figure is one of the finest of Gallant's recurring portraits of characters who work as actors in films about the war — portraits which show the ways in which the past is reconstructed according to the next generation's needs. And nowhere in her fiction do we get as revealing or as fully developed a contrast between the original and the derivative, the real and the imitative, as we do in the contrast this story draws between Alec and Wilkinson.

Of all the stories in *From the Fifteenth District*, "The Moslem Wife" exemplifies most powerfully Gallant's vision of how history sweeps over individual lives, how postwar memory works to conserve a sense of the past denied everywhere in the present, and how the imagination creates intense moments of convergence in which individuals might see how the past is reflected in the present. Most importantly, the "light of imagination" which so vividly illuminates the story's final scene also reflects across the entire range of Gallant's canon, providing us not only with insight into this story's art, but also with a deeper understanding of the significances of the past in all of Gallant's fiction.

In "The Moslem Wife," Netta Asher confronts memory's paradox. She discovers memory's potential to realize the self within history, but she is also imprisoned by memory's passive function as a repository—a vault which entombs the individual within an ossified tradition of exile, isolated from history, oblivious to the present moment. Netta Asher and Jack Ross are first cousins, children of English hotel-keepers on the Ligurian coast whose families have become "plaited like hair" over the years.[8] They marry in the early 1930s, separate during the war, and reunite when Jack returns to France from America. In place of a conventional plot, Gallant stretches a fabric of recurring detail over the framework of their relationship, knitting up these details in a pattern of opposed images of light and darkness, sunlight and shadow. She sets the "light-drenched" landscape of history over against the shaded, "deeply mirrored" hotel room Jack and Netta live in (44, 43); as long as the glare of history is dispersed by the "pure white awning" which shades the hotel room, Netta can watch the peaceful reflection of sunlight in the room's mirrors; she can remain "unnaturally happy," watching her image in the mirror rather than seeing herself as a "Moslem wife" (37, 43). But Netta is exposed to the direct glare of history when the war breaks out; she survives the war alone, but she finally assents, like a Moslem wife once again, to a reunion with Jack when he returns after the war. Their reunion denies what Netta senses—the reality of both history's and memory's ghosts, and the presence of the past in both public and private worlds.

In the story's opening allusion to Katherine Mansfield's story, "The Daughters of the Late Colonel," we can see how Gallant focusses on history at a double remove here to structure her fiction:

In the south of France, in the business room of a hotel quite near to the house where Katherine Mansfield (whom no one in this hotel had ever heard of) was writing "The Daughters of the Late Colonel," Netta Asher's father announced that there would never be a man-made catastrophe in Europe again. The dead of that recent war, the doomed nonsense of the Russian Bolsheviks had finally knocked sense into European heads. What people wanted now was to get on with life. When he said "life," he meant its commercial business.

Who would have contradicted Mr. Asher? Certainly not Netta. (36)

Gallant frames her story in Mansfield's fiction, which is about the fall of Empire, among other things; this fall is projected in both stories through its effects on families living, like the Webb family in "The Remission," within an outworn tradition. Mansfield's story deals with two daughters' lifelong subservience to their father, the (late) Colonel. Constantia and Josephine are incapable of assuming independent lives, even after the Colonel's death, because they have lived in his shadow for so long—the same shadow cast by the sun setting on the Empire. Netta appears to be nominally more independent, but she, too, lives as a "Moslem wife" in Jack's shadow and in the shadow of the late Mr. Asher and his one-hundred-year lease on the hotel, which would deny Netta an ordinary life span and deny history its more problematic evolution. Netta's marriage to Jack, like her reunion with him, depends upon her muffling memory's voice and assuming her role as a "Moslem wife."

Beyond these broad thematic parallels, Gallant's and Mansfield's stories share related images. Both narrators present the captive daughters with a glimmer of insight, imaged near the end of both stories as a ray of sunlight. This flicker of natural light from the historical world might illuminate the shadows of their private lives, freeing them from the "pastness" of the past—the traditions which have bound them in exile from themselves. Mansfield's sunlight "pressed through the windows, thieved its way in, flashed its light over the furniture and photographs" in the late Colonel's bedroom.[9] The sunlight sets both daughters dreaming, remembering their mother's death in Ceylon (outpost of Empire), wondering "[I]f mother had lived, might they have married? But there had been nobody for them to marry. There had been father's Anglo-Indian friends before he quarrelled with them."[10] But their moment of potential illumination, like so many similar moments in Gallant's fiction, passes without issue. Constantia, imprisoned once again in her "constancy," forgets what she had been about to say to Josephine; Josephine stares "at a big cloud where the sun had been," and says that she has forgotten, too.[11] Netta's last, troubling flash of insight takes place in the "last light of the long afternoon," which "strikes" a mirror in a café. This sunlight is a "flash in a tunnel, hands juggling with fire"; its "play" on the mirror will tell "anyone who could stare without blinking" a "complete story" (73). Gallant's sunlight is harsher than Mansfield's, more explicitly a historical light, and Netta is in a more public place—a café in a square—although she wishes she were in her hotel room. And Gallant, more than Mansfield, calls attention to the process of transformation from sunlight to insight. Netta cannot be sure which light, which version of reality, is "real"—the sunlight from the square, or its image on the mirror. Gallant's image raises the issue, more than Mansfield's, of where this light might be coming from: Gallant's image also resolves this issue momentarily, evoking a fusion of memory with history, converging in the "light of imagination." Mansfield's image transforms sunlight (and the chirping of baby sparrows, which Josephine interiorizes as the cries of her fledgling self) without comment, while Gallant frees Netta momentarily to seek the implications of a double vision. Netta is inquiring into the nature of imagination—and in this sense anticipating one of Linnet Muir's formulations in the stories collected in *Home Truths,* of fiction as a "variety of exile." But Netta cannot free herself into history, out of exile in an expatriate tradition, by articulating the "reliable counter-event" in memory which would oppose Jack's recollection of their reunion as the happiest moment in his life (74).

As the narrator of Gallant's story makes clear, Netta, like her father, does not know who Katherine Mansfield is, and she will not read "Daughters of the Late Colonel." Therefore she is fated to act out a similar story and suffer related consequences. Because history will prove Mr. Asher's confident "announcement" to be wishful thinking, Netta, who "certainly" cannot contradict her father will have to live through history's contradiction.

The hotel which Netta inherits is more English than England itself. Its name, "The Prince Albert and Albion," announces its status as a monolith of Empire, but Gallant does not stop at this level of irony. Through style and sentence structure, as well as through detail, she places the hotel as a monument to an English leisured class of another era. The grounds are ordered into a landscape of formalized tranquillity ("tennis courts, a lily pond, a sheltered winter garden, a formal rose garden, and trees full of nightingales" [37]), while Netta and Jack's life at the hotel moves in rhythms of leisurely repose: "[F]rom the rose garden one might have seen the twin pulse of cigarettes on a balcony, where Jack and Netta sat drinking a last brandy-and-soda before turning in" (37). Victorian mirrors in the dining room reflect "glossy walls and blown curtains and nineteenth-century views of the Ligurian coast, the work of an Asher great-uncle"; the hotel's upkeep is described in a sentence that itemizes the work of refurbishing in an unbroken monotony, enacting the repetitive nature of Netta's off-season tasks in the face of "next year's sun": "Netta also had the boiler overhauled and the linen mended and new monograms embroidered and the looking glasses resilvered and the shutters taken off their hinges and scraped and made spruce green for next year's sun to fade . . . " (38).

Because they have been raised in hotels rather than in real homes, Jack and Netta's cultural milieu is perpetually expatriate, adopted rather than inherited. They are swaddled in tradition, English at a remove from themselves. "Born abroad, they worked hard at an Englishness that was innocently inaccurate, rooted mostly in attitudes" (39); much like the three Webb children in "The Remission," Netta "talk[s] the English of expatriate children, as if reading aloud," and she and Jack use a "spoken shorthand" with each other (39). Death itself is a stilted formality in the hotel, a gentlemanly exit from life, so that Netta remembers the dead as "cold, heavy furniture" (39). The hotel is a shuttered sanctuary, a shaded mortuary, but for Netta, as for Jack, it is also home.

Within this ambience her relationship with Jack forms a second, more intimate enclosure. Their uniformity of manner, their "spoken shorthand," masks important differences. Netta, unlike Jack, has no feeling that she belongs to a culture that extends beyond the hotel grounds; Jack, unlike Netta, has no sense of their relationship defined by anything but her physical presence. As the narrator remarks in a comment which reverberates in the story's ending, but also echoes beyond this story to redefine our sense of memory and relationships throughout Gallant's fiction: "Love was memory, and he [Jack] was no good at the memory game; he needed Netta there. The instant he saw her he knew all he had missed" (42). Netta has no idea whether the two families are related to the Italian poet, Montale, while Jack wishes that they were (40); when she hears Jack playing some "deeply alien music (alien even when her memory automatically gave her a composer's name), she [is] reminded that here the dead had never been allowed to corrupt the living" (38). Netta's "automatic" memory, which throws up bits of disembodied information (a memory which is the individual incarnation of a culturally expatriate, "automatic" history), is thus distinguished from Jack's more vital memory at this early stage of the story. Jack, the "fighter," reaches out to try and make connections, however flimsy and dilettantish, with the larger world beyond the hotel; Netta, without knowing the reason for her action, kicks him savagely, unbalancing him for life (40–41). In the early years of their marriage, Jack tries to translate pages of St. John Perse's verse; to Netta, poetry is "as blank as the garage wall . . . in any tongue" (38). As "The Moslem Wife" develops, these attitudes will reverse themselves, showing us the effects of the hotel's occupation during the war, the effects of Netta's direct encounter with history. In Gallant's stories, the impact of history, particularly of the war, has often swept away characters' traditions and values along with their past. In the Pegnitz stories, many of the characters experience this impact as destruction, as obliteration. But through her depiction of Netta, Gallant explores the war's destruction in different terms from those in the German stories, suggesting that there is a certain value, a certain freedom for Netta in the insights which she gains from her passage through history. For Netta, it is a release to be free from her image as a Moslem wife; Netta is one of the first of Gallant's characters to act on her sense that there is a possible value in independence.

The story's title comes from a remark Netta overhears from one of her hotel guests, Dr. Blackley, who refers to her as the "little Moslem wife" (43). This characterization takes on different meanings as Netta reflects on her status at different parts of the story. Gallant's technique of repeating, with subtle alterations, details, phrases, descriptions, and images, continues in this story—not only with Netta's name, but also with the contexts in which she repeats certain phrases. When Dr. Blackley propositions her early in the story, for example, Netta replies "Not a hope," which becomes her refrain to men's advances until just before the occupation. We can trace Netta's evolution out of her condition as a "Moslem wife" (and back into it) by tracing the evolution of her response's meanings.

Beyond the recurring details which advance Netta's transformation, longer passages also frame her evolution. In the episode at Roquebrune, for example, when Netta begins to think about the confines of her language, we also see her beginning to emerge from the confines of the hotel and from her marriage, finding herself in an expatriate colony which shows her an absurd mirror-image of her own condition. This episode (parties and gatherings in Gallant's fiction are more often than not occasions for parody and satire) develops one of Gallant's funniest set pieces of social comment. Iris Cordier, a friend of Jack's mother ("dotty" Vera) invites Jack and Netta to her father's house at Roquebrune; Netta goes unwillingly. There, she meets Sandy and Sandra Braunsweg, Anglo-Swiss twins who are unwitting caricatures, absurd images of Netta and Jack. Sandra is trying to pummel a young American into respectable Anglophilia; she kicks him for asking where the "toilet" is in London, and she forces him to wear clothes which will "harmonize" with her car on a visit to her "undeniably excellent" English school, "Mitten Todd" (52–53). The American puzzles Netta; he is trying to be a writer (an occupation which makes no sense to her at this point), living on money his father is sending him. This scene at Roquebrune has another function beyond parody as well: it shows Netta evolving a language, looking for words which will define her sense of the Roquebrune set's artificiality. When she responds to Iris Cordier's melodramatic announcement to Jack, for example, we also see her beginning to define one sense of the past as imprisonment in tradition:

> "I've no time for women," said Iris. . . . "Shall I tell you why? Because women don't tick over. They just simply don't tick over." No one disputed this. . . . Women were underinformed. One could have virile conversations only with men. Women were attached to the past through fear, whereas men had a fearless sense of history. "Men tick," she said, glaring at Jack.
> "I am not attached to a past," said Netta, slowly. "The past holds no attractions. . . . Nothing could be worse than the way we children were dressed. And our mothers—the hard waves of their hair, the white lips. I think of those pale profiles and I wonder if those women were ever young." (52)

It is Netta, not Jack, who will begin to "tick" in time, by living within history; like the Marchesa in "The Four Seasons," Jack will flee to America, to a continent which will experience the war at a remove for the most part. Netta, unlike Iris, is not "attached to the past through fear," and she is about to acquire a sense of history. In this sense Netta becomes a central figure among Gallant's expatriates, showing that these figures are expatriated and repatriated in *time*.

Netta's response at this point shows her beginning to slough off her reticence; at the same time, she is also responding internally to Sandra Braunsweg, seeking to define her appearance. The narrator tells us that Netta cannot arrive at a word for Sandra: "Netta has never in her life thought a word like 'pretty'" (53). Now she uses the new word, "pretty," in her conversation with Jack on the way home from Roquebrune. "Pretty," an important word in Gallant's fiction from the beginning (as in "The Other Paris"), next becomes a word Netta will use to suggest the superficiality of her affair with the American. First she turns aside his double request for money and sex with her characteristic "Not a hope"; the second time he asks, just before the occupation, Netta tells him, "no more than affectionately," that she's "going to show [him] a very pretty room" (60).

Another incident which occurs before the occupation prepares for one of Netta's central insights into the flaw in the structure of "everyday living" which Gallant was looking for in writing the Pegnitz stories. Three sisters—East Indians, part of what Dr. Blackley calls the "maharaja trade"—arrive at the hotel, shepherded by a governess and a chauffeur. Because they dress in blue for tennis lessons, Mrs. Blackley proclaims with obvious satisfaction that they will not be able to play on the tennis club courts. "They can't go on the courts except in white. It is a private club. Entirely white" (48). Jack teaches them on the hotel courts instead. When the middle daughter returns after the war with gifts for Netta, she tells her that she had "hated her father, her mother, her sisters, and most of all the Dutch governess" (66). Netta's reflections can be read as her own discovery of what Gallant calls the "worm" in the structure of everyday living, the flaw which brought on the general cultural collapse: "Every calamitous season between then and now," Netta thinks, "seemed to descend directly from Georgina Blackley's having said 'white' just to keep three children in their places" (66). Netta muses on the irony by which the girl's personal grievances can be more important to her than the impact of the war: "Death made death casual: she [Netta] had always known. Neither the vanquished in their flight nor the victors returning to pick over the rubble seemed half so vindictive as a tragic girl who had disliked her governess" (66). In Netta's analysis, history's currents appear to flow from the convergence of individual attitudes like Mrs. Blackley's; when the war is over, the tidal ebb leaves "tragic" individuals still caught up in their personal grievances. In "The Moslem Wife," Gallant allows these kinds of reflections to become her characters' insights—not only the narrator's or the reader's.

The hotel's occupation, first by the Italians and then by the Germans, stands as the scene of Netta's first major transformation. We can best apprehend the meaning of this transformation by attending to the recurring descriptions of Netta, first as a *watcher*, an observer of her own reflection in mirrors, and then, during the occupation, as a *reader*, by candlelight in the hotel cellar. At the beginning of the story Netta is "no reader," although she thinks that Jack reads too many books (46). She is an observer until Jack leaves: then, she finds that "the looking glasses still held their blue-and-silver-water shadows, but they lost the habit of giving back the moods and gestures of a Moslem wife" (61). After the war, Netta begins to read, leaning against the bar in Jack's habitual pre-war pose, when he had become "exhausted . . . by trying to make a world out of reading and sense out of life," Netta felt (59). Reading one of the books which Dr. Blackley has sent her, she comes to a description of two fascists in London: "'[T]wo Fascists came in, one of them tall and thin and tough looking; the other smaller, with only one arm and an empty sleeve pinned up to his shoulder. Both of them were quite young and wore black shirts'" (68). Netta responds to this description more strongly than she ever responds to other characters: "'Oh, thought Netta, I am the only one who knows all this. No one will ever realize how much I know of the truth, the truth, the truth,' and she put her head on her hands, her elbows on the scarred bar, and let the first tears of her after-war run down her wrists" (68).

Books which fictionalize recent history have become terribly relevant to Netta, because she has just lived through an experience she cannot account for as a Moslem wife. She can no longer shade herself from history's "sunlight" by speaking "shorthand" to Jack or by tacitly accepting her father's announcements. She discovers that fiction can enact experience, that reading life is also living life. Her "true" experience of the war does not conform to one of the fundamental laws governing realism as a fictional convention: it is too implausible, she decides, after trying to write a letter to Jack about her experience during the occupation (64). In the letter she does not send, Netta writes: "I suppose that you already have the fiction of all of this. The fiction must be different, oh very different, from Italians sobbing with homesickness in the night" (63). Netta describes her true but implausible experience in this letter, while in another "sensible" one, she asks "for sugar and rice and for new books; nothing must be older than 1940" (64). Netta's own story of the war is thus both expressed and silent, articulate and mute; unlike Jack, the reader is privileged to see both sides of Netta's experience. Netta herself, however, is finally confounded in her attempt to decide which experience—her own implausible, haunted, historical experience, or her relationship with Jack, who would deny that memory links past with present—is real. Unlike Carol Frazier, who closes her story by inventing a "coherent picture, accurate but untrue," Netta tries to express her incoherent experience of the occupation, to convey its truth.

Commenting on how her stories begin for her, Gallant tells Geoff Hancock about their common structure:

> I wouldn't choose a theme and write about it. A story usually begins, for me, with people seen in a situation, like that. (*Locks fingers together.*) The knot either relaxes or becomes locked in another way. Why that should be I can't tell you. But that's what occurs to me. The situation has a beginning

and as much ending as any situation has in life. The story builds around its centre, rather like a snail.[12]

The structure of "The Moslem Wife" is a good later example of Gallant's "locked situation," just as "The Other Paris" is a good early one. In "The Moslem Wife," the knot relaxes as Jack goes off to America and Netta remains behind. But the closing scene reties the knot in another way, locking Netta into her situation once again, despite the lessons she has learned in Jack's absence.

The knot begins to tighten around Netta again as her guests return from their dispersal during the war. Jack is the last to come back; the middle sister, Dr. Blackley, and Iris Cordier return before him. Netta turns down Dr. Blackley's proposal that she divorce Jack and either marry or live with him; more importantly, she tells him that she has learned how memory means. Netta has more to say about the meanings of memory than any Gallant character before her; it is Netta, and not the narrator, who tells Dr. Blackley that memory is what binds her to Jack, not sex or "faithfulness": "'What you are talking about [her purely sexual relationship with Jack] is something of which one has no specific memory. . . . Only of seasons. Places. Rooms. It is as abstract to remember as to read about. That is why it is boring in talk except as a joke, and boring in books except for poetry'" (67).

For Netta, the resources of memory (and Jack is "no good at the memory game"), not sex, and not a relationship conducted in a private code (a "spoken shorthand"), have become the inspiration for what is an essentially creative act: the imaginative sustenance of a sense of the past. But in the same breath Netta tells Dr. Blackley that memory can also act as a terribly binding and constraining force, imposing rigid interpretations on events; memory can also reduce experience to locked patterns. So when Netta sees "closed shutters," she knows "there are lovers behind them. That is how the memory works. The rest is just convention and small talk" (67). She overrides all of Dr. Blackley's objections, which are intended to force Netta to see that she cannot interpret everyone's experience by using her own memory's code. But such are the twists and turns of dialogue in this story that, just as Dr. Blackley is trying to educate Netta, she tells him that she survived the occupation by sleeping with the Italian commander billeted at the hotel. He was "not a guest," and so she was "not breaking a rule" (68). Memory will trap Netta into subservience to Jack, and yet she has survived alone; she tells Dr. Blackley that Jack's absence "was like a cancer [she is] sure has taken root, and of which [she is] bound to die" (68).

In depicting Netta's and Jack's reunion in the Place Masséna, Gallant completes Netta's return to her earlier status as a Moslem wife, but not before confronting her with the "light of imagination." It is worth considering this closing scene in some detail to see how Gallant suggests the inevitability of their reunion. By working a web of correspondences between early and late detail,

Gallant evokes the inevitably recurrent patterns of a life governed only by memory: "Memory," Netta muses in this scene, "is what ought to prevent you from buying a dog after the first dog dies, but it never does. It should at least keep you from saying yes twice to the same person" (73). Netta shows here how much she understands—and yet cannot avoid—the ways in which her memory molds her life into patterns which reflect earlier configurations, so that her relationship becomes "the same voyage, at the same rate of speed" (73).

The Place Masséna recalls—for Netta—the earlier setting of her marriage, the hotel. But the similarities are crucially qualified. In the Place, "[T]here was a deep-blue late-afternoon sky and pale sunlight. She could hear birds from the public gardens nearby. The Place was as she had always seen it, like an elegant drawing room with a blue ceiling" (69). Jack and Netta are meeting out in the historical, public world, near a public garden where unnamed birds sing, rather than in their hotel room, in the shade and near the hotel's private gardens and its trees "full of nightingales" (37). The Place is sunlit (although the sunlight is "pale"); it is part of that "light-drenched" landscape which, earlier in the story the narrator had told us was outside the "fenced area" of their relationship, and so "too open" for "serious talk" (44). But now history has cast a palpable shadow over the landscape. The Place may *seem* as Netta had always seen it, as an extension of the hotel, an "elegant drawing room" with a ceiling, but it cannot be that drawing room: Netta and Jack walk across a square haunted by historical ghosts, "under the arches where partisans had been hanged" (70). History has become uncomfortably immediate for Netta: "[I]t seemed to Netta the bodies had been taken down only a day or so before" (70). Jack remains at a more comfortable remove; he knows "about this way of dying only from hearsay," and he unknowingly chooses a table "nearly under a poor lad's bound, dangling feet" (70). Netta is haunted by both history and memory in the square; just as she "sees" (an important, recurring term in Gallant's fictional idiom) the partisan's bound feet, she also "feels" the clasp of an invisible hand from the past when Jack takes her wrist. Netta has become vulnerable, transparent, blessed and cursed with the life of memory. Her memory, she thinks, is "dark . . . accurate . . . deadly"; for his part, Jack has a "short memory," and so a "comfortable" imagination (72). Netta's memory no longer yields up "automatic bits of memory"; it has become more visceral and more painful. Netta (not only the narrator and the reader) now understands that for Jack, there simply is no past. Netta herself looks like "a burnt-out child who has been told a ghost-story"; the ghost story is the spectral past, haunting the present.

It is at this point, when Netta is in despair over Jack's obliviousness to the past (and over her own acute sense of being haunted by it) that she sees the sunlight "strike" the mirror behind them in the café. Earlier in the story, the sunlight in her "deeply mirrored" hotel room had become a "play of light . . . as green as a forest on the walls, and as blue as seawater on the glass" (43). Now, the sunlight is far more active, its play more "unexpected":

> Desperately seeking the waiter, she turned to the café behind them and saw the last light of the long afternoon strike the mirror above the bar—a flash in a tunnel; hands juggling with fire. That unexpected play, at a remove, borne indoors, displayed to anyone who could stare without blinking, was a complete story. It was the brightness on the looking glass, the only part of a life, or a love, or a promise, that could never be concealed, changed, or corrupted. (73)

This image represents the "light of imagination," fusing sunlight with insight, history with memory. It is a *"brightness* on the *looking* glass," rather than simply a flat image on a mirror. This light could tell Netta a complete story if she could stare at it without blinking, but Netta does not quite understand what she sees. She still insists on separating her own memories from European history, despite the flash of illumination she sees before her. She insists that only *her own* experience is "real": "The dark, the ghosts, the candlelight, her tears on the scarred bar—*they* were real" (73). But "[S]till, whether she wanted to see it or not, the light of imagination danced all over the square" (73). If "The Moslem Wife" is a key story in Gallant's canon, then this "light of imagination" is a crucial phrase in her fiction's language. The moment of this light is a moment of illumination, of self in sunlight, a less ironic, more resonant version of Carol's moment with Felix in the Métro station. Natural light (sunlight, light in the world, historical light) "strikes" at the mirror of self; it is "borne indoors" to re-emerge in a fusion of self in world. The "light of imagination" could resolve the apparent dualities of self against world, subject against object, by fusing history with memory, sunlight with insight, diachronic with synchronic time. Early in the story, the narrator tells us that Netta "knew about the difference between darkness and brightness, but neither affected her" (39). Now she learns much more about darkness and brightness, but finds that she cannot stare into history's "brightness" with a naked eye. Netta perceives herself to be caught between two realities, each denying the other. Her yearning for a simpler metaphysics reveals itself when she thinks that "a pure white awning on a cross street seemed ... to be of indestructible beauty. The window it sheltered was hollowed with sadness and shadow" (73). The image of the awning has occurred twice earlier: Jack and Netta's hotel room has "white awnings," and Netta orders "new white awnings" for the hotel when everyone is fleeing the war (37, 59). From the Place, she is looking back at the fenced area of her marriage, recognizing its "sadness and shadow"; she is looking at the hotel window from the outside now, from the sunlit square. Earlier, she had looked out onto the "light-drenched" landscape from within the shuttered, "deeply mirrored" hotel room. Now, with the "same deep sadness" that she sees in the window, she tells Jack that she believes his statement—"announced [like Mr. Asher's opening announcement] in a new voice which stated nothing but facts"—that he loves her (73). Her belief is a response to a "wave" of feeling, a "powerful adolescent craving for something simple, such as true love" (73). This wave succeeds the original "wave" of revulsion she had felt when Jack stepped down from the bus at the beginning of this scene.

Netta's reunion with Jack seems inevitable, given that she does not have the resources to live more constantly with her insights; she needs the "shade" of her relationship with Jack, the shadow provided by the white awning. But Netta, more than any other Gallant character before her, lives a double life, one within this shaded area, and one in the sunlight. In the process of tracing Netta's return to Jack and her "locked situation," the story shows us Netta exploring these two lives. Jack's "buoyant" attitude supervenes, but language alerts us to the nature of his victory. Jack, the "practical romantic," is "dying to get Netta to bed right away"; all he hears is the "blood in his veins and his loud, happy thought" (73). When Netta says, for the last time, "not a hope," the phrase's meaning has reversed itself. There isn't a hope that she will be able to live with the "brightness on the looking glass," the "complete story." With the relationship reestablished, Jack is as "buoyant as morning. This *was* his morning—the first light on the mirror, the first cigarette" (74). But it is, in fact, late afternoon; the war and their separation have taken place. Jack's "first light on the mirror" is his saving delusion, an escape from Netta's fuller vision in the late afternoon sunlight. And since Netta cannot present a "reliable counter-event" to Jack's memory of this reunion as the "happiest event of his life" (74), she must let his memory stand.

The stories of *From the Fifteenth District* represent Gallant's finest achievements in evoking the climate of feeling so suddenly transformed in the thirties and forties in Western Europe. They also show Gallant at the height of her control over her art; the language, detail, and structure of these stories are exquisitely shaped and balanced to present fictions which seem at once seamless works of art and also inseparable from the realities they so vividly evoke. It seems only fitting that after *From the Fifteenth District,* Gallant's next book should return to one of her home grounds—Montreal—and to the evocations of Canadians in Europe which so many of her stories, early and late, take as their points of departure.

6

Home Truths
The Districts of Imagination

From the beginning, Gallant's stories have developed and sustained her exploration of the past as time misapprehended. *Home Truths* (1981) provides several
complementary perspectives on this extended exploration of time. Gallant's "An
Introduction" (1981) establishes some of the foundations of her fictional practices, and four stories originally published between 1963 and 1971 offer four related insights into how Gallant's fiction evokes the past. "Saturday" (1968) invites readers to consider once again the vital connections between memory, language, and voice which so much of Gallant's fiction brings to light; and "Bonaventure" (1966) is one of Gallant's most powerful stories to explore time in relation to life and art. "Virus X" (1965) depicts, in one of its most radical forms,
the distance between Gallant's postwar North American and European senses of
history; "In the Tunnel" (1971) develops in new ways the familiar Gallant story
of young North American women in Europe looking for love; and "The Ice
Wagon Going Down the Street" (1963) reminds us of how early in Gallant's fiction, and to what effects, her stories develop the tensions between worldly and
naive Canadians abroad.[1] Finally, the Linnet Muir stories collected in *Home
Truths* enrich the significance of returns to a home ground in Gallant's fiction,
both through their location of Montreal as a city in which Linnet revisits her
past in order to free herself from it, and as stories which create an autobiographical voice resonant with many of the ambiguities attendant on this form.

In a 1982 CBC interview, Gallant refers to literary criticism as "another
voice. It's like a window flung open in another landscape."[2] The first voice in
Home Truths is Gallant's, and the first window onto her fiction is her own. She
opens "An Introduction" with her reflections on Canadian art, on what is expected of Canadian writers and writing, on Canadian readers and their distrust

of imagination, and on that most sacred of Canadian conundrums—our most pervasive national myth—the Lost Canadian Identity:

> I take it for granted that "Canadian stories" has a specific meaning. In contradiction to everything said above, I am constantly assured that Canadians no longer know who they are, or what to be Canadian should mean; for want of a satisfactory definition, a national identity has been mislaid. The most polite thing I can say about this is that I don't believe it. A Canadian who did not know what it was to be Canadian would not know anything else: he would have to be told his own name.[3]

Gallant's comment here recalls her earlier remarks to Geoff Hancock on the same issue: "I have no identity problem concerning Canada. . . . In fact, I don't believe anyone has. It's something people like to imagine about themselves because it sounds tense and stormy and romantic."[4]

Prefaced by Boris Pasternak's observation that "only personal independence matters," Gallant's introduction undercuts any assumption that the "Selected Canadian Stories" of Home Truths differ (in content, in form, in style, in anything other than setting, if setting is understood in the narrowest sense of time and place) from her other ("American"? "European"? "French"? "Italian"? Rivieran"?) stories. Home Truths is important, not because its stories are "Canadian," but because among them are some of Gallant's finest, most representative stories. The German stories of The Pegnitz Junction are most important for their exploration of Fascism's small possibilities in people—possibilities which Gallant explores in German settings and characters, with all the unsettling resonances and associations that postwar German literary, historical, political, and cultural contexts carry with them. One important function of the Canadian material in Home Truths, particularly in the section entitled "Canadians Abroad," is that it adds a density of allusion to Gallant's "Canada" (a distinct part of Gallant's "North America") and Gallant's "Europe." But the most important emphases in Gallant's introduction—and in the stories themselves—fall on memory's manners of conveying the truth. The importance of the stories' Canadian setting is secondary, subsumed as it should be in the issue of the development of a writer's form.

"An Introduction" closes with Gallant's detailed recollection of how she came to write the Linnet Muir stories, an account which suggests important connections between a city's history (and that history's reconstruction in fiction) and a character's memory (and memory's recreative, formal impulse). Ending as it does with Cocteau's enigmatic formulation of the writer's calling ("Je suis un mensonge qui dit la vérité"), "An Introduction" reminds us that fiction lies to tell the truth, and that even in the case of a writer like Gallant, so meticulously concerned with accurate representation, it is the powers of invention which finally shape her fiction; as Gallant puts it, "memory can spell a name wrong and still convey the truth."[5] "An Introduction" comprises, along with her recent essay "What Is Style?" and sections of her *Canadian Fiction Magazine* interview, Gallant's most important reflections on the practice and purpose of writing fiction.[6]

In "An Introduction," Gallant comments: "Memory is something that cannot be subsidized or ordained. It can, however, be destroyed; and it is inseparable from language."[7] We have already witnessed memory's expatriation in history in the German stories; "Saturday" (1968) presents a more particular exploration of the kind of loss suffered by a character who has lost his home language. "Gérard's hatred of English in 'Saturday'," writes Gallant, "is not blind and irrational. Deprived of the all-important first language, he is intellectually maimed. The most his mind can do is to hobble along." She goes on to say that, re-reading "Saturday," she "see[s] that it is not about a family or a society in conflict, but about language; or so it seems to [her] now."[8] Gallant leads up to this crucial statement by making the same point about reading "Saturday" that she makes in her letter to Robert Weaver about reading "The Other Paris": "Like every story in this collection, "Saturday" needs to be read against its own time—the Montreal of about 1960."[9] This story's primary focus is on language and loss, as seen in its 1960 Montreal setting—and not the other way around. In fact, "Saturday," with its depiction of a French-Canadian mother determined to wrest her family free from their roots in French and in Catholicism, illustrates all too well Gallant's thesis that "to wrench your life and beliefs in a new direction you have to be a saint or a schizophrenic."[10] She is referring specifically to the German stories, but her comment applies to "Saturday" as well. Gérard lives in a reality that is half-dream, half-nightmare, in a confusion of languages through which he cannot find direction. "Saturday" is one of the few stories Gallant revised between its first appearance in *The New Yorker* and its republication thirteen years later; significantly, virtually all of her revisions consist of cuts in the expository passages which had clarified the distinction between Gérard's dreams and his waking reality. Compare, for example, the two versions of the passage which follows Gérard's opening "dream": the first is *The New Yorker* version (8 June 1968, p. 33), the second the *Home Truths* version:

Jazz from an all-night program invaded the house until Gérard's mother, discovering its source in the kitchen, turned the radio off. She supposed Gérard had walked in his sleep. What else could she think when she found him kneeling, in the dark, with his head against the refrigerator door? He had gone out, earlier, to see the girl his mother hated. He had promised he would tell the girl it was finished; that he was too young to be deeply involved. His parents had not heard him when he came in. Beside him was a smashed plate and the leftover ham that had been on it, and an overturned stool. His mother knelt too, and drew his head on her shoulder. "I ran into this funeral," he whispered. "In the East End. Some very rich English guy being buried in a cardboard box. Somebody's father." His own father stood in the doorway. The long underwear he wore at all times and in every season showed at his wrists and ankles, where the pajamas stopped.

Jazz from an all-night program invaded the house until Gérard's mother, discovering its source in the kitchen, turned the radio off. She supposed Gérard had walked in his sleep. What else could she think when she found him kneeling, in the dark, with his head against the refrigerator door? Beside him was a smashed plate and the leftover ham that had been on it, and an overturned stool. She knelt too, and drew his head on her shoulder. His father stood in the doorway. The long underwear he wore at all times and in every season showed at his wrists and ankles, where the pajamas stopped. (31–32)

The revised "Saturday" in *Home Truths* dramatizes more acutely Gérard's exile from a home in language in order to prevent readers from deciding too quickly which events really "happen" in the story as opposed to those which happen only in Gérard's mind. In this sense, the revised story immerses readers in a disorientation similar to Gérard's.

"Saturday" also clarifies the meaning of an important word in Gallant's fictional idiom. "Invention," as we saw in "About Geneva," is a key word for Gallant's narrators and characters, a word whose meanings shade into connotations such as "made up," created," and "untruthful." When Gallant herself uses the word, it usually means "made up" as opposed to "actual," or "composed" as distinct from "reported."[11] In "Saturday," "invention" is linked quite explicitly with acts of imagination which realize the past, creative acts which momentarily free two characters from their isolation in English into communion in French. Léopold, Gérard's nine-year-old brother, and his aging father are the family's twin eccentrics; the five sisters have all married identical Anglo-Protestant husbands with interchangeable faces and names, and their marriages have produced interchangeable grandchildren. The mother's dream of saving her family from a traditional French-Canadian fate has been shattered into banality. Only Léopold and his father live beyond this exile in banality, an exile predicated on the loss of a home language; Léopold can, "if he likes, say anything in a French more limpid and accurate than anything they are used to hearing."[12] The story gravitates away from Gérard's expatriation in English towards Léopold's and his father's homecoming in French; this moment of homecoming at the close of the story is a moment created by the father's realization that he, too, can "invent." Walking the family bassett, the father experiences "a sudden absence of fear" brought on by a sudden drop in the wind:

> He could dream as well as Gérard. He invented: he and Don Carlos went through the gap of a fence and were in a large sloping pasture. He trod on wildflowers. From the spongy spring soil grew crab apple trees and choke cherries, and a hedge of something he no longer remembered, that was sweet and white. Presently they—he and the dog—looked down on a village and the two silvery spires of a church. He saw the date over the door: 1885. The hills on the other side of the water were green and black with shadows. He had never seen such a blue and green day. But he was still here, on the street, and had not forgotten it for a second. Imagination was as good as sleepwalking any day. (47–48)

This moment of recovery does not displace the narrative present; the father (unlike Gérard) knows exactly where he is and his arrival, through invention, in this moment counterpoints Léopold's arrival in the same time and place. Léopold has been purposefully playing with a camera he has been given that day for his birthday. Now Léopold, who decides earlier that none of his nieces and nephews is "worth an inch of film," focusses on his father walking towards him on the porch: "He seemed to be walking straight into Léopold's camera, magically reduced in size" (48). The ambiguities of a camera-eye vision which stops time, framing it in order to capture a telling moment, are appropriate to this moment in "Saturday." The moment is framed for readers as it is for Léo and his father; it is a moment focussed in time, a moment prefiguring loss but also announcing communion. Léo has refused to go to his sister Pauline's for supper, and so he and his father are left alone, much to his father's pleasure. The narrator teaches us that memory's living moments, moments in which the past touches the present alive, consist of these kinds of meetings: "One day he [Léo] would have the assurance of a real street, a real father, a real afternoon" (48). Finally, this moment's life is translated from vision into utterance, into language given voice—Léopold's voice. Léopold closes the story by telling his father that the others are gone: "All gone. *Il n'y a que moi*" (48). *English* is "all gone"—all of its incursions, all of its inflections, gone—all gone. Gérard tries vainly to dream in French but his mind bedevils him with allusions to English literary exiles, to poetic love and illness in a foreign country, casting "Elizabeth Barrett" up to the surface (31, 33). Léopold banishes English and affirms himself, nobody but himself, no one but a French voice. "There is nothing but me," nothing but the French tongue; there are no other words. In this moment, a moment Léo will remember, he touches his father's hand. It is a moment Léo has created: time becomes his subject; momentarily he is not subjected to time. Within this moment of affirmation, Léo is free to touch, to affirm someone else's existence. In this story, memory's invention creates imaginative vision, and vision gives birth to voice: giving voice to the only home he can live in, it is only natural for Léopold to touch his father's hand.

"Saturday" is collected in the section of *Home Truths* entitled "At Home," the first of the book's three subdivisions. "In the Tunnel," "The Ice Wagon Going Down the Street," "Bonaventure," and "Virus X" comprise the second section, "Canadians Abroad." But the fact that these are stories about young Canadians adrift in Europe is of secondary importance to their place in Gallant's canon as stories about ambiguous or ironic initiation, stories which set North American varieties of innocence over against European versions of experience. "In the Tunnel," for example, charts the progress of Sarah, a young Canadian woman sent to Grenoble for a summer by her widowed father to learn about French civilization. But like other similar excursions in Gallant's stories, this one goes awry. Europe will never stand still for the "objective" scrutiny that various North American, college-educated characters bring with them; in Sarah's case, her affair with Roy Cooper teaches her a hard lesson about various failures to love. Cooper, a British inspector of prisons in Asia whose job vanished with the fading Empire, has kept from his former calling an obsession with order and sterility which has translated itself into an abstract, totalitarian tidiness in the prison of his personal life. He picks up Sarah in Nice and takes her to the "tunnel," the cottage he rents on the property of the Reeves, British expatriates suffused in the haze of a bygone era. Like "Cooper," their name is an appropriate sign for their function; they are absurdly parochial, and yet pathetic parents to two small dogs they pamper with "chockie bits," and to Roy himself; walled off in their bungalow, from which they refuse to even look at the Mediterranean, they are parodies of the stock image of the retired English couple in southern France, just as Roy represents a particularly unpalatable incarnation of the former British official, left stranded without a fiefdom to administer in the postwar decline of Empire. In this sense Cooper's portrait provides us with a sinister postwar sequel to some of Orwell's personae—the narrators of "Shooting an Elephant" or "A Hanging," for example. But in Gallant's imagination, Cooper's predations on young women in Europe and his childlike dependence on the Reeves, surrogate parents and psychological accomplices, become reflections and extensions of his former position and of his failure to adapt to the new order. In the postwar era, Cooper and the Reeves live imprisoned in a past they will not surrender, in an Empire which no longer exists.

Under the tutelage of this trio, Sarah learns too much about characters who have carefully shut themselves off from any real contact with the world or with others. The Reeves' marriage is an inert alliance against love, a dead tapestry of habit which has stultified them and provides an appropriate canopy for Roy's operations, as he lives out the death sentence of his sterility by preying on young women like Sarah who come to Europe to learn about love. Sarah brings on the beginning of the end of the affair by hurting her ankle; Roy, in one of the many manifestations of his obsession with maintaining and legislating a world free of impurities of any kind, cannot tolerate any sign of illness or injury. The connections between Roy's present life and his former position, the Reeves' version of the death of Empire, and Sarah's dawning perception of her preordained sacrificial function in this sealed-off universe, are sharply outlined in the exchange between Meg Reeves and Sarah near the end of the story:

> Meg said to her, "He misses that job of his. It came to nothing. He tried to give a lot of natives a sense of right and wrong, and then some Socialist let them vote."
> "Yes, he liked that job," Sarah said slowly. "One day he'd watch a hanging, and the next he'd measure the exercise yard to see if it was up to standard." She said suddenly and for no reason she knew, "I've disappointed him."[13]

Roy's behaviour with Sarah becomes inextricably bound up with his worldview as his attitude towards women becomes ominously linked with his attitudes towards his former "subjects"; finally, Roy becomes an early example of the Gallant characters who depict the rise of Fascism's "small possibilities in people," and Sarah begins to save herself by perceiving her situation as she listens to Roy inventing a revealing version of himself to Lisbet, the Reeves' niece:

> Roy was telling Lisbet a lie: he said he had been a magistrate and was writing his memoirs. Next he told her of hangings he'd seen. He said in his soft voice, "Don't you think some people are better out of the way?" Sarah knew by heart the amber eyes and the pupils so small they seemed a mistake sometimes. She was not Sarah but a prisoner impaled on a foreign language, seeing bright, light, foreign eyes offering something nobody wanted —death. "Flawed people, born rotten," Roy went on (98).

Sarah emerges from the "tunnel" with at least a veiled perception of the lesson she's learned from its inhabitants. She keeps as a reminder of a disastrous picnic with Lisbet and Roy, a card with "a picture of Judas with his guts spilling and with his soul (a shrimp of a man, a lesser Judas) reaching out for the Devil" (105). She is still confused about whom Judas should represent—Roy, Lisbet (who has figured in Sarah's imagination as a competitor for Roy), or even herself, "the victim, who felt guilty and maimed" (105). But she is still trapped somewhere between the abstract categories of "objective" and "subjective" being which demarcate the battleground of her relationship with her father in the story's opening paragraph and which framed her attempts in Europe to come to terms with her first long-term affair with a man. The "objective" Sarah that she has meant to flaunt in her father's face would be a "psychosociologist. Life would then be a tribal village through which she would stalk soft-footed and disguised: that would show him who was subjective" (72). The "subjective" Sarah, however, is "a natural *amoureuse*, as some girls were natural actresses, and she soon discovered that love refused all forms of fancy dress. In love she had to show her own face, and speak in a true voice, and she was visible from all directions" (72). This opening prediction has been borne out by the course of Sarah's affair with Roy, and the "tunnel" of the story's title thus takes on an additional psychological significance, referring to the dark and narrow dimensions of Sarah's constrained identity. This is a tunnel in which she is bound to live her life; she may have emerged from her affair with Roy Cooper, but she is in some measure destined to repeat versions of this first experience, and in some measure to assume Roy Cooper's role herself, as her confusion over whom Judas might represent suggests, and as the story's closing makes clear. She writes a dinner invitation on the Judas card to a man she is chasing, and comes to a moment of insight; but this perception, like so many other similar moments in Gallant's endings, is insufficient to change the pattern of her life:

> She looked at the words for seconds before hearing another voice. Then she remembered where the card was from, and she understood what the entire message was about. She could have changed it, but it was too late to change anything much. She was more of an *amoureuse* than a psycho-anything, she would never use up her capital, and some summer or other would always be walking on her grave. (106)

It is too late to change either the wording of the invitation or the course of her experience; she will always perceive herself as a "natural actress"—an *amoureuse*, with all of the ironies implied by this contradiction in terms and by the mantle of romance she wears in another language, from another era. And because she still has "capital" to spend, the spectre of her summer with Roy Cooper and the Reeves—or of some other future summer—will continue to haunt her. Sarah has escaped Roy Cooper, but emergence from the tunnel of her own condition remains a more problematic adventure.

"The Ice Wagon Going Down the Street" is a remarkable story on several counts. Like "The Other Paris," it dramatizes a revealing opposition between a conventional marriage, its partners only apparently suited to each other, and an improbable relationship between partners only apparently mismatched. Its Canadian characters, Peter Frazier and Agnes Brusen, act out typically Canadian parts in Europe in their conceptions of their central and western Canadian origins, respectively; and the story's central image, which gives it its title and its imaginative form, is one of Gallant's finest evocations of a child's sense of identity as inseparable from a familiar universe—a sense which will be shattered in adulthood, but which remains in memory as a vivid and troubling trace of a lost unity.

Peter and Sheilah Frazier have journeyed through Europe, Ceylon, and Hong Kong with their two daughters in search of a job worthy of Peter's supposedly aristocratic Canadian background; it is Peter's perennial delusion that his career is being manoeuvred into its preordained shape by unnamed higher-ups in Canadian diplomatic circles. But Peter's career has gone sour and the family is back in Toronto at the opening of the story in Peter's sister's apartment, where they have been living for four months while they decide their next move. The story looks back to the failure of their European sojourn, focussing most sharply on Peter's stint in Geneva, where he had an obscure clerical job filing photographs for the information service of an international agency. His boss there was Agnes Brusen, a western Canadian of Norwegian descent who in every way epitomizes what is apparently utterly foreign to Peter. She is from a large family in small-town Saskatchewan, terra incognita for Peter; she has been educated at great sacrifice to better her lot and take her place in the larger world which Peter feels is his birthright; and she is, in contrast to Peter's stunning wife, a "mole . . . small and brown, and round-shouldered as if she had always carried parcels or younger children in her arms."[14]

And yet, to Peter's and Sheilah's chagrin, Agnes has succeeded in climbing the social ladder they have fallen from in Geneva; for reasons they cannot fathom, Agnes is on the Burleighs' guest list. Mike Burleigh, an old friend of Peter's, is a "serious liberal who had married a serious heiress" (112), and before they were dropped, the Fraziers spent weekends at the Burleighs' country house outside of Geneva—a privilege now extended to Agnes. When the Burleighs throw a Mardi Gras costume party for all their friends, both those current and out of favour, Peter and Agnes are thrown together in a moment which reveals their affinities. Sheilah charms another guest, Simpson, into suggesting the possibility of a job for Peter in Ceylon; Peter is delegated to see Agnes, who is drunk, safely home. She is as miserably out of place at the party (and in the larger social world crystallized in the Burleighs' party) as he is, but for entirely different reasons. Peter escorts her to her room, where he narrowly avoids a "disaster," he thinks, and goes home to Sheilah. Agnes has suffered the revelation that the society she has aspired to all her life is a sham; she tells this to Peter in the office a few days later, in their only serious conversation:

"What can I think when I see these people? All my life I heard, Educated people don't do this, educated people don't do that. And now I'm here, and you're all educated people, and you're nothing but pigs. You're educated and you drink and do everything wrong and you know what you're doing, and that makes you worse than pigs. My family worked to make me an educated person, but they didn't know you. But what if I didn't see and hear and expect anything any more? It wouldn't change anything. You'd all be still the same. Only *you* might have thought it was your fault. You might have thought you were to blame. It could worry you all your life. It would have been wrong for me to worry you." (132)

Confronted with Agnes's insight, Peter feels threatened, as if for his part he might confess his vulnerability to her, against his will. His apparent social impregnability, the veneer of an "educated" person, is also a sham; Peter is just as abandoned and alone as Agnes, but from a different quarter. His essential sense of insecurity, masked by his charming demeanour, issues from his family's fall from their position in Canada and from his upbringing, so different from Agnes's, as a child whose "patrimony was squandered under his nose," who "remembers seeing and nearly understanding adultery" at one of his father's parties, and who was read Beatrix Potter by his sister while the adults downstairs made noise like "the roar of the crouched lion" in a fairy tale (114). Orphans from the social and the familial world respectively, Agnes and Peter recognize in each other the isolation and the attraction of opposites, and for the rest of that day they talk quietly to each other, like "old friends" (133); this may be the only intimate conversation either of them has had, or will have, in their lives. Nothing "happens" but their mutual recognition; after that day, they never talk again, and soon Peter leaves for Ceylon. But what is inescapable and unforgettable for Peter is Agnes's childhood memory of being up before the rest of the family and alone in the universe, a memory she first recounts to him on the night of the party and then again in the office. It is a vision of being unalterably alone which captures, first, a child's communion with the world, and then an adult's oppressive sense of isolation. On the way to her room, Agnes tells Peter:

"I've never been alone before. When I was a kid I would get up in the summer before the others, and I'd see the ice wagon going down the street. I'm alone now. Mrs. Burleigh's found me an apartment. It's only one room. She likes it because it's in the old part of town. I don't like old houses. Old houses are dirty. You don't know who was there before." (128)

In the Burleighs', and Peter's version of the social world, Agnes must feel isolated, adrift; and in Agnes's version of childhood, Peter must feel utterly lost. The significance of Agnes's childhood memory frames the story, uniting Agnes and Peter in the distance each has travelled, over such separate routes, from such separate origins. Peter's memory of Agnes, years later in his sister's Toronto apartment with Sheilah, closes the story and reaffirms at once the identification he feels with Agnes and his denial of this kinship. In one of the realignments of relationships familiar in Gallant's stories, Peter reflects that Sheilah really has much more in common with his father, whom he imagines "with Sheilah, in a crowd"; Peter imagines that he and Agnes had almost "once run away together, silly as children, irresponsible as lovers" (132). But even though he is then given a vision of completion, of Agnes as a child in Western Canada, and the ice-wagon, and finally of himself, this is a "true Sunday morning . . . and this is life," and so the magically vivid image of the ice wagon must remain an indecipherable sign to him. The real story, as the title suggests and as the closing image confirms, is not about Peter and Sheilah's marriage, or their failed quests in Europe and the East to strike it rich in "the international thing" (107); rather, the story's plot is formed by Agnes's compelling memory, so that Peter's closing assertions ring hollow, and the last word must be Agnes's:

> Everything works out, somehow or other. Let Agnes have the start of day. Let Agnes think it was invented for her. Who wants to be alone in the universe? No, begin at the beginning. Peter lost Agnes. Agnes says to herself somewhere, Peter is lost. (134)

In "Bonaventure," we move from Peter's and Agnes's contrasted visions of isolation to a sharply defined separation between natural time and timeless art. Douglas Ramsay, a twenty-one-year-old Canadian on a music scholarship in Europe, tells his Swiss host and confessor, Katharine Moser, that everything her famous husband did "was intellectual. He was divorced from nature by intention."[15] He explains his view of art to her: "Painters learn to paint by looking at pictures, not at hills and valleys, and musicians listen to music, not the wind in the trees. Everything Moser said and wrote was unnatural. It was unnatural because he was sophisticated" (152). Gallant juxtaposes Ramsay's home in art with Katharine Moser's home in the natural world, whose parts she names and whose laws, particularly the laws of time, sexuality, and mortality, she lives by. Douglas Ramsay's initiation (which he flees from, as Carol Frazier flees from hers) is an initiation into the world of time and so into the meaning of the past—particularly his father's past, which resurfaces at several points and gives the story its title. The father's return from the war to Bonaventure station in Montreal is a set scene whose significance Douglas Ramsay cannot make out.[16]

Ramsay believes that through art he can escape time and the past altogether; his frame of reference establishes several ironic antitheses between natural and civilized worlds, time and eternity, mortality and immortality, life and art. In this story, Ramsay's attitude to nature reveals his ignorance of the nature of time; although nature makes only brief appearances in Gallant's fiction, it often serves important symbolic and allusive functions. Netta Asher's historical sunlight in "The Moslem Wife" is as significant as the perpetual drizzle Carol

Frazier encounters in "The Other Paris"; Gallant repeatedly uses flowers (irises, anemones, nasturtiums, lilacs, lilies, the orchis in this story) and trees (Christine's larches in "The Pegnitz Junction," for example) as well as wasps like the one which threatens the commissioner in "The Old Friends" to allude to the significance of individual gestures or to the nuances in dialogue.

Identifying as he does with Adrian Moser, Douglas Ramsay imagines that art is completely self-referential, a home divorced from nature and free of time. Art may be timeless, but artists' lives are not, and Ramsay cannot make this distinction. It is fitting that the story closes with Ramsay imagining that he has freed himself from the effects of the "weather . . . outside" (172), but we are shown that his sense of liberation is spurious. Ramsay, who has fled from the Moser chalet, addresses "the remains of Katharine's letter" in an interior monologue, remembering driving with Katharine: "We drove slowly, crawling, because Katharine had seen a white orchis somewhere. Did anyone dare say this was a waste of time? The orchis was a scraggly poor thing with sparse anemic flowers. . . . Surely he had passed a test safely and shown he was immune to the inherited blight?" (172).

But Katharine Moser's love for flowers is in reality no waste of time, but a celebration of time; if Douglas Ramsay knew as much about flowers as Katharine does, he would recognize that the orchis (named from the Greek for the testicle, which it resembles), is a natural fertility symbol; he would not be so certain that he was "immune to the inherited blight." The story closes by revealing Ramsay's escape as an ironic one; he cannot flee time through art any more than Carol Frazier can flee history's facts through memory's fictions. As Katharine Moser tells him, "Nothing can be divorced from nature and survive" (152); and the closing paragraph shows that Ramsay's temporary triumph will only last as long as he keeps his eyes closed to the natural passage of time: "Only afterward did he think that he might be mistaken, but that day, the day he arrived in Berlin, he was triumphant because he sat with his back to the window and did not know or care what the weather was like outside"(172). That Douglas Ramsay is one of Gallant's "Canadians Abroad" should not distract us from the story's relevance as an exploration of a character's attempt to escape time. "Bonaventure" is more important as a story of ironic initiation than as a story about a young Canadian away from home.

"Virus X" explores more particularly the double pull that Canadians (ex-Europeans themselves—in Lottie Benz's case, only one generation out of Germany) feel returning after the war to an Old World which no longer exists anywhere except in their minds. Yet "Virus X," like "Bonaventure," is finally best read as an ironic or failed initiation. Through her depiction of Lottie Benz, Gallant plays upon the same false sense of history which Carol Frazier brings to Paris. Lottie, a bookish Canadian sociology student comically adrift in a postwar Europe she cannot place, is set over against "Vera," a Ukrainian classmate from Winnipeg. Lottie, on a Royal Society scholarship, is less successful at reading actual European sociology than is Vera, who, having flunked out of high school, has a vision unimpeded by the pages of sociology texts or the theories of Lottie's supervisor, Dr. Keller. The story is rich with send-ups of "Canadian problems of national identity," developed mainly at the expense of Lottie's prim theoretical excursions into the issue of ethnic minorities' comparative assimilation in Canada, the United States, and Europe: Kevin, Lottie's Canadian fiancé, has a cousin in Paris who begins "bemoaning his own Canadian problems of national identity, which Lottie thought a sign of weakness in a man. Moreover, she learned nothing new. What he was telling her was part of Dr. Keller's course in Winnipeg Culture Patterns."[17]

"Virus X" also calls attention to homes in and exiles from language. In Strasbourg, Lottie speaks German, her "secret language"; she thinks the words will remain, engraven, to condemn her" (189). Her ambivalent attitude towards languages and native tongues coalesces with her attraction to and repulsion from her parents' birthplace: "So this was the place she loathed and craved, and never mentioned. It was the place where her mother and father had been born, and which they seemed unable to imagine, forgive or describe" (195). Through Lottie and Vera, Gallant recreates the North American ambiguity towards what postwar European history entails—towards its immediately visible historical scars, towards half-forgotten, half-suppressed native tongues, cultures, and countries, towards the inexplicably civilized contours (to a Canadian eye) of the European natural landscape. This ambiguity constitutes a major theme in Gallant's fiction from the early fifties onward; "Virus X" marks one of its funniest incarnations.

In "Virus X" as in "The Other Paris," larger social themes find expression through the structure of a relationship. In this story, Lottie's long-distance engagement to Kevin counterpoints Vera's more clandestine affair with the peripatetic Al Wiczinski, "sort of a Canadian," who has been offered a hazily defined teaching job in Strasbourg: Vera calls it "politics, in a way... but mostly the culture racket. After all, teaching Slav lit to a bunch of Slavs was what, culture or politics?" (190) Like Carol Frazier, Lottie returns to North America with her North American fiancé; like Netta Asher, Lottie stops composing letters in her head—letters to Kevin which we read but which she never sends. Like Carol's and like Netta's, her return to her relationship represents a defeat, a turn away from initiation. "Virus X" takes its title from an epidemic which European newspapers report is sweeping across Europe, an epidemic to which hypochondriac Lottie has evidently succumbed. In a minor key, and with less extensively developed implications, this metaphor for Europe's postwar malaise anticipates the more fully developed metaphor of the aimless train ride in "The Pegnitz Junction." Lottie recovers from her illness without quite graduating from her fevered sociological theorizing. Even though she discovers that most of what her thesis advisor has told her about cultural patterns—in Europe as well as in Canada—bears little resemblance to what she encounters in her actual field research, she is finally unable to translate her insights into vision, and so she returns to Canada with Kevin.

"Virus X" also anticipates "The Pegnitz Junction" in its tongue-in-cheek sallies into literary history. Vera drags Lottie to Katherine Mansfield's grave for a commemorative Christmas visit; in the ensuing spoof of the Katherine Mansfield legend on the thirtieth anniversary of her death (while Lottie worries over her consumptive symptoms in a nearby hotel room), the story anticipates the play with literary figures and traditions in "The Pegnitz Junction," as well as the use of Mansfield's "The Daughters of the Late Colonel" in "The Moslem Wife." As is the case with most of Gallant's literary allusions, this play is also serious. Mansfield represents the legendary expatriate literary tradition, and her story also figures as a ghostly mirror-image, as a literary and historical (and more sombre) version of Lottie's European education. But unlike Mansfield's (and unlike Gallant's), Lottie's attempts to articulate what she actually sees in Europe never make it out of her notebooks. We read one of her "composed" descriptions as she recovers from "Virus X" toward the end of the story; the passage teaches us how clearly she has come to see the realities which so disappointed her at the story's opening, and it also shows us that she has some promise as a writer: "Last night, just at the edge of the night, the sky and the air were white as milk. Snow had fallen and a thick low fog lay in the streets and on the water, filling every crack between the houses. The cathedral bells were iron and muffled in snow. I heard drunks up and down the sidewalk most of the night" (216).

But Lottie's clear-eyed report on the Europe she sees before her eyes does not instil in her enough of a sense of "personal independence," the independence gained from a more clear-eyed vision of what postwar European cities really look like, with their new Arab quarters, their bombed railway stations, their ubiquitous (and unpopular) American soldiers, and above all, their distinctive light—an unromantic, wintry, iron gray. Her return to Canada with Kevin is a consequence of her thinking that her composition "was not a letter to anyone. There was no sense to what she was doing. She would never do it again. That was the first of many changes" (216). Lottie cannot live with her vision any more than Carol Frazier, or Christine, or Netta Asher can. She cannot live in the space she clears, the moment she inhabits by describing what she has learned to see, and so she returns to Canada in retreat from education, in retreat from an initiation into history.

As a story which extends the implications of reading the discontinuities between Gallant's postwar European and North American worlds, "Virus X" instructs readers principally by calling attention to the depiction of European settings as historical foregrounds which refute North American characters' naive worldviews. "Virus X" stands in the line of development which begins with "The Other Paris" and ends with Linnet Muir's militant return to a home city.

The six "Montreal stories" collected in *Home Truths* present Linnet Muir, Gallant's most gifted reporter on memory. By reconstructing a city Linnet re-creates its history, but she also moves beyond these reports to explore the workings and meanings of her memories. Linnet needs above all to "re-member" herself; unlike most Gallant characters before her, however, she realizes that to do so she must start with the world, not with the self. Her memories thus take shape around the most prominent character in all of these stories, the Montreal of her childhood and adolescence. "In Youth Is Pleasure" opens the Montreal cycle with a first-person narrator returning to Montreal, home ground, from New York; she is also travelling into the past towards her childhood in order to gain her autonomy. Linnet Muir is an articulate, politicized reporter on her past, and also, in part, a version of a younger Mavis Gallant; as Gallant puts it, "The girl (Linnet Muir) is obviously close to me. She isn't *myself,* but a kind of summary of some of the things I once was. . . . Straight autobiography would be boring. It would bore me. It would bore the reader. The stories are a kind of reality *necessarily* transformed."[18]

Gallant is well aware of the ambiguities attendant upon the "truth" of autobiography and, therefore, attendant upon Linnet's "autobiographical" reconstructions of her past—particularly, Linnet's recurrent insistence upon the truth and the relevance of what she sees before her eyes. Linnet returns to Montreal armed with her own sacred texts, which are leftist, not liberal, about socialism, not love. We have come a long distance from "The Other Paris," in which Carol Frazier affirms her romantic conception of love by sentimentalizing her experience; Linnet affirms her independence by imagining it as a political revolution. Looking down a receding row of younger selves, Linnet reports on her memory's inventions, demythologizing her past, deconstructing memory's fictions in order to name herself.

It is probably much more than coincidence that the recovered memories which form the Linnet Muir stories should have come to Gallant when she was doing research for one of the major projects she had been working on for several years, a history of the Dreyfus affair. In her introduction to *Home Truths,* Gallant writes that, unlike her usual experience with her fiction, she knows "exactly how the [Linnet Muir] stories came to be written, and why."[19] She explains that in the mid-seventies she had been doing research for the Dreyfus book, "reading virtually nothing for two years except documents and books about the Dreyfus case" (xx). She describes the enormous differences between herself and Dreyfus, but she finishes by establishing their one common bond: they "had both resolved upon a way of life at an early age and had pursued [their] aims with overwhelming singlemindedness" (xxii). Having recognized her bond with Dreyfus, Gallant "moved with greater sureness into the book [she] wanted to write" (xxii). She had been working on the Dreyfus book by "restoring . . . his Paris, his life," walking the route Dreyfus walked on the morning of his betrayal, looking at "all the paintings and photographs [she] could find of that particular Paris" (xxii). She began, at the same time, to recover a "lost" Montreal; perhaps it is in order to explore her own singular resolve that Gallant has restored the lost Montreal of her childhood. As with her history of Dreyfus, so with her Linnet Muir stories: Gallant restores cities to evoke personalities and characters. Gallant begins by describing the image of Montreal she recovered, but she ends by describing the function of memory—a progression parallelled by that of the Linnet Muir stories:

> At the same time—I suppose about then—there began to be restored in some underground river of the mind a lost Montreal. An image of Sherbrooke Street, at night, with the soft gaslight and leaf shadows on the sidewalk—so far back in childhood that it is more a sensation than a picture—was the starting point. Behind this image was a fictional structure of several stories, in the order in which they are presented here—three wartime stories, then the rest.
>
> The character I called Linnet Muir is not an exact reflection. I saw her as quite another person, but it would be untrue to say that I invented everything. I can vouch for the city: my Montreal is as accurate as memory can make it. I looked nothing up, feeling that if I made a mistake with a street name it had to stand. Memory can spell a name wrong and still convey the truth. (xxii)

Gallant's language often resembles her characters' language; here, she uses a word which recurs in her fiction, "invented," as opposed to "reported." Linnet is not an exact "reflection" (a usage which recalls Gallant's repeated use of mirrors, mirror-images, and reflections in her fiction) but she is in some measure an autobiographical character. But what seems to most concern Gallant here is that readers understand that her Montreal is as "accurate as *memory* can make it," and that therefore this kind of accuracy has less to do with facts than with fictions; the spelling of a name does not have that much to do with the kinds of truths that memory, like fiction, conveys.

The first three Linnet Muir stories are roughly chronological; Linnet is eighteen or a few years older and working in Montreal just before and then during the war. The last two stories to appear in *The New Yorker* double back to focus on Linnet as a child, and "With a Capital T" returns to Linnet working as a reporter in Montreal. "In Youth Is Pleasure" (1975), the first story, presents Linnet Muir remembering her break from her mother in a successful bid for independence. Returning from Montreal to New York, she stays with her old French-Canadian governess, Olivia, finds a job, and tries to discover the truth about her father's death; he had died in unexplained circumstances when she was a child. As she asks his old Montreal friends about his death, she remembers how she had remembered Montreal when she *was* that child. She discovers that the Montreal she lives in is and is not the place she remembers: this discovery, which frees her out of adolescence but only into the new bondage of adulthood, involves her in resituating her memory within a wider, less mythological or private, historical framework. Linnet learns that memory makes necessary fictions, and that it then becomes necessary to understand that these are indeed fictions, just as they are necessary.

Linnet leaves New York as a politicized romantic—recalling the "passionately left-wing political romantic" Gallant describes herself as in the 1978 *Canadian Fiction Magazine* interview.[20] Linnet has taken her politics to heart via literature, and they are passionately personal ideals, more important to her than her mother's obsession—"the entirely private and possibly trivial matter of [her] virginity."[21] She is pursuing a concretely economic independence, and yet this quest sets her searching into her memories of the Montreal of her childhood. The fusion of her objective odyssey with its subjective counterpart begins to suggest one completion of Gallant's interrupted dialogues between self and world by immersing one in the other: Linnet's journey is at once "into a new life and a dream past" (228).

Linnet goes from one of her father's old friends to the next, frustrated each time by their inability (or refusal) to give her straight answers to her questions about his death. This line of the plot particularizes Linnet's general critique of Canadian impassivity and reticence, contrasted with the more openly emotional behaviour she had seen in America. While she tries to discover the truth about her father, a subterranean process of recollection begins to take place. She recounts that she had lived the first ten years of her life in Montreal before moving to a city in Ontario, "a place full of mean judgements and grudging minds, of paranoid Protestants and slovenly Catholics" (223). In Ontario, her memory of Montreal "took shape":

It was not a random jumble of rooms and summers and my mother singing "We've Come to See Miss Jenny Jones," but the faithful record of the true survivor. I retained, I rebuilt a superior civilization. In that drowned world, Sherbrooke Street seemed to be glittering and white; the vision of a house upon that street was so painful that I was obliged to banish it from the memorial. The small hot rooms of a summer cottage became enormous and cool. If I say that Cleopatra floated down the Chateauguay River, that the

Winter Palace was stormed on Sherbrooke Street, that Trafalgar was fought on Lake St. Louis, I mean it naturally; they were the natural backgrounds of my exile and fidelity. (223)

Linnet has a double perspective on her memory. She remembers the raw "content" of her experience (the "random jumble of rooms and summers," for example) and also the formed "memorial" which "took shape" once she had left Montreal and moved to Ontario. The work of memory, to "retain" and "rebuild," goes on in exile from its object, and the "fidelity" of the narrator's efforts (which recalls Netta Asher's equation of memory with faith, a connection which Linnet will make at the end of this story), attests to her aim: to build a work of art, a memorial, a fiction. Her literary and historical lore (Cleopatra, the Winter Palace, the Battle of Trafalgar) becomes the "natural" background of her subjective sense of exile and fidelity.

But at the same time that she goes through this reflexive process, remembering what she had remembered, Linnet also begins to demythologize, to reconstruct memory—and to affirm, by the very force of her naming its parts, her "fidelity" to memory. Standing in Windsor Station, just off the train from New York, Linnet sees a statue of Lord Mount Stephen, founder of Canadian Pacific: everyone in her childhood had taken the statue to be a monument to Edward VII. This is a cutting, comic moment, depicting how Canadians' allegiance to Empire has blinded them to the identity of one of their own national figures; but it is also a moment in which Linnet sees "true" evidence, in the world as well as in memory, of her past: "Angus, Charlotte and the smaller Linnet had truly been: this was my proof; once upon a time my instructions had been to make my way to the Windsor Station should I ever be lost and to stand at the foot of Edward VII and wait for someone to find me" (224).

In the stories before the Montreal sequence, Gallant's characters had often been passive, acted upon rather than acting: this is especially, but not exclusively true of Gallant's women. Linnet gathers strength by acting. She leaves New York and enters her "dream past"; it does not immobilize her, as fragments from the past immobilize characters like Christine in "The Pegnitz Junction." Her memory is an active force which recreates the past by investing it with shape and meaning. This shaping force is ongoing: "[E]ven now," remarks Linnet the narrator—even as she remembers what her sensations were at eighteen—she forms her recollection with imagery suggesting her militancy, her march toward independence. She remembers the June morning of her arrival in Montreal "like a roll of drums in the mind" (225). Like Gallant, Linnet begins to make fiction by remembering and like Gallant, as she remembers she becomes, necessarily, involved in the process itself, asking herself how memory means. Linnet does not mimetically "copy" her past: she "sees" it rather than "watching" it, expresses it rather than reflecting it. She embodies her past as insight rather than observing herself in it at a distance, as if the past were a mirror which stopped time. In the same way that her "memorial" Montreal was fashioned from images taken from history, so her memories of herself at eighteen are structured upon images of rebellion and revolution (225–26).

When Linnet closes her inquiry into her father's death, her dream past begins to "evaporate," and she finds herself standing on the street corner of a purely historical Montreal. But even this discovery, that the only "real" Montreal is the one she sees before her eyes, is one that she must balance against the insistent images of the Montreal that she lived in as a child. She insists that there can be only one Montreal, but she remembers another at the same time: "[O]ne day, standing at a corner, waiting for the light to change, I understood that the Sherbrooke Street of my exile—my Mecca, my Jerusalem—was this. It had to be: there could not be two. It was *only* this" (235). She then goes through the same process she went through earlier, remembering twin Montreals; she sees that she will have to give up one of the chief pleasures of youth, the "natural" fidelity to images in memory. Montreal can no longer be a holy city because her pilgrimage has become timebound, secular, historical. Linnet's closing thought, as she watches a "crocodile" of little girls coming out of her old school, plays upon the ambiguity of time's faithfulness to youth; looking at the children, she thinks: "I should have felt pity, but at eighteen all that came to me was thankfulness that I had been correct about one thing throughout my youth, which I now considered ended: time had been on my side, faithfully, and unless you died you were bound to escape" (236–37).

Linnet escapes childhood by realizing the nature of time; the crocodile of little girls she sees will have to split up into individuals, each of whom will have to create herself by remembering herself in time, by being active with her memory. Unlike those whom God loves, Linnet will not die young, and so she is indeed "bound" by time to "escape" her youth: this is the ironic sense in which time is "faithful" to her in her drive towards independence. The pleasure of youth for Linnet was not in the days, months, and years of childhood, in which she felt herself imprisoned, but in the capacious memorials she could retain and rebuild, structures in which, as in fiction, time is fluid, history at her disposal. But even as the historical world becomes inexorably more contingent, and Linnet perceives that reality, "as always, [is] narrow and dull," she discovers the way in which memory, like fiction, can "spell a name wrong and still convey the truth." "Bound to escape" from youth into adulthood, Linnet "remembers" Linnet by calling the past into being.

In "Varieties of Exile" (1976), Linnet repatriates herself from her exile in various romances to a home as a writer of realist fiction by telling a story about the nature of romance. In doing so, she invites us to read "out" from her story to two worlds—the historical world to which all of Gallant's fiction refers, and the imaginatively constituted world of Gallant's fiction. This second world's autonomous structure forms itself upon those moments at which Gallant's characters "see" in the "light of imagination." By the time Gallant writes "Varieties of Exile," these moments of insight—into the world's "natural" historical sunlight, as it is reflected in fiction's "natural" mirrors ("looking glasses")—have developed from slim possibilities, through perplexing impasses, into verifying perceptions. Both "In Youth Is Pleasure" and "Varieties of Exile" close with Linnet's clear-sighted descriptions of such a moment. The "situation" Linnet is locked into is principally a dialogue with her own powers of perception, with memory and imagination; Linnet's "situation" evolves into insight.

The plot of "Varieties of Exile" traces the course of Linnet's wartime fascination with refugees. She romanticizes these figures and writes stories "about people in exile" in her spare time; she's "entirely at home with foreigners" because "the home [is] all in [her] head."[22] She meets Frank Cairns, a special kind of refugee—a remittance man; Linnet then writes a devastating chapter-by-chapter account of the standard "RM" story (she calls this a "romance") and debunks it in favour of a simpler story, the "classic struggle for dominance" between "strong father, pliant son" (267). Cairns, a "Socialist RM" as she calls him in notes she makes for the story, personifies a type, but when he enlists and then is killed in action in Italy, Linnet's reaction to his death leads her to a moment of insight into writing certain kinds of fiction as a variety of exile. Linnet moves through several of these varieties of exile as she romanticizes and then realizes her experience. She self-consciously subverts her own efforts—her romances about exiles, her recital of the standard "RM" essay and finally a novel about a "RM" which she can't remember having written.

Frank Cairns's variety of exile is knit up with Linnet's variety: Cairns lives a romance, while Linnet writes romances. Both romanticizations cover over realities which Linnet presents during the course of the story, instructing us in the connections between romance and romanticized reality. Both romances are shattered into historical fragments by Cairns's death. "Varieties of Exile" is in this sense a fiction about fiction: one of its subjects is a writer's progress and a literary imagination's encounter with the literal world. For Linnet, fiction begins as a way of decoding experience. As she says early in the story, "Anything I could not decipher I turned into fiction, which was my way of untangling knots" (261). Looking back at herself, Linnet sees that she was living in her head, in a romance: she populated her imagination with refugees, believing them to be incarnations "straight out of the twilit Socialist-literary landscape of [her] reading and . . . desires" (261).

By debunking her report on remittance men, Linnet takes a step out of her twilit literary landscape; she reports the conventional romance first, and then, as if she were a Freudian critic, explicates the story by referring us to the conflict between father and son. When Frank Cairns enlists, Linnet is forced into a more direct encounter with her romanticized "Socialist RM." By this time, Linnet is engaged to another man, but her engagements, unlike Carol Frazier's, are peripheral to the central impetus of her stories, which is her drive towards independence through her insights into how fiction means. Linnet is constantly engaged and constantly breaking engagements in these stories; in "Varieties," she does marry, but her husband is never an important figure. Marriage has been a variety of exile throughout Gallant's fiction, a variety which Linnet brushes up against just once.

Linnet's shock at reading Frank Cairns's name among those of the war dead precipitates her destruction of the novel she finds in her picnic hamper. Her description of the moment of insight with which she ends this story is revealing:

> In the picnic hamper . . . I also found a brief novel I had no memory of having written, about a Scot from Aberdeen, a left-wing civil servant in Ceylon—a man from somewhere, living elsewhere, confident that another world was entirely possible, since he had got it all down. It had shape, density, voice, but I destroyed it too. I never felt guilty about forgetting the dead or the living, but I minded about that one manuscript for a time. All this business of putting life through a sieve and then discarding it was another variety of exile: I knew that even then, but it seemed quite right and perfectly natural. (281)

Like "Varieties of Exile," the novel is a first-person fiction with "shape, density, voice," which realizes a world by "getting it all down." The civil servant's voice articulates Frank Cairns's and Linnet's socialist dream, making it an "entirely possible" world.

As she destroys the manuscript, Linnet imagines the imagination as a "sieve," a filter. Passing life through this filter is a variety of exile, and yet to a writer, this process, like the process of building (and then demolishing) memorial Montreals in memory, seemed at that point in her life "perfectly natural." It is "quite right" because this process is necessary to convey the kind of truth that Linnet (not necessarily Gallant) was after, a truth which documents and verifies her imaginative report on the way she "sees." Gallant's focus here is not on Linnet's self-consciousness per se, but on her growing awareness of how she sees, an awareness reflected in her report on the details she sees. In "Varieties of Exile," Linnet sees romantic types, then real figures, and finally the relations between the two, a relation most fully established, she reports, in the novel she destroys.

Linnet's progress in this story completes one passage in the journey of Gallant's characters through her fictional world. Linnet returns to the "home" at the heart of all of Gallant's homes, a home which is a process: for a writer, the "natural," ongoing process of imagining a home and then "discarding" it *is* "home." The imagination "naturally" turns reality into that "other reality called fiction."[23]

Gallant's images of imagination constitute moments of synthesis and convergence. They illuminate the dialogues between the various subjective and objective constituents we have noted throughout her fiction: self and world, memory and history, invention and report, insight and sunlight, image and mirror. When these moments, in all their variety, "take place" (it is difficult to ignore how we spatialize time—and so texts—to discuss them), Gallant's figures live in Netta's "light of imagination." Linnet's insight into fiction as a variety of exile is another of these moments, but it is also in one sense the moment of all of Gallant's fiction. As we learn that it is "quite right and perfectly natural" for Linnet to realize her world by remembering her past, we also learn to read other characters' excursions into history in all their variety.

More than any other stories in Gallant's canon, the Linnet Muir cycle affirms many of the home truths about time, memory, history, voice, and imagination at the heart of Gallant's fiction. Throughout her fiction, we can read the broken dialogue between memory and history as failures of voice which have called attention to themselves when inarticulate characters have stammered at time, and at each other out of time. Their assertions have been suspect, their disclaimers disingenuous; their stories, particularly the first-person narratives, have often ended in an awkward silence following on bewildered defeat. Many of Gallant's characters seem to speak this language defeated by time; to tell time's stories, Linnet Muir must learn memory's place within history by returning home. Her homecoming confers upon her that most elusive of qualities, in Gallant's fiction as in life, the sound of a voice with its own timbre. Linnet's voice resonates within human time, time measured by memory's pulse and heartbeat, time placed in history's districts, in a reconstructed Montreal whose historical ambience is as tangible as weather. An imagination which realizes memory in history thus gives voice to the Linnet who haunts the Mavis who remembers her. Linnet sees the past in the light of her imagination; listening to the clear cadences of her voice, we might well find ourselves at home in the districts of Gallant's imagination, its streets scarred by history, its houses haunted by memory.

The pattern which begins with Carol Frazier and then ends by beginning again with Linnet Muir can help to shape our reading of the development of Gallant's fiction. First Gallant writes stories in which expatriates are defined in terms of what they have lost, where they have exiled themselves from, what they were in another time and place. "Home" is variously a set of values, a class context, a pitch of voice, a manner of speech; or, again, an encircling family or relationship. As Gallant's characters begin to explore European settings, their sense of being on alien ground strikes their domestic codes into sharp relief; in exile,

finally, from full identity, even her European characters live at a remove from history and culture, in memory and manners.

With Linnet Muir, Gallant begins with a character self-consciously journeying home from exile into identity, rather than the other way around. This journey is a return, and the past—which up to this point Gallant has imagined essentially as an absence, a trap, a vacuum, or a historical nightmare—becomes a potentially more fertile presence in an "underground river" in Gallant's imagination, as well as in Linnet Muir's. Behind this image, Gallant "sees" a "whole fictional structure." Recreating the past becomes a route into history, into Linnet's independence in the world. Reading Gallant's stories in this framework, we might understand the "light of imagination" which perplexes Netta as a version of Gallant's synthesis of memory and history in a moment of presence. Linnet Muir, through her art of remembering herself, brings Netta's moment, and the moment of all of Gallant's fiction into clearer focus. We can pass Linnet's fiction through the "sieve" of our previous reading; "naturally," we can imagine Linnet as another variety of Netta, Christine, Erika ("An Autobiography"), Jean Price ("Its Image on the Mirror"), Puss ("The Cost of Living"), or Carol Frazier. To relate her to these other figures does not mean, however, that Linnet should be understood only in a reincarnative function as a Gallant "type." Gallant's characters, like her stories, vary as much as they recur; the lines of development begin to curve into elliptical orbits of expatriation and recreation. Linnet does not stand at the head of one of these lines as much as she completes a cycle, by taking one direction, through memory, from the ironic "junction" at which history and memory seem to stand still in the *Pegnitz Junction* stories. Linnet's exploration of memory and fiction, then, can illuminate Netta's missed moment of inspiration; Linnet speaks from within the historical world that Carol Frazier flees. Linnet's reportorial eye enables her to begin speaking as a revelatory "I," because she can look and articulate in two directions—towards "revolutionary" independence and back into her own "dream past." Her discovery of where these directions converge teaches her how and why she writes fiction; we can draw on Linnet's discovery to help teach us how and why to read Gallant's stories.

7

Overhead in a Balloon
Another Paris

French culture, and in particular, Paris, have served from the beginning of Gallant's career as settings for North American encounters with European postwar experience. But in the eighties—thirty years after the appearance of *The Other Paris*—the twelve stories collected in *Overhead in a Balloon: Stories of Paris* do not conceive of the capital through the perspective of a naive North American woman looking for love amidst romantic monuments, but more centrally through the imaginations of native or long-time Parisians. Paris becomes another kind of home ground in this book. It is no longer the city to which Gallant's North American characters travel, searching for a setting for their romantic visions; instead, it is the setting for explorations of characters as inseparable from Paris as (a continent and a worldview away) some of Margaret Laurence's characters are inseparable from Manawaka. Many of the characters in these stories see Paris as the centre and the circumference of the universe: in the title story, for example, a Swiss character notices that a Parisian speaks of "'Paris' instead of 'life,' or 'manners,' or 'people'."[1]

The "Paris" of *Overhead in a Balloon* shows to exquisite effect Gallant's intimate familiarity with the Paris of the late seventies and eighties, and in this sense complements the vision of the city and the long view of developments in Parisian architecture in her essay "Paris: The Taste of a New Age."[2] Everywhere, older buildings are being demolished, trees cut down, whole blocks gutted to make way for parkades or shopping centres. The politics of the late seventies and eighties have also invaded the city: the promise or the threat (depending on characters' inherited allegiances, which often function like religious convictions) of a socialist government is on most characters' minds most of the time; right-wing thugs bomb allegedly left-wing bookstores, left-wing students burn

allegedly right-wing novels, and the epithet "Fascist!" has acquired a broader, more diffuse cultural and personal significance as its particular historical origin fades in the collective memory. The new scarcity and the straitened economy of the eighties have generated a pervasive anxiety which permeates the social atmosphere, and the physical atmosphere itself is also changing; the "gassy air of cities," which ominously recalled a more specific era in *The Pegnitz Junction,*[3] is now simply gaseous with urban effluvia, affecting the shades of light which Gallant has always rendered so carefully in the stories she has set in Paris.

But in *Overhead in a Balloon,* the city that Gallant has realized in such close detail figures most importantly as the setting for a purpose which has always been felt to some degree in her fiction—an exploration of the various significances of culture itself. Many of these stories take an overview of culture—of its meanings, its uses, its position in contemporary French society—as their explicit subject. To this end, several of the book's opening stories are populated with the denizens of the contemporary cultural milieu—gallery owners, critics, painters and writers, patrons of the arts—seen intimately from the inside, but also from a mock-Olympian perspective, comically distanced, "overhead." The cumulative effect of this group of five of the book's twelve stories is the most fully sustained exploration to date in Gallant's fiction of the uses, the sources, and ultimately the value of the imagination in contemporary Western society.

Save for the obvious exception of *The Pegnitz Junction,* no other book of Gallant's develops so many different kinds of connections between individual stories. *Overhead in A Balloon* is unified first by the stories' common settings in Paris, as the book's subtitle suggests, but the links are more complex than this. The first two stories, for example—"Speck's Idea" and "Overhead in a Balloon"—are connected in several important ways. First, they focus respectively on Sandor Speck, curator of an art gallery, and on Walter, his assistant; second, both stories take as one of their most important themes the place and purpose of art in French society; third, both stories approach this exploration through characters' positions in French society and through their private relationships— in Speck's case, through his failed second marriage and his "courtship" of Lydia Cruche, widow of the painter Hubert Cruche; in Walter's case, through his term of residence in a warren of rooms belonging to two generations of a French family which goes through several contortions to accommodate its quirky members' changing status and aspirations. And finally, both place their respective characters' reflections on art and its uses in the context of their political, ideological, and religious convictions—or lack of same—so that their conceptions of art and its uses also become comments on relations between church and state, on secular humanism, the culture industry, and the loss of any metaphysical bearings, and on the interior landscapes of their private lives.

"Speck's Idea," the book's longest story, is also its fullest and most comical development of a character struggling to stay afloat in the swirling eddies of the

culture industry, rather than languish in one of its backwaters. Speck's "idea" is to perpetrate a revival of the reputation and the paintings (the order is crucial) of Hubert Cruche by designing a Cruche retrospective. Of course, the "objective" or "authentic" merit of Cruche's art is a moot point, as the story makes clear. First we see Speck in a restaurant drawing up the catalogue notes and introduction for an artist who does not exist; it is the "idea"—the plot, the scheme, what advertisers would call the "concept"—that is important. The painter and art to flesh out the "idea" will come later. "Idea" also effectively signals the disembodied and abstract (but not disinterested) nature of Speck's plan, which is ultimately designed to put Speck, not Cruche, and Speck's failing gallery, not Cruche's paintings, back on the cultural map.

In these stories, culture always figures as the reflection of social fashion rather than as the product of personal or social expression or vision; if culture is envisioned as a commodity in a market—and that is certainly the vision of culture in this opening story—then its patterns of consumption will be reflected first in the venues of its "appreciation." Fittingly, then, the location of Speck's gallery has been dictated by the various and volatile political forces which have recently manifested themselves on the streets. In the last few months, he's moved first from the Right Bank (where the entire block has been "wiped off the map to make way for a five-story garage") to a "picturesque slum protected by law from demolition" on the other side of the Seine; when Basque separatists blow up the slum, he moves to the Faubourg Saint-Germain, where he is scheming to save his business and pay the exorbitant rent.[4]

Although Speck's "vision" of art is an idea set squarely on the foundations of his perception of culture as a commodity, he has scant insight into either the political determinants which condition cultural values, or into the ways in which his own values determine his pursuit of this commodity. For Speck, politics have always seemed trivial: "Nothing political had ever struck Speck as being above the level of a low-grade comic strip" (6). And yet it is "politics" in their contemporary social, guerrilla-style expression that most violently threaten his gallery's physical existence; and it is in "political" language—although now the term has shaded into different connotations—that his wife Henriette finally dismisses him, shouting "Fascist!" at him in a thrice-repeated chorus from a departing taxi. Hilarious on several counts, the scene also prefigures the story's ending, when Speck himself will hurl this epithet three times at Lydia Cruche. But this use of the term also alerts us to the ways in which a "Fascist" ordering of reality has determined Speck's totalitarian, abstract, and self-interested perception of the culture industry, which he would like to manipulate to promote his own reputation.

Like many of the characters in these stories, Speck has negotiated a worldview for himself which carefully skirts religious or metaphysical considerations; one traditional context for the imagination—the numinous—is therefore either

inaccessible or incomprehensible to these characters. A determined rationalist and agnostic, Speck has adopted a wholly finite, secular view of the universe in which the church has absolutely no say in the affairs of state, the imagination, or the heart; Speck owes all of his success and his prospects as a cultural middleman to the modern expropriation of art from its former position as an expression, distillation, or crystallization of beauty, grace, inspiration, or spiritual values, and to its relocation as a medium of purely material value to the consumer—a tangible medium which might appreciate over time, a collectible which is subject to the vagaries of the market, or of investors, or of brokers like Speck himself. In this sense Speck is, indeed, a "Fascist" in the art world, dictating and regulating taste to advance his own abstract "idea," a speck of an idea which is ultimately revealed to issue solely from Speck's own need for recognition.

When Speck hears a wealthy fellow Mason mention the Cruche collection that he has assembled over the years, he puts his plan in motion to woo Cruche's widow. His arduous courtship of Lydia Cruche, however, appears to stall at her vision of orthodoxy; she is a Japhethite, and believes that the Bible forbids the show, telling Speck that "God doesn't want it" (31). And yet Lydia Cruche proves to be just as calculating in her own way as Speck: at first she appears to have sold Speck's idea to an Italian entrepreneur, to whom she has promised a Cruche show in Milan. Betrayed and defeated, Speck is about to board a bus from Lydia's gritty suburb into Paris when she catches up with him and concedes that he was, indeed, the originator of the idea and should have first crack at the show. But Speck realizes that Lydia has outmanipulated him and will now be able to bargain for better terms: his parting cries of "Fascist!" at her deftly complete the story's symmetrical shape as a comment on several kinds of "fascism"—Speck's and Lydia's—in relation to their interests in the world of art.

In Walter, Speck's Swiss-born assistant, Gallant offers an alternative of sorts to Speck's explicit worldliness; Walter is worriedly travelling down all of the contemporary avenues of salvation, from analysis, to his hopes of conversion to various faiths, to faith in art. Walter is a minor character in the opening story, but in "Overhead in a Balloon," his view of art and his struggles to gain a foothold in French society become more central.

Walter's trials are situated squarely in the midst of Gallant's depiction of a French middle-class milieu; Speck (Walter's mortal enemy) and the gallery become faint backdrops as Walter tries to establish himself in an extended French family as bizzare in its way as the Maurels of *A Fairly Good Time.* Walter's first contract with this family is through Aymeric, a very minor portrait painter fallen on hard times who has resorted to painting family villas in the area around Paris. Walter moves into the apartment which Aymeric's cousin Roger presides over and attempts to assimilate into the family.

In Roger, however, Walter meets a formidable obstacle, and the book's funniest evocation of a character whose every living moment is orchestrated by a detached passion for order and routine. Roger's perspective on his family—his elderly mother, his separated sister, Monique, his bride-to-be, Brigitte, and Aymeric—is serenely benign, and he listens to Walter's various confessions with a similar, apparently benign detachment. The boundaries of Robert's detachment are circumscribed by his job and his hobbies. He works with biological fragments of human material in his position as supervisor of a small laboratory, where he sits "counting blood cells in a basement room,"[5] and his "favorite topic was not God but the administration of the city of Paris, to which he felt bound by the ownership of so many square metres of urban space" (61).

Roger's perspective is, as the title suggests, a gaze which looks down from "overhead"; one of Roger's pastimes is hot-air ballooning, and when he tells the family that he is getting married for the second time (because "his first marriage had been so happy that he could hardly wait to start over" [67]), Walter silently wonders whether Roger will get married "overhead in a balloon" (67). Walter's frustration at his inability to get through to Roger, or to Aymeric, who drops Walter early in the story, becomes a measure of the impenetrability of the family, and by extension a comic indictment of the serene insularity of the French Catholic middle class. Walter will never be able to become a part of this enclosed and complacent universe, and so his estrangement from art becomes compounded by his continuing estrangement from the French milieu he would like to merge with. His original conception of God as art undergoes a succession of diminutions, and Roger rebuffs Waler's confessions with the serenity of the true believer, member of a faith to which Walter cannot be admitted:

> Years before, when he was still training Walter, his employer had sent him to museums, with a list of things to examine and ponder. God is in art, Walter had decided; then, God *is* art. Today, he understood: art is God's enemy. God hates art, the trifling rival creation.
>   . . . Robert listened. His blue gaze never wavered from a point just above Walter's head. When Walter had finished, Robert said that as a native Catholic he did not have to worry about God and art, or God and anything. All the worrying had already been done for him. (60)

Finally, Walter will be displaced by Brigitte and evicted from his room in the family's apartment. With the aid of a "dream book," Roger acts as the family analyst of dreams, but of course his interpretations are always dictated by self-interest; even expressions from the unconscious will be adapted to Roger's plans. When Walter returns from a summer holiday at his parents' home in Switzerland, Roger interprets Walter's madcap dream, about a badger taking Walter's employer hostage at the art gallery, to mean "a change of residence, for which the dreamer should be prepared" (71). The ordered and removed perspective from which Roger can survey the whole city also suggests another kind of "fascist" overview, which will not admit Walter and his worries over art, salvation, or even simply friendship.

The story which most directly explores the connections between a writer's imagination and his society is "Grippes and Poche." The character of Henri Grippes, French critic and man of letters, is the principal link between this story and the two others in which he appears, "A Painful Affair" and "A Flying Start"; those stories are further linked, and connected as well with another story, "Larry," by the recurrence of a character named Mary Margaret Pugh, a rich American patron of the arts. Through her character we are afforded a comic vision of the short history of American postwar influence on French letters; as Grippes writes, after the war benefactresses like Miss Pugh lived "in tumbledown houses . . . that were really fairy castles."

> The moat was flooded with American generosity and American contrition. Probably no moat in history was ever so easy to bridge. (Any young European thinking of making that crossing today should be warned that the contrition silted up in the early nineteen-seventies, after which the castle was abandoned).[6]

Another link in this group of stories is the character of Victor Prism, Grippe's English rival and counterpart; through Prism Gallant develops a series of comic contrasts between French and English writers and critics in matters ranging from conduct and dress to more literary questions of taste and style. Shortly after Miss Pugh's death, Grippes writes Prism inquiring about the possibility of his moving to London and sharing a flat with Prism:

> Prism responded with a strange and terrifying account of gang wars, with pimps and blackmailers shot dead on the steps of the National Gallery. In Paris, Prism wrote, Grippes could be recognized on sight as a literary odd-jobs man with style. No one would call him a climber—at least, not to his face. . . . In England, where caste signs were radically different, he might give the false impression that he was a procurer or a drug pusher and be gunned down at a bus stop.[7]

Prism's progress also provides us with what must be one of the shortest accounts of the birth of a literary critic. In "A Flying Start," Grippes, who has been asked to write a memoir of Prism's sojourn in France as a young man, recounts Prism's arrival on Miss Pugh's doorstep with the manuscript of part of a novel and describes Miss Pugh's patronage. But when Prism cannot continue with the novel, he writes on one of the blank manuscript pages: "'Are we to take it for granted that the artist thinks he knows what he is doing?' At that moment, Prism the critic was born."[8]

The composite portrait of Grippes—which includes sketches of his two-year residence in a California university, and of his Paris apartment, overrun with roaches and with his collection of stray cats—parodies many of the stock images of the French writer. But finally, the most compelling aspect of Grippes' character emerges in "Grippes and Poche," where Grippes is entangled in a protracted battle with the French income tax system; he is suspected of defrauding the government by not reporting returns on one of his failed novels, but his bigger secret is the three apartments he owns in Paris, inherited from "an American patroness of the arts"—another legacy from Miss Pugh.[9] In a contemporary world where the imagination can no longer draw on its traditional sources of inspiration in the past, the novels Grippes writes will mirror the uneasy, attenuated connections between the writer's creations and the writer's life. Soon after his first meeting with Poche, Grippes begins to write a long series of novels, each of them with a protagonist derived in large part from Poche. Grippes' most vital human contact, it appears, is with his tax inspector; their relationship becomes his guiding inspiration.

Grippes fails in his two attempts to use his own life as a source for fiction; his California novel, about his affair with a student named Karen-Sue, fizzles on both sides of the Atlantic, and the entire first edition of his autobiographical novel is burned on the barricades in "les événements" of May 1968. Poche provides him with an apparently inexhaustible source of material, although all of the characters are necessarily thin derivations of the original, and none of the novels "grows under the pen" of Grippes; rather, the characters appear to him as if they had been provided with dossiers by the income tax division of an otherworldly civil service, so that Grippes himself begins to assume the role of a tax inspector:

> It was about this time that a series of novels offered themselves to Grippes—shadowy outlines behind a frosted-glass pane. He knew he must not let them crowd in all together, or keep them waiting too long. His foot against the door he admitted, one by one, a number of shadows that turned into young men, each bringing his own name and address, his native region of France portrayed in color postcards, and an index of information about his tastes in clothes, love, food and philosophers, his bent of character, his tics of speech, his attitudes toward God and money, his political bias, and the intimation of a crisis about to explode underfoot. (136)

These formulaic characters and plots suggest how and what Grippes must write, given the position of the writer in contemporary French society and given the de-

mands of his readers—representative among them, Poche. Grippes has promised himself never again to use his own past in his fiction, and has built his reputation upon his images of Poche and his politically correct fusion of style with
conviction: "The shoreline of the eighties, barely in sight, was ready to welcome
Grippes, who had re-established the male as hero, whose left-wing heartbeat
could be heard, loyally thumping, behind the armor of his traditional right-wing
prose" (141).

In a further irony, Poche, avid reader of Grippes's novels, never recognizes
himself in Grippes's characters; at their last meeting, before passing Grippes on
to another inspector, Poche tells him that "[M]uch of your autobiographical
creation could apply to other lives of our time, believe me" (144). If Grippes the
novelist must work with what his imagination gives him in the manner of a civil
servant—admitting his characters one by one as they present themselves with
their files behind the frosted-glass pane—then Poche begins to manifest signs of
his own creativity, both by bending rules to grant Grippes exemptions to which
he is not legally entitled and, more mysteriously, by quoting to Grippes lines that
Grippes is certain he never composed.

Throughout the story, the political atmosphere has always been a tangible
element in Grippes's Paris; the story begins when de Gaulle has been in power
for five years, and ends at the beginning of the eighties, when the resurgence of
right-wing brutality is evident in the streets; returning to his apartment, Grippes
sees four plainclothes policemen beating up two pickpockets. It is difficult for
Grippes to reincarnate another Poche character in this atmosphere, in which
"[A] fashion for having well-behaved Nazi officers shore up Western culture"
had developed (145).

In this new atmosphere, Grippes's imagination begins to offer him an image
he does not know what to do with, of a woman from an earlier era, dressed in
gray, who "prayed constantly into the past" (148); she seems to be a ghost from
Grippes's own anticlerical background, recalling the "lapsed agnostics [who]
sometimes crossed enemy lines and started going to church. One glimpsed them,
all in gray, creeping along a gray-walled street" (135). Earlier, Grippes "could
swear that in his string of novels nothing had been chipped out of his own past"
(137); the novels which have established his reputation have been anachronis-
tic, "a slice of French writing about life as it had been carved up and served a
generation before," and therefore "quietly insurrectional" (137). But now,
given the ways in which his imagination has offered him his material, he does
not know how to use fragments of his own past; the age demands formula fiction suited to the ideological temper of the times, a "sturdy right-wing novel,"
for which the only requisite is a "pessimistic rhythm" (148). The fatalistic, inexorably plodding rhythms of this kind of fiction would produce a linear plot
ending with only one possible ending: "and then, and then, and then, and
death" (148).

The only way in which Grippes will be able to use his past is to harass this image of the woman as if he were a public official; other avenues of inspiration have been closed off to him, both by the way he has written fiction, and by the way in which the age he lives in has read it. To the complaint, "[W]hy don't they write about real life anymore?" that he reads in an article used for wrapping food for his cats, Grippes silently replies: "Because to depict life is to attract its ill-fortune" (146). With this credo, it will be difficult to evoke the figure of the woman in gray; he will have to resort to the tactics of harassment described in the story's closing sentence: "He had got the woman from church to dining room, and he would keep her there, trapped, cornered, threatened, watched, until she yielded to Grippes and told her name, as, in his several incarnations, good Poche had always done" (150).

The images presented in these stories of writers and their public, and of the general condition of culture and cultural responses in an increasingly politicized right-wing society, are wryly, comically apposite comments on the contemporary fate of the imagination's attempts to recover the past. Complementing this composite exploration of the position of the artist in contemporary culture are four linked stories which provide, through a first-person narrator's account of his two marriages, a reflection of the last forty years of France's history. These stories—"A Recollection," "Rue de Lille," "The Colonel's Child," and "Lena"—treat character as an individual emanation of historical forces, so that the stories' common narrator, unnamed until the last story, finally seems to encompass his country's passage through its recent history, and his actions to represent aspects of the attitudes of his nation. The connections between these stories also provide further insight into how Gallant uses the links between stories to develop different but related perspectives on a single subject. The narrator's "recollections" on his marriages provide a metaphorical frame of reference for France's recent history which functions in a manner similar to the presentation of Christine's relationship with Herbert in "The Pegnitz Junction," except that the separation of these four stories helps to create the sense that different facets of a common experience are being recreated as the subject is recalled each time from a different temporal frame.

The strongest link between the stories is the narrator, whose memories form the surface plot of the narrative. In 1940, at the age of twenty-two, he marries Magdalena, a beautiful Jewish woman of thirty-six who has converted to Catholicism. He marries her to provide her with the safety of his French name and protect her from the deportations which are beginning. Throughout all four stories, Magdalena incarnates several aspects of France's troubled history. She is an Eastern European from Budapest who was brought to Paris between the wars by a Frenchman who has abandoned her for a count's daughter; the narrator intends to protect her from the resurgence of anti-Semitism, when "anti-Jewish thoughts and feelings had suddenly hardened into laws."[10] Magdalena is an exotic foreigner whose voice "sang a foreign tune" (158), who enjoys the privileges of the rich, and who survives the war in Cannes, where she is admired by famous collaborators and by German officers. She is also maddeningly naive, and as such she is a potential victim: when the Jews of Paris are lined up to be identified and issued yellow stars, she stays in bed, and later picks one up from the gutter in the street to show her friends in Cannes. When Germans stop the train she and Édouard are travelling on and check passengers' papers, Édouard just manages to slip the star up his sleeve before it is discovered where Magdalena has left it in her luggage. Édouard's marriage to Magdalena—a marriage, not as an act of love, but as an idealistic gesture, an act of conscience—represents one French attitude to Eastern European émigrés during and after the war; other women of Magdalena's acquaintance call her "senseless things" such as "'Central European whore' and 'Jewish adventuress'. "[11]

But this alliance has more troubling ramifications which haunt Édouard for the rest of his life. From the beginning, Magdalena fascinates him as no other woman ever has, as he tells her in "Lena," the last story, when she is in her eighties and his second wife has died; but this fascination has a steep price. Édouard is the child of anticlerical republican parents, schoolteachers who underwrite his education and instil in him his fierce sense of patriotism; after leaving Magdalena in Marseilles, he is bound from there to Algeria and then to London, where he hopes to join de Gaulle and the Free French. But his fervent nationalism has its blind side, too; he is not quite sure why he is impelled to put Algerian soil in an envelope and take it with him to London, and his ambition to join the Free French is comically sidetracked when he crashes his motorcycle into a wall on his first training ride. In Édouard, we see an individual incarnation of French impulses during the war; his impulsive but ambiguous actions reflect several conflicting French attitudes during these years.

Édouard's marriage to Magdalena forms the plot of the first story, "A Recollection," which is narrated from a perspective set in the early eighties in Paris. The second story, "Rue de Lille," recalls the death of Juliette, Édouard's second wife, some time after 1976; "The Colonel's Child" then reaches further into the past to narrate Édouard's meeting Juliette in London during the war; and "Lena" returns to the present to focus on Édouard after Juliette's death, with Magdalena still alive in her eighties. The departures from chronology implied in the stories' order—the same order as that of their original appearances in *The New Yorker*—reinforce the pervasive influence of Magdalena in Édouard's life, an influence which reflects the persistence of France's wartime ghosts.

Édouard's wartime experience is further complicated during his recovery from his injuries in a London hospital, where he is tended by Juliette, the daughter of a French colonel who is in France behind enemy lines, and who is eventually caught and sent to a concentration camp. Juliette is a young expatriate dressed like an English girl by her mother, and the native of another class in

French society, hitherto unknown to Édouard—an upper-class Protestant. Typical of the ways in which differences of class and status are demarcated in Gallant's stories, it is only out of France, exiled in London, that Édouard can meet someone so foreign to him in his own country that at first he thinks her French accent is something learned. When Juliette discovers through her mother's contacts in France that Édouard is already married to Magdalena, the results of Édouard's idealism begin their lifelong history of haunting his marriage to Juliette. But their marriage will also be haunted by other ghosts of Édouard's youthful patriotism, which Édouard later describes as being "like metaphysical frenzy";[12] as a token of their engagement, he gives Juliette some of the Algerian soil he has saved. Fittingly, Juliette does not know what to do with this increasingly troubling sign of French dominion in North Africa.

The nature and the persistence of Magdalena's presence in Édouard's and Juliette's marriage provides a revelatory perspective on France's troubled view of its recent past. Because Édouard is still married to Magdalena, he cannot have legitimate children with Juliette. It is as if the events of the past, having never been understood, will never cease to trouble the present; although Juliette tries to bring the three of them together over lunch in the early fifties so that Édouard can try to convince Magdalena to grant him a divorce, Magdalena—dressed in bridal white—remains serenely oblivious and the attempt fails. And when Édouard finally obtains the divorce years later, Juliette has already gone through menopause.

The most powerful indication of Magdalena's perennial influence comes in "Rue de Lille," when during a conversation with Juliette Édouard stumbles over his unintentional admission that he has seen Magdalena not once, but several times in the thirty years since the war. The force of Juliette's reaction to this revelation indicates its devastating effect:

> Viewing me at close range, as if I were a novel she had to translate, Juliette replied that one ought to be spared unexpected visions. Just now, it was as if three walls of the court outside had been bombed flat. Through a bright new gap she saw straight through to my first marriage. We—my first wife and I—postured in the distance, like characters in fiction.[13]

Juliette's job as a translator of American fiction, responsible for bringing American literature to France after the war, signals one of France's postwar directions; but Édouard, who has himself become a celebrated radio and television personality catering to the French fascination with their own literary figures, cannot free himself from the image of France's European legacy, embodied in Magdalena.

Finally, Magdalena's troubling influence on Édouard cannot be resolved or forgotten. The end of "Lena" leaves her on her deathbed, but she has refused to die, reviving twice after her doctor has given up hope. Édouard cannot bring himself to look at her after these resurrections; but in exchange for the "fascination" which he has confessed to her, she would leave him, if he looked at her, with a more troubling spiritual and devotional "imposition": "the encounter with her blue, enduring look of pure love."[14]

The city of Paris imagined and reflected in *Overhead in a Balloon* and the "other" Paris of Carol Frazier's invention might seem to be two quite different creations, marking the beginning and, for the time being, one conceivable end of Gallant's canon. On the surface, they seem to serve very different fictional purposes, and the historical city itself has not stood still over the last thirty-five years, any more than has Linnet Muir's or Mavis Gallant's Montreal. But as striking as the differences might seem between the Paris of the fifties and the eighties in Gallant's stories, the familiarity of the city evoked in *Overhead in a Balloon* provides even more striking confirmation of the formal and stylistic unity which circumscribes the whole imaginative world of Gallant's fiction.

As we have seen from the beginning, Gallant's stylistic, structural, and thematic signatures are not separable qualities; they form the manner and the matter of her stories into the "conformation of whatever the author has to say," as Gallant has put it.[15] Her style, arguably the first quality to strike Gallant's readers, is marked by precision, by reliance on simile rather than metaphor, and by its effectiveness as a vehicle for irony. The voices of Gallant's stories are consequences of her style; they communicate through indirection, through suggestive silences, abrupt but oblique observations, and sudden, sharp variations in tone.

Gallant's style demands that readers believe in the world it so faithfully renders—hence its precision and Gallant's consistent concern with verisimilitude—but it also calls attention to itself, to the ordering of words which forms the language of Gallant's fiction. This language has its recurring pairs of words ("pretty" and "shabby," "watching" and "seeing") and single words ("inventing," for example) as well as its recurring structures. The most obvious of these is the insistent and ironic series of "ands" linking lists which mean both less and more than the sum of their parts; the most powerful example to date of this structure forms the ending of "The Other Paris."

These aspects of language and syntax refer readers not only out to the worlds which Gallant's words render so tangibly, but in to the structures which form Gallant's stories. The most significant structural unity in Gallant's fiction is her stories' recurrent evocations of returns—returns via juxtaposed details, repeated phrases with opposed meanings, scenes set over against each other, characters' attitudes and situations reversed. These returns are structural figurations of Gallant's fundamental concern with time. They do not imply a cyclical repetition of history; rather, they imply subtle alteration, variations within each repetition, each return to a "locked situation." The structure of Gallant's stories often suggests that because neither memory nor history proceeds along straightforward narrative lines, the repetitions implied in her stories' returns to crucial moments must be studied for their variation. These variations constitute what amounts to change for Gallant's characters: crucial changes in perception, in attitude, in manner, in relationships. Returns to a "locked situation," be it a moment in history or in a relationship, imply both inertia and the search for a new direction, both paralysis and the possibility of reconstituting moments stopped in time.

The structures of Gallant's stories, through their insistent reference to the forms of characters' and cultures' returns to moments in the past, constitute variations on Gallant's major theme, which is the paradoxical nature of time. In Gallant's stories, the past often threatens the present with the ironic revelation that time has faltered and stopped—that characters and cultures have been arrested in memory, frozen in history—that there is no direction home because there is insufficient sense of where home was. The most cataclysmic rupture of the present from the past (and of North America from Europe) results from the upheavals of the war; but history's violence is also evident on a smaller and more intimate scale in Gallant's fiction, in the essentially private bewilderment of characters who return to a continent, or a city, or a family which history has rendered alien ground. Gallant's characters must learn to live on this ground, to make it into home ground by reconstructing memory's intersections with history in the districts of imagination. Imaginative returns to the past in Gallant's stories give birth to voices capable of inventing the present, of declaring, like Léopold in "Saturday," "Il n'y a que moi," or affirming, like Linnet Muir, that the variety of exile called writing was, at least for a time, "quite right and perfectly natural" because in her writing Linnet begins to memorialize the past.

Gallant opens her 1973 essay on the life of Paul Léautaud with a comment which could serve well as the lead entry in a book of maxims for aspiring writers of fiction: "All lives are interesting; no one life is more interesting than another. Its fascination depends on how much is revealed, and in what manner."[16] The second entry might be her cautionary remark, in a review of Günter Grass's *From the Diary of a Snail,* on the difficulties of reporting—and hence, of narrating: "Writers nearly always imagine it is easy to be a reporter, not to speak of a moral philosopher. The latter is simpler. One of the hardest things in the world is to describe what happened next."[17] The manner in which Gallant's fiction reveals ordinary lives is to quicken still moments with sudden light. The promise of meaning in Gallant's stories is always an elusive spark, flashing out from tiny collisions of detail, flickering quickly over nuances, lighting up a phrase, a state of mind, a landscape for a moment—and then subsiding into the steady glimmer of her fiction's surface and style. The illumination of the "complete story" which eludes Netta Asher in "The Moslem Wife"—a "flash in a tunnel," "displayed to anyone who could stare without blinking"—finds its analogue in the complete illumination which necessarily eludes Gallant's readers. We cannot read texts without blinking; Gallant's fiction demands that we recognize how significance plays over her stories in flashes and sparks, and that we develop the imaginative agility to respond to these moments of light. Netta Asher's light of imagination "danced all over the square": reading in the light of imagination, seeing its inventions, its dance of illumination across the moments of Gallant's fiction, we might hear voices keeping time in memory's histories of home.

Notes

NOTES TO CHAPTER ONE

1. "Memory, Imagination, Artifice: The Late Short Fiction of Mavis Gallant," *Canadian Fiction Magazine* 28 (1978): 88.
2. Geoff Hancock, "An Interview with Mavis Gallant," *Canadian Fiction Magazine* 28 (1978): 23.
3. Susan Leslie, "An Interview with Mavis Gallant," *Audience*, CBC FM, 6 February 1982.
4. Hancock, *CFM* interview, p. 41.
5. See Douglas Malcolm's and Judith Skelton-Grant's *ABCMA* bibliography for comprehensive listings of the *Standard* material.
6. For reviews of the play's production at Tarragon Theatre, see Mark Czarnecki, "Daughters of the Revolution," *Maclean's*, 22 November 1982, p. 78; Carole Corbeil, "Mavis Gallant's Elusive Drama," *The Globe and Mail* [Ontario ed.], 13 November 1982, p. E6; Gina Mallet, "*What Is To Be Done?* A Treat at Tarragon," *Toronto Star*, 12 November 1982, p. D1; for a review of the published playscript (Dunvegan, Ontario: Quadrant, 1983), see Neil Besner, "Reading Plays," *Canadian Literature* 104 (Spring 1985): 128–30.
7. *Standard Magazine*, 29 March 1947, pp. 3, 14. Gallant tells Fletcher Markle: "I was brought up partly by a psychiatrist who was an assistant of Freud—had been analyzed by Freud." She says that Freud was "gospel" for her at certain periods in her life, that she "went through a great period of Freud" and thought of his work "almost like a code." (*Telescope*, Channel 6, Toronto, 22 January 1969).
8. "Duncan & MacLennan: Writers," *Rotogravure*, 9 June 1945, pp. 16–19; "On the Air," 9 April 1949, p. 13; "Sarah of Saskatchewan," *Standard Magazine*, 17 April 1948, pp. 7, 14, 17; "The Town Below," *Standard Magazine*, 17 July 1948, pp. 11, 15; "Maria Chapdelaine," *Rotogravure*, 13 January 1945, pp. 6, 8, 9–11; "Canadian Story," *Rotogravure*, 2 March 1946, pp. 3–6, 8–9.
9. "Canadian Story," *Rotogravure*, 2 March 1946.
10. *Harper's Bazaar* 80 (July 1946): 58–59, 128–29.
11. "Report on a Repat," *Rotogravure*, 23 July 1945, pp. 2–6, 8–9; "These Are the First Impressions the War Brides Formed of Canada," *Rotogravure*, 13 October 1945, pp. 4–6, 8–9; "Don't Call Me War Bride," *Standard Magazine*, 2 March 1946, pp. 5, 13; "DP Test Case—A Failure," *Standard Magazine*, 28 August 1948, pp. 3, 16–17, 22; "I Don't Cry Anymore," *Standard Magazine*, 22 April 1950, pp. 5, 14, 28; "Report on a Repat, Part II," *Rotogravure*, 29 July 1950, pp. 16–17.
12. "Bringing Up Baby," *Standard Magazine*, 8 February 1947, pp. 4–5; "Problem Chil-

dren," *Rotogravure*, 25 October 1947, pp. 16–17, 19–20; "Your Child Looks at You," *Standard Magazine*, 18 December 1948, pp. 3–4.

13. "On the Air," 21 February 1948, p. 4.
14. "On the Air," 26 March 1949, p. 7.
15. "On the Air," 22 January 1949, p. 5.
16. Hancock, *CFM* interview, p. 39.
17. "On the Air," 5 March 1949, p. 4.
18. *Paris Notebooks: Essays & Reviews* (Toronto: Macmillan, 1986).
19. Hancock, *CFM* interview, p. 32.
20. Graeme Gibson, "Interview with Mavis Gallant," *Anthology*, CBC Radio, 31 August 1974.
21. Gibson interview.
22. Earl Beattie, "Interview with Mavis Gallant," *Anthology*, CBC Radio, 24 May 1969.
23. "Good Morning and Goodbye," *Preview* 22 (December 1944): 2.
24. "Madeline's Birthday," *The New Yorker*, 11 September 1951, p. 24.
25. "The Other Paris," in *The Other Paris* (Boston: Houghton Mifflin, 1956), p. 30. All subsequent references to this story appear in parentheses in the text.
26. *Structuralist Poetics: Structuralism, Linguistics and the Study of Literature* (London and Henley: Routledge & Kegan Paul, 1975, reprinted 1977), p. 221.
27. *Structuralist Poetics*, p. 221.
28. "Wing's Chips," in *The Other Paris*, p. 141.
29. "The Deceptions of Marie-Blanche," in *The Other Paris*, pp. 122–23.
30. "Señor Pinedo," in *The Other Paris*, p. 199. All subsequent references to this story appear in parentheses in the text.
31. "When We Were Nearly Young," *The New Yorker*, 15 October 1960, p. 42.
32. "The Picnic," in *The Other Paris*, p. 106.
33. Shirley, the central figure in Gallant's novel *A Fairly Good Time* (1970), "never failed to expect her mother's letters to contain magical solutions, and never failed to be disappointed. The correspondence between mother and daughter, Montreal and Paris, was an uninterrupted dialogue of the deaf" (45). See chapter 3.
34. The mother thinks her daughter's memories of Geneva will "crystallize" around two characters the girl has created in a play ("About Geneva," in *The Other Paris*, p. 196). All subsequent references to this story appear in parentheses in the text.

NOTES TO CHAPTER TWO

1. Jean Price, the narrator of "Its Image on the Mirror," calls her opening memory "a tableau"; in "An Unmarried Man's Summer," Walter Henderson composes his life in a "mosaic image." Both stories appear in *My Heart Is Broken* (New York: Random House, 1964); published in England as *An Unmarried Man's Summer* (London: Heinemann, 1965).
2. In *My Heart Is Broken*, pp. 157–93.
3. "An Introduction," in *Home Truths: Selected Canadian Stories* (Toronto: Macmillan, 1981), p. xii.
4. In an interview with Graeme Gibson, Gallant comments on "Its Image": "I had an idea about time and memory and I was really trying to do something. I don't know whether I succeeded or not, perhaps not." *Anthology*, CBC Radio, 31 August 1974. For a detailed discussion of time and memory in *Its Image on the Mirror* see D. B.

Jewison's "Speaking of Mirrors: Imagery and Narration in Two Novellas by Mavis Gallant," *Studies in Canadian Literature* 10, 1 & 2 (1985): 94–109.

5. The excerpt is from Yeats's verse drama, *The Shadowy Waters* (1906). This late romantic play tells of Forgael, a seeker after "love . . . /But of a beautiful, unheard of kind/That is not in the world" (410). Forgael is looking for "Miracle, ecstasy, the impossible hope,/The flagstone under all, the fire of fires,/The roots of the world" (408). In the poem which prefaces the drama, the speaker asks:

> Do our woods
> And winds and ponds cover more quiet woods,
> More shining winds, more star-glimmering ponds?
> Is Eden out of time and out of space?

Gallant quotes from one of Forgael's speeches to Aibric, a loyal follower:

> Forgael: All would be well
> Could we but give us wholly to the dreams
> And get into their world that to the sense
> Is shadow, and not linger wretchedly
> Among substantial things; for it is dreams
> That lift us to the flowing, changing world
> That the heart longs for. What is love itself,
> Even though it be the lightest of light love. . . .
>
> Aibric: While
> We're in the body that's impossible. (411)

All page references are to *The Collected Poems of W. B. Yeats* (New York: Macmillan, 1956, reprinted 1976).

6. Gallant tells Fletcher Markle: "[I] love mirrors, I have a book about them." *Telescope*, Channel 6, Toronto, 29 January 1969.

7. Jean's memories are arranged in seven sections; the narrative present is some time shortly after 1958. The opening section (57–70) recalls events very close to Jean's narrative present; she remembers helping her parents move from the Allenton home to Montreal. She then begins to fill in the past, recalling details from Frank's, Isobel's, and her own childhoods. The family reunion at the summer cottage, recalled in the second section (70–80), takes place after the move from Allenton. In the third section (81–90), Jean returns to her childhood, but then she shifts to her memories of living and working in wartime Montreal and pursuing Isobel there. Section four (100–12) recalls Jean's meeting Tom Price, their marriage, and his departure for overseas. In the fifth section (113–30) Jean remembers learning of Frank's death, and recalls her return to Allenton with Isobel. Section six (130–47) backtracks from section five, recording Frank's stay with his sisters in Montreal just before he leaves for England. The last section (147–55) recalls Jean's encounter with Isa in Allenton after Frank's death. Thus, at the end of the novel, Jean is remembering events which take place before those recorded in the first section. The effect of this structure is to call attention to the ways in which the process of memory instructs Jean.

8. Commenting on Gallant's two-part article, "The Events in May: A Paris Notebook," George Woodcock remarks that this piece shows "the same sharp observation of action, speech and setting that one finds in Gallant's stories. There were parts, one felt, that only needed to be taken out of the linear diary form and reshaped by the helical

patterning of memory for them to become the nuclei of excellent stories" ("Memory,
Imagination, Artifice: The Late Short Fiction of Mavis Gallant," *Canadian Fiction
Magazine* 28 [1978]: 74).

9. "Style and Its Image," in *Literary Style: A Symposium,* ed. and trans. by Seymour
   Chatman (London & New York: Oxford University Press, 1971), pp. 6, 10.
10. Gallant tells Fletcher Markle that she began work on "Its Image on the Mirror" in
    1956, then "put the whole thing away." Then, says Gallant, "I tried the same idea in
    a shorter form, it was a short story called 'The Cost of Living'; I tried it in another
    way"; she was writing about the "same relationship between sisters, one attempting
    to enter into the life of another. The theme of both is domination." *Telescope,* Chan-
    nel 6, Toronto, 29 January 1969.
11. "The Moabitess," p. 54.
12. "Acceptance of Their Ways," p. 13.
13. "Bernadette," p. 41.
14. "My Heart Is Broken," in *My Heart Is Broken,* p. 195. All subsequent references to
    this story appear in parentheses in the text.
15. In *My Heart Is Broken,* pp. 203–17. All subsequent references to this story appear in
    parentheses in the text.

NOTES TO CHAPTER THREE

1. Frank O'Connor, *The Lonely Voice: A Study of the Short Story* (Cleveland and New
   York: The World Publishing Company, 1962).
2. The most helpful discussions of *Green Water, Green Sky* are D. B. Jewison's "Speaking of Mirrors: Imagery and Narration in Two Novellas by Mavis Gallant," *Studies in
   Canadian Literature* 10, 1–2 (1985): 94–110; and Ronald Hatch's "Mavis Gallant
   and the Creation of Consciousness" in *The Canadian Novel: A Critical Anthology,*
   vol. 4, *Present Tense,* ed. John Moss (Toronto: NC Press, 1985), pp. 45–71. Hatch's
   article also presents a fine treatment of *A Fairly Good Time.* For another comprehensive analysis of *A Fairly Good Time,* see Donna Coates's unpublished M.A. thesis,
   "Family Relationships in the Fiction of Mavis Gallant" (University of Calgary, 1982),
   chapter 5, "An Uninterrupted Dialogue of the Deaf" (pp. 117–45).
3. "Green Water, Green Sky," *The New Yorker,* 27 June 1959, pp. 22–29; "August,"
   The New Yorker, 29 August 1959, pp. 26–36, 38, 41–42, 44, 46, 51–52, 54, 56,
   59–60, 62–63; "Travellers Must Be Content," *The New Yorker,* 11 July 1959, pp.
   27–34, 36, 38, 43–46, 48–49, 52.
4. Gallant's linked stories include those linked by shared characters or narrators, as well
   as stories more generally connected through broader thematic parallels. Leaving aside
   the more problematic connections of the latter group (in which some readers would
   include the "German stories" collected in *The Pegnitz Junction*), there are several
   other groups of explicitly linked stories in the Gallant canon:
   a. "Good Morning and Goodbye," *Preview* 22 (December 1944): 1–3; and "Three
      Brick Walls," *Preview* (December 1944): 4–6.
   b. The six "Linnet Muir" stories (collected in *Home Truths*; see chapter 6).
   c. "Speck's Idea" and "Overhead in a Balloon" (collected in *Overhead in a Balloon*;
      see chapter 7).
   d. "A Painful Affair," "A Flying Start," and "Grippes and Poche" (collected in *Over-
      head in a Balloon;* see chapter 7).

e. "A Recollection," "Rue de Lille," "The Colonel's Child," and "Lena" (collected in *Overhead in a Balloon;* see chapter 7).

f. "The Chosen Husband," *The New Yorker,* 15 April 1985, pp. 40–49; "From Cloud to Cloud," *The New Yorker,* 22 July 1985, pp. 22–25; "Florida," *The New Yorker,* 26 August 1985, pp. 24–27.

5. There are a few revisions in the versions of the stories published as parts of the novel. Most are slight changes in punctuation. Perhaps the most significant revision makes it clearer that George's memory (rather than someone else's) can distort his experience:

Original *New Yorker* version (p. 24): "The gardener heard the splash and fished him out, and he said that George was not on his back at all but on his face, splashing and floundering."

Revised version (*Green Water, Green Sky,* p. 7): "The gardener heard the splash and fished him out and he was perfectly fine; not on his back at all but on his face, splashing and floundering."

6. Susan Leslie, "An Interview with Mavis Gallant," *Audience,* CBC FM, 6 February 1982.

7. *Green Water, Green Sky* (Boston: Houghton Mifflin, 1959), p. 5. All subsequent references to this novel appear in parentheses in the text.

8. Fletcher Markle, "Interview with Mavis Gallant," *Telescope,* Channel 6, Toronto, 22 January 1969.

9. Geoff Hancock, "An Interview with Mavis Gallant," *Canadian Fiction Magazine* 28 (1978): 58.

10. *A Fairly Good Time* (New York: Random House, 1970), p. 45. All subsequent references to this novel appear in parentheses in the text.

11. "Jorinda and Jorindel," *The New Yorker,* 19 September 1959, pp. 38–42.

12. *Overhead in a Balloon: Stories of Paris* (Toronto: Macmillan, 1985).

13. For another French character who collects Nazi war memorabilia, see Monnerot in "A Report," *The New Yorker,* 3 December 1966, pp. 62–65.

NOTES TO CHAPTER FOUR

1. George Woodcock takes a different view: "In my view what Mavis Gallant really discovered, and what she presents in these stories is not where 'Fascism' (I would prefer the exacter with *Nazism* [sic]) came from, since that world of Nazi origins hardly exists in the memories of Germans who are not historians, but rather the emerging world of modern Germany which the Nazi age has cut off like a black curtain from the traditional past, so that only men in their eighties talk of 'the good old Kaiserzeit' and nobody talks of the Weimar age" ("Memory, Imagination, Artifice: The Late Short Fiction of Mavis Gallant," *Canadian Fiction Magazine* 28 [1978]: 83).

2. *CFM* interview, pp. 39–41.

3. *CFM* interview, p. 40.

4. Gallant tells Geoff Hancock that " a great deal of conversation in it ['The Pegnitz Junction'] is cut off, short circuited." *CFM* interview, p. 65.

5. "The Old Friends," in *The Pegnitz Junction* (New York: Random House, 1973), p. 89. All subsequent references to this story appear in parentheses in the text.

6. "Ernst in Civilian Clothes" is the only one of these stories republished in *The Pegnitz Junction.* The others appeared in *The New Yorker:* "Willi," 5 January 1963, pp. 29–31; "A Report," 3 December 1966, pp. 62–65.

7. "Ernst in Civilian Clothes," in *The Pegnitz Junction,* p. 141. All subsequent refer-

ences to this story appear in parentheses in the text.

8. "A Report," p. 65. All subsequent references to this story appear in parentheses in the text.
9. "One Aspect of a Rainy Day," in *The New Yorker,* 14 April 1962, pp. 62–65.
10. "Willi," p. 30. All subsequent references to this story appear in parentheses in the text.
11. "The Latehomecomer," in *From the Fifteenth District* (Toronto: Macmillan, 1979), p. 134. All subsequent references to this story appear in parentheses in the text.
12. "O Lasting Peace," in *The Pegnitz Junction,* p. 163. All subsequent references to this story appear in parentheses in the text.
13. "An Autobiography," in *The Pegnitz Junction,* p. 109. All subsequent references to this story appear in parentheses in the text.
14. See Ronald Hatch's discussion of "An Autobiography" in his article "Mavis Gallant and the expatriate character," *Zeitschrift der Gesellschaft für Kanada-Studien* 1 (January 1981): 133–43; see in particular pp. 139–41.
15. "The Pegnitz Junction," in *The Pegnitz Junction,* pp. 15, 16. All subsequent references to this story appear in parentheses in the text.
16. *CFM* interview, p. 65.
17. Ibid.
18. Ibid., p. 51.
19. Ronald Hatch suggests that Gallant's "later sense of character is one in which people seem to 'float' in a pond of historical forces." "The Three Stages of Mavis Gallant's Short Fiction," *CFM* 28 (1978): 99.

NOTES TO CHAPTER FIVE

1. *From the Fifteenth District: A Novella and Eight Short Stories* (Toronto: Macmillan, 1979). The five Linnet Muir stories appeared in *The New Yorker* as follows: "In Youth Is Pleasure," 24 November 1975; "Between Zero and One," 8 December 1975; "Varieties of Exile," 19 January 1976; "Voices Lost in Snow," 5 April 1976; "The Doctor," 20 June 1977.
2. *Home Truths: Selected Canadian Stories* (Toronto: Macmillan, 1981). The sixth Linnet Muir story, "With a Capital T," was first published in *Canadian Fiction Magazine* 28 (1978): 8–17.
3. For a discussion of all of the stories in this book, see D. B. Jewison, "Children of the Wars: A Discussion of *From the Fifteenth District,*" *Commonwealth* 9, 1 (Autumn 1986): 112–20; for a detailed discussion of "Irina," see Ronald Hatch, "The Three Stages of Mavis Gallant's Short Fiction," *Canadian Fiction Magazine* 28 (1978): 92–114; for discussions of "The Four Seasons," see George Woodcock, "Memory, Imagination, Artifice: The Late Short Fiction of Mavis Gallant," *Canadian Fiction Magazine* 28 (1978): 74–91, and Janice Kulyk Keefer, "Mavis Gallant and the Angel of History," *University of Toronto Quarterly* 55, 3 (Spring 1986): 282–301.
4. "Potter," in *From the Fifteenth District,* p. 169. All subsequent references to this story appear in parentheses in the text.
5. Geoff Hancock, "An Interview with Mavis Gallant," *Canadian Fiction Magazine* 28 (1978): 53.
6. "The Four Seasons," in *From the Fifteenth District,* p. 3. All subsequent references to this story appear in parentheses in the text.
7. "The Remission," in *From the Fifteenth District,* p. 89. All subsequent references to

this story appear in parentheses in the text.

8. "The Moslem Wife," in *From the Fifteenth District*, p. 39. All subsequent references to this story appear in parentheses in the text.
9. "The Daughters of the Late Colonel," in *Katherine Mansfield: Selected Stories*, ed. Dan Davin (Oxford: Oxford University Press, 1969, reprinted 1978), p. 270.
10. "Daughters," pp. 270–71.
11. "Daughters," p. 272.
12. *CFM* interview, p. 45.

NOTES TO CHAPTER SIX

1. "The Ice Wagon Going Down the Street" first appeared in *The New Yorker*, 12 October 1963, and was first collected in *My Heart Is Broken* (1964); "Virus X" in *The New Yorker*, 31 January 1965; "Bonaventure" in *The New Yorker*, 30 July 1966; "Saturday" in *The New Yorker*, 8 June 1968; and "In the Tunnel" in *The New Yorker*, 18 September 1971 (first collected in *The End of the World and Other Stories* [Toronto: McClelland and Stewart, 1974; NCL 91]).
2. Interview with Susan Leslie, *Audience*, CBC Radio, 6 February 1982. In another interview, Gallant comments that "every language is a window." Interview with Earl Beattie, *Anthology*, CBC Radio, 24 May 1969.
3. "An Introduction," in *Home Truths: Selected Canadian Stories* (Toronto: Macmillan, 1981), p. xiii.
4. Interview in *Canadian Fiction Magazine* 28 (1978): 26.
5. "An Introduction," p. xxii.
6. "What Is Style?" in *Canadian Forum* 62, 721 (September 1982): 6, 37. Reprinted in *Making It New: Contemporary Canadian Stories*, ed. John Metcalf (Toronto: Methuen, 1982), 72–75.
7. "An Introduction," p. xv.
8. Ibid., p. xviii.
9. Ibid.
10. *CFM* interview, p. 51.
11. Consider, for example, Gallant's use of the word in "An Introduction": "The character I called Linnet Muir is not an exact reflection. I saw her as quite another person, but it would be untrue to say that I invented everything" (xxii). Again, she comments to Earl Beattie on Canada as a country where there was a large gap between "reality and dream": "The people's lives didn't match up to what they seem to think they were and the people invent things or they invent backgrounds or they invent families.... I'm not talking about lies, which is something else... everybody lies... I mean inventions... invention of reality, fabrication of history" (*Anthology*, CBC radio, 24 May 1969).
12. "Saturday," in *Home Truths*, p. 39. All subsequent references to this story appear in parentheses in the text.
13. "In the Tunnel," in *Home Truths*, p. 99. All subsequent references to this story appear in parentheses in the text.
14. "The Ice Wagon Going Down the Street," in *Home Truths*, p. 116. All subsequent references to this story appear in parentheses in the text.
15. "Bonaventure," in *Home Truths*, p. 151. All subsequent references to this story appear in parentheses in the text.
16. This scene, set in Bonaventure station, recalls Gallant's description of the station in

her *Standard* article, "Report on a Repat," *Rotogravure*, 28 July 1945, pp. 2–6, 8–9.

17. "Virus X," in *Home Truths*, p. 181. All subsequent references to this story appear in parentheses in the text.
18. Geoff Hancock, "An Interview with Mavis Gallant," *Canadian Fiction Magazine* 28 (1978): 28.
19. "An Introduction," p. xx. All subsequent references to this section of *Home Truths* appear in parentheses in the text.
20. *CFM* interview, p. 39.
21. "In Youth Is Pleasure," in *Home Truths*, p. 219. All subsequent references to this story appear in parentheses in the text.
22. "Varieties of Exile," in *Home Truths*, pp. 261–62. All subsequent references to this story appear in parentheses in the text.
23. Gallant discusses the relation between reality and fiction using imagery similar to Linnet's: "Once you have put reality through the filter and turned it into that other reality called fiction, the original ingredient ceases to exist. Ceases to exist in memory, that is."(*CFM* Interview, p. 28)

NOTES TO CHAPTER SEVEN

1. "Overhead in a Balloon," in *Overhead in a Balloon: Stories of Paris* (Toronto: Macmillan, 1985), p. 53.
2. "Paris: The Taste of a New Age," collected in *Paris Notebooks: Essays and Reviews* (Toronto: Macmillan, 1986), pp. 161–75.
3. "The Pegnitz Junction," in *The Pegnitz Junction: A Novella and Five Short Stories* (New York: Random House, 1973), p. 5.
4. "Speck's Idea," in *Overhead in a Balloon*, p. 1. All subsequent references to this story appear in parentheses in the text.
5. "Overhead in a Balloon," p. 57. All subsequent references to this story appear in parentheses in the text.
6. "A Flying Start," in *Overhead in a Balloon*, p. 123. All subsequent references to this story appear in parentheses in the text.
7. "A Painful Affair," in *Overhead in a Balloon*, p. 103–4. All subsequent references to this story appear in parentheses in the text.
8. "A Flying Start," p. 128.
9. "Grippes and Poche," in *Overhead in a Balloon*, p. 132. All subsequent references to this story appear in parentheses in the text.
10. "A Recollection," in *Overhead in a Balloon*, p. 151. All subsequent references to this story appear in parentheses in the text.
11. "Lena," in *Overhead in a Balloon*, p. 176.
12. "The Colonel's Child," in *Overhead in a Balloon*, p. 166.
13. "Rue de Lille," in *Overhead in a Balloon*, p. 165.
14. "Lena," in *Overhead in a Balloon*, p. 187.
15. "What Is Style?" in *Canadian Forum* 62, 721 (September 1982): 6.
16. "Paul Léautaud, 1872–1956," in *Paris Notebooks*, p. 142.
17. Review of *From the Diary of a Snail* in *Paris Notebooks*, p. 206.

Bibliography

Ackroyd, Peter. *Notes For a New Culture: An Essay on Modernism*. London: Vision Press Ltd., 1976.

Alter, Robert. *Partial Magic: The Novel as a Self-Conscious Genre*. Berkeley and Los Angeles: University of California Press, 1975.

Auerbach, Erich. *Mimesis: The Representation of Reality in Modern Literature*. Princeton, N.J.: Princeton University Press, 1953; reprinted 1971.

Atwood, Margaret. *Survival: A Thematic Guide to Canadian Literature*. Toronto: Anansi, 1972.

Barthes, Roland. "Style and Its Image." In *Literary Style: A Symposium*. Ed. and trans. (in part) by Seymour Chatman. London and New York: Oxford University Press, 1971, pp. 3–10.

———. *Critical Essays*. Trans. Richard Howard. Evanston, Ill.: Northwestern University Press, 1972.

———. *Writing Degree Zero*. Trans. Annette Lavers and Colin Smith. New York: Hill & Wang, 1968; reprinted 1977.

———. *The Pleasures of the Text*. Trans. Richard Howard. New York: Hill & Wang, 1975.

Bates, H. E. *The Modern Short Story: A Critical Survey*. London and New York: T. Nelson & Sons, 1945.

Beattie, Earl. "Interview with Mavis Gallant." *Telescope,* Channel 6, Toronto, 22 and 29 January 1969.

Becker, George G., ed. *Documents of Modern Literary Realism*. Princeton, N.J.: Princeton University Press, 1963.

Besner, N. "A Broken Dialogue: History and Memory in Mavis Gallant's Short Fiction." *Essays on Canadian Writing* 33 (Fall 1986): 89–99.

———. "Reading Plays." *Canadian Literature* 104 (Spring 1985): 128–130.

———. "Mavis Gallant's Short Fiction: History and Memory in the Light of Imagination." Unpublished dissertation, University of British Columbia, 1983.

Bonheim, Helmut. *The Narrative Modes: Techniques of the Short Story*. Cambridge: D. S. Brewer, Boydell & Brewer, 1982.

Bonhoeffer, Dietrich. *Letters and Papers from Prison*. Ed. Eberhard Bethge. Trans. Reginald H. Fuller. New York: Macmillan, 1953; reprinted 1962, 1965.

Booth, Wayne C. *The Rhetoric of Fiction*. Chicago: University of Chicago Press, 1961.

Bradbury, Malcolm and James McFarlane, eds. *Modernism: 1890–1930.* Harmondsworth, Engl. and New York: Penguin, 1976.

Chatman, Seymour. "On the Formalist-Structuralist Theory of Character." *Journal of Literary Semantics* 1 (1972): 57–79.

Chiari, Joseph. *The Aesthetics of Modernism.* London: Vision Press, 1970.

Coldwell, Joan. "Memory Organized: The Novels of Audrey Thomas." *Canadian Literature* 92 (Spring 1982): 46–56.

Crosland, Margaret. *Beyond the Lighthouse: English Women Novelists in the Twentieth Century.* London: Constable, 1981.

Culler, Jonathon. *Structuralist Poetics: Structuralism, Linguistics, and the Study of Literature.* London and Henley: Routledge and Kegan Paul, 1975; reprinted 1977.

Dahlie, Hallvard. *Varieties of Exile: The Canadian Experience.* Vancouver: University of British Columbia Press, 1986.

Davies, Robertson. "The Novels of Mavis Gallant." *Canadian Fiction Magazine* 28 (1978): 69–73.

Eakin, John Paul. *Fictions in Autobiography: Studies in the Art of Self–Invention.* Princeton: Princeton University Press, 1985.

Fabre, Michel. "'Orphan's Progress,' Reader's Progress: Le 'on-dit' et le 'non-dit' chez Mavis Gallant." *Recherches Anglaises et Américaines* 16 (1983): 57–67.

Ferguson, Suzanne C. "Defining the Short Story: Impressionism and Form." *Modern Fiction Studies* 28, 1 (Spring 1982): 13–24.

Frye, Northrop. *Anatomy of Criticism: Four Essays.* Princeton, N.J.: Princeton University Press, 1957; reprinted 1971.

Gabriel, Barbara. "Fairly Good Times: An Interview with Mavis Gallant." *Canadian Forum* 66, 766 (Feb. 1987): 23–27.

Gallant, Mavis. *The Other Paris.* Boston: Houghton Mifflin, 1956. London: André Deutsch, 1957. Reprinted, Freeport, N.Y.: Books for Libraries Press, 1970. [Includes: "The Other Paris"; "Autumn Day"; "Poor Franzi"; "Going Ashore"; "The Picnic"; "The Deceptions of Marie-Blanche"; "Wing's Chips"; "The Legacy"; "One Morning in June"; "About Geneva"; "Señor Pinedo"; "A Day Like Any Other."]

———. *Green Water, Green Sky.* Boston: Houghton Mifflin, 1959. London: André Deutsch, 1960.

———. *My Heart Is Broken: Eight Stories and a Short Novel.* New York: Random House, 1964. London: Heinemann, 1965 (Title: *An Unmarried Man's Summer*). [Includes: "Acceptance of Their Ways"; "Bernadette"; "The Moabitess"; "Its Image on the Mirror"—a short novel; "The Cost of Living"; "My Heart Is Broken"; "Sunday Afternoon"; "An Unmarried Man's Summer"; "The Ice Wagon Going Down the Street."]

———. *A Fairly Good Time.* New York: Random House, 1970. London: Heinemann, 1970.

———. *The Pegnitz Junction: A Novella and Five Short Stories.* New York: Random House, 1973. London: Jonathan Cape, 1974. [Includes: "The Pegnitz Junction"; "The Old Friends"; "An Autobiography"; "Ernst in Civilian Clothes"; "O Lasting Peace"; "An Alien Flower."]

———. *The End of the World and Other Stories.* Toronto: McClelland and Stewart,

1974 (NCL 91), intro. Robert Weaver. [Includes: "The Other Paris"; "The Picnic"; "About Geneva"; "An Unmarried Man's Summer"; "The End of the World"; "The Accident"; "Malcolm and Bea"; "The Prodigal Parent"; "The Wedding Ring"; "New Year's Eve"; "In the Tunnel."]

——. *From the Fifteenth District: A Novella and Eight Short Stories.* Toronto: Macmillan, 1979. London: Jonathan Cape, 1980. [Includes: "The Four Seasons"; "The Moslem Wife"; "The Remission"; "The Latehomecomer"; "Baum, Gabriel, 1935– ( )"; "From the Fifteenth District"; "Potter"; "His Mother"; "Irina."]

——. *Home Truths: Selected Canadian Stories.* Toronto: Macmillan, 1981. [Includes: ("An Introduction," M. Gallant); "Thank You for the Lovely Tea"; "Jorinda and Jorindel"; "Saturday"; "Up North"; "Orphan's Progress"; "The Prodigal Parent"; "In the Tunnel"; "Bonaventure"; "Virus X"; "In Youth Is Pleasure"; "Between Zero and One"; "Varieties of Exile"; "Voices Lost in Snow"; "The Doctor"; "With a Capital T."]

——. *What Is To Be Done?* Dunvegan, Ont.: Quadrant, 1983.

——. *Overhead in a Balloon: Stories of Paris.* Toronto: Macmillan, 1985. [Includes: "Speck's Idea"; "Overhead in a Balloon"; "Luc and His Father"; "A Painful Affair"; "Larry"; "A Flying Start"; "Grippes and Poche"; "A Recollection"; "Rue de Lille"; "The Colonel's Child"; "Lena"; "The Assembly."]

——. *Paris Notebooks: Essays and Reviews.* Toronto: Macmillan, 1986.

Gibson, Graeme. "Interview with Mavis Gallant." *Anthology,* CBC Radio, 31 August 1974.

Gom, Leona M. "Laurence and the Uses of Memory." *Canadian Literature* 71 (Winter 1976): 48–58.

Good, Graham. "Notes on the Novella." *Novel* 10, 3 (Spring 1977): 197–211.

Graff, Gerald. *Literature Against Itself: Literary Ideas in Modern Society.* Chicago and London: University of Chicago Press, 1979.

Hancock, Geoffrey. "An Interview with Mavis Gallant." *Canadian Fiction Magazine* 28 (1978): 19–67.

Hatch, Ronald B. "Mavis Gallant: Returning Home." *Atlantis* 4, 1 (Fall 1978): 95–102.

——. "The Three Stages of Mavis Gallant's Short Fiction." *Canadian Fiction Magazine* 28 (1978): 92–114.

——. "Mavis Gallant and the Expatriate Character." *Zeitschrift der Gesellschaft für Kanada-Studien* 1 (Jan. 1981): 133–42.

——. "Mavis Gallant and the Creation of Consciousness." In *The Canadian Novel: A Critical Anthology,* vol. 4, *Present Tense,* ed. John Moss. Toronto: NC Press, 1985, pp. 45–71.

——. "Mavis Gallant." In *Dictionary of Literary Biography,* vol. 53, *Canadian Writers Since 1960: First Series,* ed. W. H. New. Detroit: Gale Research, 1986, pp. 195–204.

Hirsch, E. D., Jr. *The Aims of Interpretation.* Chicago and London: University of Chicago Press, 1976; reprinted 1978.

Howe, Irving, ed. *The Idea of the Modern in Literature and the Arts.* New York: Horizon Press, 1976; reprinted 1978.

Irvine, Lorna. *Sub/Version.* Toronto: ECW Press, 1986.

Jewison, D. B. "Speaking of Mirrors: Imagery and Narration in Two Novellas by Mavis Gallant." *Studies in Canadian Literature* 10, 1 & 2 (1985): 94–109.

——. "Children of the Wars: A Discussion of *From the Fifteenth District.*" *Commonwealth* 9, 1 (Autumn 1986): 112–20.

Keefer, Janice Kulyk. "Strange Fashions of Forsaking: Criticism and the Fiction of Mavis Gallant." *Dalhousie Review* 64, 4 (Winter 1984–85): 721–35.

——. "Mavis Gallant and the Angel of History." *University of Toronto Quarterly* 55, 3 (Spring 1986): 282–301.

——. "Mavis Gallant's World of Women: A Feminist Perspective." *Atlantis* 10, 2 (Spring 1985): 11–29.

Keith, W. *Canadian Literature in English.* London & New York: Longman, 1985.

Kermode, Frank. *The Sense of an Ending: Studies in the Theory of Fiction.* New York: Oxford University Press, 1967.

Lentricchia, Frank. *After the New Criticism.* Chicago: University of Chicago Press, 1980.

Leslie, Susan. "An Interview with Mavis Gallant." *Audience,* CBC FM, 6 February 1982.

Levin, Harry. *The Gates of Horn: A Study of Five French Realists.* New York: Oxford University Press, 1963.

Lodge, David. *The Modes of Modern Writing: Metaphor, Metonymy, and the Typology of Modern Literature.* Ithaca, N.Y.: Cornell University Press, 1977.

——. *Modernism, Antimodernism, and Postmodernism.* Birmingham: University of Birmingham Press, 1977.

——. *Working with Structuralism: Essays and Reviews on Nineteenth and Twentieth-Century Literature.* Boston, London, and Henley: Routledge & Kegan Paul, 1981.

Lohafer, Susan. *Coming to Terms with the Short Story.* Baton Rouge and London: Louisiana State University Press, 1983.

Lukács, Georg. *Realism in Our Time: Literature and the Class Struggle.* New York & Evanston, Ill.: Harper and Row, 1964.

Malcolm, Douglas, and Judith Skelton Grant. "Mavis Gallant: An Annotated Bibliography." In *The Annotated Bibliography of Canada's Major Authors,* vol. 5, ed. Robert Lecker and Jack David. Downsview, Ont.: ECW Press, 1984, pp. 179–230.

Markle, Fletcher. "Interview with Mavis Gallant." *Telescope,* Channel 6, Toronto, 22 and 29 January 1969.

Martens, Debra. "An Interview with Mavis Gallant." *Rubicon* (Winter 1984–85): 151–182.

May, Charles E., ed. *Short Story Theories.* Athens, Ohio: Ohio University Press, 1976.

McLean, Stuart. "Interview with Mavis Gallant." *Sunday Morning,* CBC Radio, 19 April 1981.

Mendilow, A. A. *Time and the Novel.* New York: Humanities Press, 1952; reprinted 1972.

Merler, Grazia. *Mavis Gallant: Narrative Patterns and Devices.* Ottawa: Tecumseh Press, 1975.

Meyerhoff, Hans. *Time in Literature.* Berkeley and Los Angeles: University of California Press, 1955.

Moss, John. *A Reader's Guide to the Canadian Novel.* Toronto: McClelland and Stewart, 1981.

New, William H. *Among Worlds: An Introduction to Modern Commonwealth and South African Fiction.* Erin, Ont.: Porcépic Press, 1975.

————. "Fiction." In *Literary History of Canada: Canadian Literature in English.* Ed. Carl F. Klinck. 2nd ed. Toronto: University of Toronto Press, 1976.

O'Connor, Frank. *The Lonely Voice: A Study of the Short Story.* Cleveland and New York: The World Publishing Co., 1962.

O'Rourke, David. "Exiles in Time: Gallant's *My Heart Is Broken.*" *Canadian Literature* 93 (Summer 1982): 98–107.

Pratt, Mary Louise. "The Short Story: The Long and the Short of It." *Poetics* 10, 2/3 (June 1981): 175–94.

Proust, Marcel. *Remembrance of Things Past.* Trans. C. Scott Moncrieff and Terence Kilmartin. New York: Random House, 1981.

Reid, Ian. *The Short Story.* London: Methuen; New York: Barnes & Noble, 1977.

Shaw, Valerie. *The Short Story: A Critical Introduction.* London and New York: Longman, 1983.

Stevens, Peter. "Perils of Compassion." *Canadian Literature* 56 (Spring 1973): 61–70.

Tobin, Patricia Dreschel. *Time and the Novel: The Genealogical Imperative.* Princeton, N.J.: Princeton University Press, 1978.

Watt, Ian. *The Rise of the Novel: Studies in Defoe, Richardson and Fielding.* London: Chatto & Windus, 1957; reprinted 1977.

Wilson, Edmund. *O Canada: An American's Notes on Canadian Culture.* New York: Farrar, Straus, and Giroux, 1964.

Woodcock, George. "Memory, Imagination, Artifice: The Late Short Fiction of Mavis Gallant." *Canadian Fiction Magazine* 28 (1978): 74–91.

Index